Segregated Time

Segregated Time

P.J. BRENDESE

OXFORD
UNIVERSITY PRESS

Oxford University Press is a department of the University of Oxford. It furthers the University's objective of excellence in research, scholarship, and education by publishing worldwide. Oxford is a registered trade mark of Oxford University Press in the UK and certain other countries.

Published in the United States of America by Oxford University Press
198 Madison Avenue, New York, NY 10016, United States of America.

© Oxford University Press 2023

All rights reserved. No part of this publication may be reproduced, stored in a retrieval system, or transmitted, in any form or by any means, without the prior permission in writing of Oxford University Press, or as expressly permitted by law, by license, or under terms agreed with the appropriate reproduction rights organization. Inquiries concerning reproduction outside the scope of the above should be sent to the Rights Department, Oxford University Press, at the address above.

You must not circulate this work in any other form
and you must impose this same condition on any acquirer.

Library of Congress Control Number: 2021953387
ISBN 978–0–19–753574–5

DOI: 10.1093/oso/9780197535745.001.0001

Printed by Integrated Books International, United States of America

For those out of time
On borrowed time
Acting in time they do not have
For untimely Souls
who make time
to inhabit time
Otherwise

Contents

Prelude and Acknowledgments   ix

Introduction: Whose Time Is It?   1

1. White Time: The Race of Segregated Time   19
2. Doing Time: Carceral Temporality   43

Interlude 1: The Part That Has No Time   73

3. Killing Time: Imminent Immigrants and the Temporal Borders of Racial Biopolitics   79
4. Borrowed Time: Life and Debt on Subprime Time   105

Interlude 2: Time Travel   135

5. End Times: The Segregated Apocalypse Now   149

Epilogue: Other Times   173
Notes   187
Index   241

Prelude and Acknowledgments

This book about the racial politics of time was written under multiple shortages of time and layers of duress that were political, professional, and personal. Politically, it took shape in an atmosphere shot through with incessant displays of murderous white supremacy, the uptick of militant nativism, and an acceleration of transnational fascism—and that is hardly an exhaustive list. As if the situation were not dire enough, the project unfolded amid an encroachment of an apocalypse wrought by a climate crisis that many white nationalists disavow. Remarkably, a critical mass of whites ignore planetary catastrophe while mobilizing against what they take to be the *real* end times: the end of white supremacy. On another level, everyday forms of stealing time have long been taken for granted by too many white people. Here is James Baldwin:

> What is it that you wanted me to reconcile? I was born here almost sixty years ago. I am not going to live another sixty years. You always told me it takes time. It has taken my father's time, my mother's time, my uncle's time. My brothers' and my sisters' time. My nieces' and my nephews' time. How much time do you want for your progress?[1]

When Baldwin asks how much of his and his family's time *you* want for *your* progress, he intimates a segregated white time as that which defines its progress and seeks its advance by way of racialized temporal theft. As a kid, I remember being puzzled hearing adults marvel at just how far "the Blacks" had come "in such a short time." I wondered how four centuries could be considered a short time. The more precise question would have been, a short time *for whom*? Years went by before I read texts like Martin Luther King Jr.'s "Negroes Are Not Moving Too Fast" and *Why We Can't Wait*. Still more time passed until I wrote this book grappling with what I will conceptualize and refer to as white time and white temporality. Back then it just seemed strange. Today, it still seems strange. Just not in the same way. Alluding to the strangeness of the disconnect I explore in this study, Baldwin argued that whites "do not relate to the present any more than they relate to the person."[2]

It is no revelation that different people have different senses of the present and diverse experiences of time's passage. The subjective aspects of duration are at least part of what makes it difficult to talk about time. Nevertheless, the myriad ways that humans experience temporal duration should not prevent us from grappling with how power influences how time is understood and inhabited. Another flashback from my childhood helps to make the point less abstract. My parents own a funeral home, and because death is always untimely, we couldn't go away on vacation when we were kids. Instead, they bought a shack on a nearby lake so rustic it felt like it was held together by duct tape, prayer, and profanity. Six of us shared one little bathroom. We got water from the lake using a claptrap of a pump that my father would somehow ingeniously MacGyver into life each summer. My sister—the only girl of four—would occupy that bathroom for what seemed like eternities on end, taking showers the lengths of which the world hadn't seen since the time of Cleopatra. So my mother hung a sign outside the bathroom that said "How long a minute is depends on which side of this door you are on." Intended as a joke at the expense of those of us waiting, the sign also expressed something important about the relationship between privilege, duration, temporality, and biological necessity resonant in this study of segregated time. As we shall see, the ability to make others wait is but one way time can be weaponized.

The anecdote illuminates segregated time in another way as well. Only belatedly did I come to learn the Native American history of that lake as being on unceded Mohawk hunting grounds. Indigenous presence had largely been segregated from the public memory that I absorbed growing up. Native American history was supplanted by a version of the past that supposedly only *really* got started around the time of the American Revolution. Perhaps if I had been more aware of the willful erasure of Mohawk histories and Indigenous relationships to that land, I might have questioned segregated memory and segregated time. Perhaps I might have sooner come to ask why it is that, here, there, and elsewhere, those who have lived on the land the longest tend to be least likely to be in positions of power there now. In popular culture Native Americans were racialized as belonging to the past, and I—like many other white kids—learned that Indians were always already destined for extinction. Of course, the supposed inevitability of their vanishing was no accident, but part of a settler colonial project designed to facilitate the extermination and dispossession of Native Americans. Likewise, it is no accident that the very absence of Native histories, themes, and questions only fortifies forms of colonial unknowing that benefit white power. In what follows, I suggest that dynamic is also part of a prevailing temporal order—a way of understanding and experiencing time—that is racialized as well.

As indicated above, I am neither Indigenous nor a person of color. Dealing with segregation in terms of time—as opposed to just space—requires us to deal with whiteness *as race*, and not the absence thereof. One aspect of what I will conceptualize and critique as segregated "white time" is the prerogative to impose a universal understanding of what (capital *T*) Time is, and how it is, and should be, inhabited by Others. All the more reason to be clear from the outset that I make no attempts in that direction. During the course of writing this book, I learned a great deal about the vast differences across experiences and understandings of what is called time. Disappearing into the richness of myriad studies made me appreciate the foolishness of any project that would pretend to advance a "grand theory of time" or *the one thought* inside of which all thinking about time must take place. As I discuss in these pages, that impulse is itself a force of colonial imposition I associate with white time. From another angle, the flux and dynamism of ongoing race-making projects raises a different set of challenges, as do the continuities of white supremacy. With this in mind, the chapters offer entry points into segregated time without the pretense of claiming the universality or comprehensive timelessness the book contests. Simply put, my treatment of what I call white time does not presume that all subjects racially coded as white experience or understand time in the same way across all times. Nor do I think it is the case that one can (or should) essentialize or ontologize something called "Indigenous time," or "Black time," and so on. Rather, I want to contemplate the racial ordering of time in general, and white time and white temporality especially, as normative and normalizing disciplinary forces with the power to influence what allegedly was, is, and ought to be.

Speaking of disciplines, this work emerges from within political theory, but it is resolutely interdisciplinary. My primary focus is not how the field's parochial shortfalls reverberate across its academic echo chambers, though these surface intermittently. To the extent those diagnostic shortcomings radiate politically, I explore them by working across the intersection of race and time. This is particularly salient with respect to where political theory's belated grappling with entanglements of race and empire intersects with more mainstream political problems and silences. This study also departs from many prevailing norms of doing political theory insofar as it is not a work of intellectual history, or a compare-and-contrast situating authors to be reconciled or alienated.[3] Nor does the book take the tack that reading one or more theorists "properly" in the interpretive manner that I (as author) might suggest could resolve perennial philosophical-political questions. Lastly, this is not a work of ideal theory. It wrestles in the muck and mire of nonideal worlds where racial hierarchy exists and persists. I am fluent in the dominant conventions and I continue to learn from, and with, scholars immersed in them. Respectfully, I take a decidedly different path. Mine is a question-driven, exploratory, experimental approach that comes with its own liabilities and limitations.

The book challenges the linearity of time in its form as well as its content. In practice, this means I deliberately move asynchronously between levels of analysis, terrains, authors, and tempos in an effort to bring what the text does performatively closer to the argument.[4] My own time limitations made it impossible to expand the individual chapters into multiple manuscript-length studies. Instead, I lay down a series of markers in order to draw together a constellation of inflection points around the political and theoretical stakes of segregated time. In an effort to achieve a modicum of concision and to concretize what might otherwise remain abstract about time and temporality, my political reference points are largely, if not entirely, drawn from the Americas. That said, as the range of authors from whom I draw sustenance attests, this is not intended to imply some regional centrality of importance or a default template from which to extrapolate or interpolate across time and space. In taking this approach, my intention has always been to be as ecumenical and invitational as possible, to cultivate receptivity, and to seed future inquiry. If the conceptualization of segregated time and white time put forward here proves generative and adaptable beyond the horizons of the book and its author, it will have been worth my time—and hopefully yours. My sincere wish is that it expands the scope of available inquiry by raising issues of segregated time to the level of political questions worthy of ongoing consideration. It may well be the case that political theory is fated to be perpetually out of synch. Political theory's targets, power and politics, are always in motion—so there is no having the last word. This is certainly the case when it comes to issues of race since, as Malcolm X put it, "Racism is like a Cadillac, each year they introduce a new model."[5]

Although the book actively resists a definitional account of "our time," the political urgency and frenetic tenor of the historical context from which the study emerged undoubtedly seeped onto these pages. Professionally, the book was written on a tenure clock that had plenty of contingencies, anxieties, and nonlinear temporal irruptions of its own. Disciplines discipline us, and the harrowing experience of having been among the itinerant labor of the academic precariat is a disciplinary force unto itself. If not for the generous support of so many who encouraged the project, all of it would read like the lyrical equivalent of a hostage video. Or it might not have been written at all. The solidarity of fellow travelers matters deeply to me personally and intellectually. I believe that having a scholarly vocation is quite different from following professional academic requirements in search of rewards and recognition. All of this only underscores my gratitude to those who, despite its attendant risks, have encouraged and supported exploratory scholarship. At Johns Hopkins University, William E. Connolly and Jane Bennett have been indispensable interlocutors, treasured critics, and trusted friends. The exceptional political theory program at Hopkins they have built over decades is truly unique and untimely in the timeliest of ways. Bill generously shared his time—and insights on time—commenting on multiple iterations of my manuscript and essays, while somehow always making time for everything else. Jennifer Culbert has been unfailingly willing to talk me through anything with penetrating insight. Her fierce hospitality and radical receptivity has been a steady source of solidarity. Sam Chambers read my work at all hours and always offered insightful feedback and expert editorial advice—even up against his own deadlines. Lester Spence and I cotaught a graduate seminar on biopolitics and the racial state of exception that left its imprint on this study, and I am grateful for his thoughtful comments on the work. Fortunately for me, Robbie Shilliam joined our department just in time to help me better see what I was up to and productively expand my horizons. Adam Sheingate and Richard Katz supported me and the project during their respective time as department chairs. Much gratitude and respect to all.

I am especially grateful to those brave and generous souls who read and commented on all, or significant parts, of the manuscript. Special thanks to Paul Apostolidis, Lawrie Balfour, Cristina Beltrán, Romand Coles, Laura Grattan, Michael Hanchard, George Shulman, Mark Reinhardt, and Roxanne Euben. Since Lawrie Balfour, Bill Connolly, Rom Coles, Laura Grattan, George Shulman, and Mark Reinhardt read too much of this more than once, it seems only appropriate to thank them twice. Michael Hanchard was not only a key inspiration for this project, he was a generous source of intellectual sustenance and support along the way. I remain deeply grateful.

Peter Euben joyfully discussed and argued with me about much of what appears in these pages, along with a great many other things. Always a steady source of insight and inspiration, I miss him dearly. Rest in peace and rest in power.

My colleagues at Johns Hopkins University within and beyond the department have been wonderfully supportive. Thanks to Bentley Allan, Erin Chung, N. D. B. Connolly, Steven David, Clara Han, Jared Hickman, Nicolas Jabko, Lawrence Jackson, Margaret Keck, Sebastian Schmidt, Stuart Schrader, Danny Scholzman, Christie Thornton, Naveeda Khan, Ali Khan, Renee Marlin-Bennett, John Marshall, Sebastián Mazzuca, Juan Obarrio, Sarah Parkinson, Vesla Weaver, Alexandre (Sasha) White, and Emily Zackin. I have been extremely fortunate to work with a superb group of graduate students with whom I discussed many of these themes in graduate seminars and in relation to their own projects. It is a pleasure to learn with such intelligent and decent people. Thanks to Udbhav Agarwal, Conor Bean, Adam Culvert, Rothin Datta, Stephanie Erev, Sheharyar Imram, David Johnson, Ty Joplin, Jiyoung "Ashley" Kim, Stephanie Saxton, Pyar Seth, Elliott Schwebach, Blaj Skerjaneck, Franziska Strack, Ben Taylor, Tvrtko Vrdoljak, Darko Vinketa, and Tulio Zille. William E. Connolly and I cotaught a terrific graduate seminar entitled *Postcolonial Ecologies and Planetary Temporalities* that remains fertile ground for my thinking. Thanks to all those who participated in that course and my other graduate seminars, especially *Indigenous Political Thought* and *Decolonizing Time and Memory*. Many thanks to Quinn Lester for preparing the index. I am especially grateful for productive discussions with Quinn, Jishnu Guha-Mujamdar, Jacob Kripp, Stephanie Najjar, Jon Masin-Peters, Thomas Mann, and Chris Forster-Smith during their progression from Hopkins graduate students to colleagues. In addition to doing excellent written work, all have enriched my graduate and undergraduate courses with their commitment to integrating teaching and research as key to participating fully in an intellectual community.

Deep gratitude to those who took the time to talk with me about these ideas and offered sustenance of all kinds over the course of the journey: Josh Arneson, Osman Bakan, Lauren Berlant, Jon Bombard, Craig Borowiak, Jon Brendese, Nick Brendese, Tom Carroll, Jill Casey, Meghan Connolly-Haupt, Dipesh Chakrabarty, Glen Sean Coulthard, Michael Dawson, Stefan Dolgert, Rebecca Donnelly, Kennan Ferguson, Rob Flynn, Jim Flynn, Jason Frank, Jill Frank, Andrew Friedman, Jack and Ella Gallagher, Tom and Elizabeth Gallagher, Eddie Glaude Jr., Jeffrey Green, Siba Grovogui, Cynthia Halpern, Bernard Harcourt, Cheryl I. Harris, Gordy Haupt, Alexander Hirsch, Kimberly Hutchings, Greg Jackson, Michael Kane, Brendan Kane, Alisa

Kessel, Claire Jean Kim, Christine Ming-Whey Lee, Matthew J. Lindstrom, Alex Livingston, Nancy S. Love, David Marinaccio, Barak Mendelsohn, Aileen Moreton-Robinson, Jeanne Morefield, Sam Okoth Opondo, Zach Oberfield, Steven Philips, Peter Raponi, Mark Rifkin, Neil Roberts, Howard Rosenfield, Andrew Schaap, Joel Schlosser, Audra Simpson, Nikhil Pal Singh, Jon "Freedom" Snyder, Gus Stadler, Jill Stauffer, and Alexander Weheliye.

My editor at Oxford University Press, Angela Chnapko, went above and beyond to see this book through to publication during ridiculous times. She is truly excellent, and her sterling reputation is well deserved. Sincere thanks to the Press and the anonymous reviewers at Oxford. Heartfelt gratitude to Katie Patricia Boone for helping to brighten the dark times that produced this work, and for keeping alive the possibility of other times. As always, infinite thanks to my parents, Philip and Gerry Brendese for being present the whole time with sustaining affirmation, support, and encouragement. Having been born to such wonderful people is an unearned blessing.

Portions of the book appeared elsewhere in earlier forms, but none have been merely reprinted. Sections of Chapter 3, "Killing Time," appeared as "Borderline Epidemics: Latino Immigration and Racial Biopolitics," *PGI: Politics, Groups and Identities* 2, no. 2 (June 2014): 168–187, and in "Double Crossed by the Crossing: On the Spaciotemporal Borders of Immigration," *Contemporary Political Theory* 12, no. 3 (August 2013): 230–241. Sections of Chapter 2, "Doing Time" and the first interlude appeared in earlier forms in "Black Noise in White Time: Segregated Temporality and Mass Incarceration," in *Radical Future Pasts: Untimely Political Theory*, ed. Romand Coles, Mark Reinhardt, and George Shulman (Lexington: University Press of Kentucky, 2014), 81–111. Gratitude is extended to the respective publishers for permission to adapt the material here.

Introduction

Whose Time Is It?

When Martin Luther King Jr. argued on behalf of civil rights, he was told that he was "too soon." Today when activists demand reparations for slavery, they are told they are "too late."[1] What time is it? Or is the appropriate question *whose* time is it? Both queries point to the theme of this study: the phenomenon of segregated time. Segregated time refers to how conceptions of time diverge across peoples, how a range of political subjects are designated as occupants of different time zones, and how these divergent temporal spheres are mutually implicated. Relatedly, segregated temporality connotes the multiple *experiences* of time that shape human subjectivities and dispositions. A closer look at these entwinements reveals how various strategies of racialized political power are imbued in segregated time and temporality. This book explores the role of segregated time in historically entrenched racial inequalities and ongoing race-making projects. As Michael Hanchard has argued, racial inequalities are frequently experienced as impositions on human time.[2] Among the most obvious is the power to define progress and the prerogative to tell others to wait for goods, services, rights, and standing—all of which have long been figured along racial lines. Importantly, resistance to incursions on human time has likewise been expressed in a temporal register; hence Martin Luther King Jr.'s sustained attention to time in *Why We Can't Wait* and "Negroes Are Not Moving Too Fast."[3]

In King's famous "Letter from Birmingham City Jail," he declared that the greatest threats to racial equality were not rabid segregationists, but white moderates who affirm a commitment to equality in theory, but not in practice. At least not yet. The outright racist is easily identified, but the white moderate clergyman who "paternalistically feels he can set the timetable for another man's freedom" is really a covert enemy disguised as a friend.[4] Storming against strategies of "temporizing," King gave full voice to the political stakes, declaring that "justice too long delayed is justice denied" and the time for justice "is always now."[5] Temporizing tactics are especially insidious

Segregated Time. P.J. Brendese, Oxford University Press. © Oxford University Press 2023.
DOI: 10.1093/oso/9780197535745.003.0001

because of their seductive appeal to self-aggrandizing "good people" who deploy the "yes, but not yet" to inoculate themselves against any challenge to their status as powerful and virtuous. Cloaking themselves in the veneer of self-righteous religiosity, white moderates respond to the suffering of African Americans with "appalling silence and indifference." They criticize the struggle for racial justice as "untimely,"[6] insisting that Black folks simply need to "wait on time."[7] By identifying the role of time as a vector of white power, King discloses key insufficiencies of liberalism while identifying political and theoretical tensions that provide an entry point to this study. Arguing that the forces of evil have used time more effectively than those working on behalf of good, he addresses two corresponding logics of power that arrive cloaked in the moral veneer of rehabilitation and uplift: white paternalism and temporizing universalism.

The fundamental structure of a paternal relationship is one in which the subordinate, immature party is understood to be at an inferior stage of development. The people or nations occupying the infantile position are regarded as in need of mature oversight to help them progress and catch up, in time. Of course, the imperative to provide help, nurture growth, and promote progress has long been understood to confer a moral obligation on the part of an adult benefactor, à la "White Man's Burden." Long before Kipling's poem, however, the signatories of the Mayflower Compact drew up their coat of arms in England depicting an American Indian with the words "Come over and help us," a sentiment prefigured by Spanish colonials before them.[8] The paternal rhetoric of salvation, rehabilitation, and uplift is readily recognizable in the logic of empire, enslavement, and missionary conquest. Indeed, civilizational-developmental discourses continue to be invoked to justify military invasion to this day.[9] Those on the receiving end of paternalist rhetoric have frequently been stigmatized as anachronistic; beings less evolved, behind the times, coded as primitive, savage, pagan, idle time-wasters, irredeemably violent, irrational/unreasonable, sexually incontinent, and so forth. Adopting the guise of assisting others in need of advancement, strategies of white paternalism attempt to conceal how time is weaponized to sustain an unequal, highly disciplinary power relationship between the supposedly advanced benefactors and their immature dependent-beneficiaries. As a paternalist tactic of Anglo-liberalism, temporizing universalism promises that liberal goods like equality, freedom, private property, and religious tolerance will be handed down by power to everyone in due time. *Just not yet.*[10]

On the ground, liberalism's imposed wait time perpetuates a segregated temporality whereby brutally illiberal practices can exist simultaneously alongside the most generous affirmations of liberal ideals. Through a circuitous temporal sleight of hand, institutions that belong "essentially to the past" can legitimate and fortify themselves in the present on the basis of "future oriented reform."[11] Those told that their political dreams must be deferred are relegated to a suspended, in-between time: caught between the original injuries of the past and the yet-unrealized promises of democracy to come. The suffering and death that happens in the interval—the multiple ways of being cast "out of time" this book takes up—underscore the urgency of exploring time as a vector of political power. As anthropologist Johannes Fabian writes, "Time is a carrier of significance, a form through which we define the content of relations between Self and Other."[12] Temporally inflected strategies have continuities and variations across time and space, yet still consign populations to what historian Dipesh Chakrabarty terms "the waiting room" of history.[13] The imposed duration of white colonialism is potent enough to seep into one's identity, prompting psychiatrist-turned-revolutionary Frantz Fanon's self-description, "I am one who waits."[14]

I begin with imposed waiting and postponement because both are recognizably relevant modalities of power by which segregated time (re)produces temporal outcasts in racialized ways. (After all, the purpose of an introduction is to suggest why the themes taken up in the book might be worth the reader's time.) The question of who has the prerogative to tell whom to wait for goods and services dramatizes the impositional structure of segregated time. To the limited extent that race and time *are* considered in the same frame of scholarly analysis, a focus on the indefinite deferral of justice is eminently understandable. Typically segregated from time and memory, however, is how the commitment to liberal justice (so frequently deferred) has long participated in a modern race-making projects operating with a logic of missionary generosity.[15] Influential colonial clerics and their followers promised to utilize nonwhite peoples as raw material available to be infused with Anglo-European notions of God, rationality, sovereignty, civilization, and humanity itself.[16] As precursors of the white moderate clergy King famously called out, their civilizational rationale is captured in the phrase "Kill the Indian, save the man," then widely believed a progressive counterpoint to the view that "the only good Indian is a dead Indian."[17] What is often concealed is how the liberal "not yet" is elemental to the legacy of cultural genocide that has itself historically been pitched as a benevolent, Christian alternative to the nevermore of *outright* genocide. All too frequently, "wait" is what temporizing says, while genocide is what it does.

The work of instructing others in how to "catch up" reflects an assimilationist politics laden with a compulsory absorption into a racial time signature. To paraphrase Fanon, this is a temporal force of whiteness as destiny (BSWM, 10). The ideas that (a) whiteness is fated and (b) becoming white is an inherently good thing were once expressed to me by a former colleague who (without a hint of irony) optimistically mused that "in time, everyone becomes white." To be sure, who counts as white has changed and is changing still. That whiteness is associated with power, however, remains an enduring feature of contemporary political times. The endurance of white supremacy compels this study's exploration into, and beyond, durational wait time as a marker of racialized inequalities of power. Once we pose the question of whose interests have been, and continue to be, served by the prevailing order of time, the topic of race becomes virtually impossible to avoid. All the more reason for us to investigate the political justifications governing temporal theft, ownership, and the redistribution of time—along with practices of excommunication from the prevailing temporal order. At the same time, I shall be especially concerned with the normalized, taken-for-granted rhythms and flows that allow impositions on others' time to proceed without justification in the first place.[18]

This brings us back to the idea of whiteness as destiny. An obvious question left unresolved by Anglo-liberalism is what happens with those for whom whiteness (variously conceived) is not phenotypically possible, economically tenable, or normatively desirable. When the predominant political order has conflated equality with sameness—to the point that it cannot deal with differences it has failed to wholly annihilate, or convert into identity, or turn into grateful subordinates, over time—what happens next? One possible answer is legible in the ongoing political nightmare of inequality and inequity. People of color are subject to being "out of time" in multiple senses of the phrase. Those perceived as anachronistic, or outside of Time, are frequently subjected to incursions upon their time that shorten and expropriate their lives to the point of having no time left.[19] Indeed, one of the most vulgar expressions of segregated time is how the extended lifetimes of racially dominant populations are parasitic on the foreshortened lives of racial others. Hence Ruth Wilson Gilmore's influential definition of racism as "state-sanctioned and/or extralegal production and exploitation of group differentiated vulnerability to premature death."[20]

Under the present order of time, residual differences are managed through a range of punitive practices taken up in these pages, including (but not limited to) racialized criminalization, the racial stigma of indebtedness, institutionalized precarity, and compulsory life on borrowed time. Part of the legacy of white supremacy is how racial others are recursively apprehended as asynchronous temporal outsiders, violating the chronology of present time and representing a threat to future time—thus vulnerable to discipline, dispossession, and extermination, fast and slow.[21]

Not So Fast

The preceding themes are also connected by a dynamic I call the *race of segregated time*, with the triple entendre of the word "race" registering race as acceleration, race as competition (a zero-sum biopolitical contest of human disposability), and race as a fluid production of ascriptive identities separating temporal insiders from outcasts. Part of my intention is to complicate the notion of ours as a shared epoch unified by a temporality of acceleration. To the extent that time figures in contemporary political analyses, temporality tends to be presented as a unidirectional force of acceleration that is all-encompassing, aggregating, and cuts across difference in a globalizing age.[22] The compression of space and time wrought by high-speed transportation, the innovations of clock time, and a raft of technological, cybernetic innovations contribute to the increasingly frenzied pace of contemporary life.[23] If one adds to that the contagious sense of temporal shortage in the face of the Great Acceleration of climate change, the focus on the consolidating elements of contemporary time might seem almost intuitive. Yet the harms of transnational legacies of (not-so-post-) colonialism and chattel slavery and the competition of racial capitalism are differentially distributed.

If we pause to consider the chronology of those first to be impacted by ecological disaster, one confronts a perversion of the biblical injunction that "the last shall be first." People last to get goods services and standing are among the first to be subsumed by the rising tides of economic crisis and ecocide. In matters of apocalypse, it seems the future is here. "It's just not evenly distributed yet."[24] The vulnerability of those positioned in the low-lying areas of economic hierarchies and geographies often coded as the "Global South" suggest a relation between climate accelerators and the acceleration of human expendability. Accordingly, theorists of postcolonial ecology have recently begun to speak of the displacement of Indigenous peoples by climate change as producing temporal refugees.[25] These are but some of the many iterations of race that challenge shared notions and experiences of "our" time under investigation in these pages.

Imperial histories are most often told in relation to space—not time.[26] The practice coincides with a popular tendency to think of racial segregation spatially and not temporally. As I intend to elucidate, both are at stake. Take the rather obvious, yet elemental, historical truth that dispossessing people of their land—and thus their means of subsistence—is a powerful compulsion to sell one's labor in the form of time. Deeper still, European orientations to time were instrumental as a civilizational distinction that set New World settlers apart from Indigenous peoples synched with cosmological forces, creation myths, and the rhythms of nonhuman nature. Native Americans were so closely associated with nature that early colonists called them the "naturals." In Australia, Aboriginal peoples were officially categorized as fauna until as recently as 1967.[27] Suffice it to say the capacity to keep to biologically racist-evolutionary, eschatological, and clock time has long been viewed as a signifier of the uniquely *human* ability to detach from the natural world and assert dominion over nature and bodies associated with it. The adherence to clock time as quantifiable, and available to be productively saved or expended, was likewise employed to distinguish settlers from Indigenous others viewed as idlers given to wasting time. This made them available to be wasted by empire, in the transitive sense of wasting as rendering disposable. To settlers, Native peoples are apprehended as those who get in the way of progress "just by staying home."[28] And it would be a gross understatement to say that the command of time was important to effectuating the horrors of chattel slavery.[29] Slavery's theft of time meant that enslaved people's resistance was figured in temporal terms; through work slowdowns, sabotage, and stoppages—up to, and including, the "general strike" W.E.B. Du Bois theorized in *Black Reconstruction* as the transfer of labor away from the Southern planters to Union forces.[30]

As we shall see, time and temporality are important ingredients to race-making as processual, fluid, and iterative. Among many imperial Europeans, the association of African subjects with rhythm made them uniquely suited for labor and distinguished them from other racial subjects like First Nations, destined for extinction.[31] Yet the racist connotations of "Black time" as slow, tardy, and retarded suggests that Afro-diasporic peoples have also been denigrated as lazy and wasting time. Analytically, this would make people of

African descent rather poor candidates for whites seeking to save their own time (and lives) by exploiting Black labor. From there, King's repeated insistence that "Negroes are not moving too fast" would seem bizarre. How is it that populations stigmatized as lazy, idling, time squanderers can alternately be accused of moving too quickly? Further, if one takes the view that a population is lesser evolved and perpetually behind the times, then the risk of being outpaced—or outraced—seems unfathomable. It seems silly that Black people supposedly incapable of progress would have to be targeted as moving too fast and forcibly kept out of the dominant flows of power and privilege. The point of this work is not, however, to catalog performative contradictions and the faulty reasoning of racist thinking—as if there were any other kind.

I want to resist the tendency to stall at the level of enumerating the many logical contradictions of racism, as if the worst thing racists were complicit in is being bad thinkers.[32] To proceed along those lines would ignore the deadly impact of what race *does*, namely the subject before us now: the coproduction of race and segregated time. Time and again, race has proven a steady site of willful unknowing not easily aligned with the analytic standards of Enlightenment reason and empirical evidence.[33] Contemplating race at any length means confronting terrifyingly maddening habits of disavowal; that is, the ways that people can both know and not know things at the same time.[34] Most teachers, myself included, are humbled by James Baldwin's observation that many whites know better than to think that they are superior to people of color, "but as you will discover, people find it very difficult to act on what they know."[35] It is not that empirical evidence of nonwhite humanity has been absent—far from it. Rather, in the context of white temporality, seeing is not believing when it comes to race matters—a point to which I return in the later section on segregated memory and segregated time. For the sake of conceptual clarity, some brief remarks are in order.

For purposes of this study, race and time are treated as mutually implicated in ways that are meaningful and even deadly. Both are political artifacts produced by human construction, which is to say that they are produced by power.[36] With respect to race, a growing body of scholarship attests that modernity has been figured in highly racialized terms.[37] Theories of "multiple modernities," "Afro-modernity," and what anthropologist Johannes Fabian has influentially criticized as a denial of coevalness, invite this investigation into the function of segregated time and its logics of power.[38] For starters, racially subordinate groups are disproportionately vulnerable to what Foucault calls the "regularization" of mass death.[39] In the chapters to come, this routinization spans demise by slow attrition, exploitation, and long-term wasting, as well as the more rapid-fire-death dealing Achille Mbembe terms "necropolitics." Foucauldian biopolitics is a structure where the line between life and death coincides with those falling within, or outside, the human race. Experiences and concepts of race are hardly exhausted by that distinction, but my own view is that the importance of the human—along with its constitutive boundaries, virtual approximations, and others—remains salient.[40] What counts as human life is meaningless without the nonhuman difference that gives the term its integrity and coherence. The same is true of progress and backwardness, also racialized categories.

From here we can see why the term "racial" is so frequently conjoined to "inequality," and why it is virtually impossible to speak of race without invoking power relations. Arguments that seek to depoliticize race are in reality advancing a political strategy.[41] When contemporary audiences hear the word "race" and think of racial others (and not the dominant whites who function as a referent against which those subordinate identities are defined), they call to mind people who have historically been denied the status of being fully human. As Didier Fassin puts it, "The 'idea of race' can also be seen as a reduction of the social to the biological, but in an inverse sense. It challenges the notion of a common humanity by differentiating among people at the deepest levels of their being, looking for the marks of origins."[42] From this vantage we can see at least some of the reasons how the repeated public dehumanization of nonwhites is ignored by many privileged, received as an emergent crisis-level event in other quarters, and experienced as everyday feature an ongoing multigenerational racial nightmare by others.[43] The disparate range of reactions points to the historical disavowal of past precedent, and how segregated memory is imbricated in segregated time, the subject to which we now turn.

Race: From Segregated Memory to Segregated Time

Time is a carrier of memory, which is to say that memories happen in and through time and they are mutually implicated—but each is not reducible to the other. Memory plays a role in shaping our experiences of time, perceptions of duration, and felt expectations of time's limitations and potentialities. Memory influences our *sense of time*, what philosophers refer to as temporality. But these mnemonic-temporal sensations often diverge strongly across peoples and even brush against prevailing political modes of timekeeping. As the Martiniquan philosopher-poet Édouard Glissant wrote, "Memory in our works is not a calendar memory; our experience of time does not keep company with the rhythms of month and year alone."[44] The fact that Glissant has to alert readers to the existence of what I am calling segregated temporalities suggests a presumption that people experience memory and time the same way, all the time. Elizabeth Freeman speaks to how institutional memory (broadly conceived) shapes temporality, writing: "Temporality is a mode of implementation through which institutional forces come to seem like somatic facts."[45] Under conditions of segregated time, alternate time zones and divergent experiences of time are taken for granted to the point that they come to seem like somatic facts. An effect *and* affect is heightened danger of political invisibility, marginality, forced disappearance, and discipline of asynchronous populations.[46] My view is that the segregation of memory is among the most frequently employed tools of white supremacy employed to effectuate segregated time.

In *The Power of Memory in Democratic Politics* I explored how power is implicated in mnemonic practices that marginalize people politically.[47] I do not reprise the book here, but some abbreviated remarks help elucidate the conceptual correspondences and tensions between segregated memory and time, why time is meaningful to issues of race, and the contributions of the present study. Segregated memory refers to how modes of relating to the past diverge across populations. Disappearing memories of colonial dispossession, slavery, and Jim Crow, for example, allow contemporary inequalities to remain encrypted in white innocence. Racial inequalities can then be passed off as the outcome of a failure to work hard or make good choices. This is the line of argumentation from political entrepreneurs who speak in the vernacular of cultural (as opposed to biological) racism. Additional strategies of power associated with segregated memory include historical bracketing, which admits that atrocities such as slavery, genocide, and colonialism happen*ed*—with the emphasis on the past tense—with the effect of ignoring the continuities between past and present injustices. The presumption of a discrete divide between past, present, and future persists as a culturally imbued habit of thought. It is also mnemonic segregation that perpetuates a view of linear time in which power is not innocent.

For instance, think of how the emergence of liberal ideals of freedom, equality, and religious tolerance is frequently taught independent of the explosion of slavery, genocide, and prohibition of Indigenous religions that were contemporaneous with liberalism's origins and descent.[48] Carving a tripartite division between past, present, and future can serve quite different political ends. After the Holocaust, Chancellor Konrad Adenauer declared Germany a *tabula rasa* (a "blank slate") to much controversy, as his invocation of amnesiac amnesty represented an *erased* slate.[49] Today, some object to the timestamp of the "post" in postcolonialism to ask: if ours is a time beyond, or after, colonialism, where did it go? When, approximately, did colonialism disappear?[50] And if North American colonial genocide can disappear so quickly, why was its extermination of Native peoples so inspirational to the Nazis as a model for their own racial cleansing?[51] To the extent the listed issues are gathered under the heading of "transitional justice," a question that follows is *from* and *to* what, precisely, are we transitioning? Is the time of slavery and colonialism over? How so?

Strategies of bracketing history and treating evil as temporary aberrations are different from the deployment of myth-historical fantasies that insist, for example, that chattel slavery was benevolent, or that slavery was not the cause of the Civil War. When lies are repeated often enough to become truth, as Goebbels would have it, over time the historical erasure effectuated by that repetition enacts a colonization of memory and temporality. This is what is at stake politically in ongoing state-sponsored prohibitions against teaching so-called critical race theory in schools. The erasure of violent histories from school curricula is a form of epistemic colonialism intended to (re)produce political subjects innocent of white supremacy and who therefore will not challenge its workings.[52]

For sure, many prefer to imagine that "all men are created equal" really included everyone from the outset and the nation originated from a virgin birth of liberal consent among equals. A somewhat different path of willful racial amnesia admits to the nation's founding imperfections, but holds the story of the United States afterward is that of its collective attempt to "catch up" to the unproblematic and sterling ideals laid down by its sanctified founders.[53] Notions that Americans are trying to "catch up to the past" point toward more nuanced forms of segregated memory calling for a multidimensional mnemonic approach. For starters, this means making distinctions between the kind of forgetting that happens by way of a poor memory and forgetting as a willful disavowal of what one knows, at least on some level, but nevertheless chooses not to acknowledge.

For instance, many know that slavery and Indigenous genocide happened but refuse to countenance the possibility that the present condition of inequality rests upon those institutions. At the level of epistemology, compulsive disavowal is implicated in racialized forms of unknowing. In terms of street-level politics where so much white supremacy is lived and experienced, this means that corrective information and better history classes alone are no panacea. It is here where the discourse of affect becomes especially important, as histories are not merely the stuff of narrative memory or historiography. To paraphrase Frantz Fanon, the past is *epidermalized* (BSWM, 11). That is, in addition to narrative memory, we possess—and are possessed by—infrasensory memories that course through our tacit presumptions, our habituated practices of aversion and attraction, our emotional registers, and even the tones of voice we employ when addressing different audiences. The ongoing segregation of space and time points to what Fanon theorized as the psychoaffective attachments of colonialism, as I shall discuss in relation to white temporalities. From the insights of Fanon and others, it follows that the work of desegregating memory also entails overcoming embodied habits of ignoring and avoiding spaces to cultivate practices of relationality by pressing the flesh with different people. This enjoins a politics of making time by using time we do not "have" in any familiar sense of sovereign ownership of territory. To approach these depths, however, it is useful to first recount some aspects the liberal colonial temporal orders to which those attachments refer.

Selective amnesia is built into modern social contract theory. Hobbes argued that people should accommodate themselves to the whole, as bricks do to a wall, by shearing off the rough edges of diversity—chiseling away at the memories that are guardians of difference.[54] The "just another brick in the wall" imagery suggests a logical equivalence between sameness and contemporaneity, while also anticipating the conflation of equality with sameness commonplace in liberal politics. Racial amnesia is especially problematic with respect to liberalism's focus on choice. A hallmark of cultural racism is the contention that the relative inequities among populations are due to the poor life decisions of people of color.[55] Free choice without the option to do otherwise is neither free nor choice. Yet a fundamental aspect of the human condition is being born into a condition of radical choicelessness. We choose approximately none of the conditions of our birth—not how we are embodied, what our physical or intellectual attributes will be, nor the where, when, how, why, or to whom we will be born. Martin Heidegger refers to this as the existential "thrown-ness" of the human condition.[56] We are thrown into this life under conditions not of our own making, to make of them what we will. Being thrown into time is what all have in common.[57] Liberalism's emphasis on choice seems rather strange given that the range of options available to differently situated (or differently "thrown") peoples is so radically divergent.[58]

If we refuse to acknowledge the reality that we all show up in spaces and times without anyone asking our consent beforehand, then the fact of our being thrown into this or that spacetime takes on both theoretical and political relevance.[59] Acknowledging thrown-ness as fundamental to the human experience of time does not necessarily entail a deterministic view that evacuates *any* agency or capacity for choice. A different way of inhabiting time might avow that we are not thrown into time the way a potter uses clay to throw a pot. People make choices, but they do not make them under conditions of their own choosing, as Tommie Shelby has cogently argued with respect to criminal justice in the ghetto.[60]

For his part, John Locke's emphasis on a rights-bearing, consenting individual takes priority over deep collective memory or a strong notion of collective debt obligation.[61] By tracing the selective memory of social contract theory through its contemporary iterations, where justice is typically treated as rights-based, distributive, or procedural, the reciprocity of the social contract frequently figured justice in present-centered ways.[62] This presentism undercuts from the start the possibility of shared liability, reparations for past wrongs, future-oriented environmental politics extending beyond one's individual lifetime, and broader notions of intergenerational justice between current and future generations. For instance, consider the radically divergent temporal horizons of political decision-making separating the present-centered calculus of Anglo-liberal settler colonialism in contrast to the Mohawk imperative to weigh the impact across fourteen generations—seven prior and seven to come.

In 1990, the Canadian government and the Mohawk had a significant land dispute over the expansion of a golf course near the city of Oka, Quebec. The Mohawk erected a barricade in protest, and the disruption to traffic and everyday rhythms and flows heightened tensions. According to John Paul Lederach, a peacemaker called upon to mediate the conflict, the negotiations with the Canadian government collapsed within a week as a result of competing notions of time.[63] For the government, the only operative question was when and how the Mohawk barricade would come down in the coming days. The Mohawk orientation to the land rested on a notion of justice that spanned transgenerational time. The past and future were alive and at issue in the Mohawk present, such that what that present moment "was" for each party was so vastly different as to entail a political conflagration of segregated time and segregated space.[64] As the Mohawk political anthropologist Audra Simpson puts it, "concepts have teeth, and teeth that bite through time."[65]

The fact that so many of these issues are dramatized by racial politics spurs this study's treatment of time as a vehicle of power imbued by contractarian forgetting, if not reducible to it. For instance, acknowledging multiple, often conflicting temporalities which are neither wholly linear nor circular means that nineteenth-century biological racism did not entirely replace the logic of social contract theory. Nor did biological racism disappear into cultural (or ethical) racism, as some presumed in the onset of the twenty-first century. That fact that so many were surprised by the recent Trump-era transnational uptick in explicit white nationalisms evinces a failure to grapple with the haunting, spectral presence of these supposedly "prior" logics. To say something is spectral is to suggest that it is, in important ways, both present and absent—and therefore irreducible to what philosophers call the metaphysics of presence.[66] Bearing that in mind, *Segregated Time* is prompted by the need to consider what is often spectral in political theory and mainstream politics. A guiding premise of the book is that a commitment to pluralism entails an agonistic relationship to difference that is receptive not just to multiple identities, but also to multiple relationships to time. Toward that end, it seems incumbent upon us to consider noxious identities in need of abolition in terms of their temporal orders—what I shall theorize as *white time* and *white temporality*.

Structure of the Book

To gain clarity on these issues and their implications, the book's chapters elucidate how time functions as a vector of political power, affect, and resistance. In Chapter 1, "White Time: The Race of Segregated Time," I examine the pull toward a unifying notion of time in theory and practice in terms of its colonial legacy and the challenges posed by its remainders. The projected universality of time as objectively neutral and always given is coincident with the ways that colonial whiteness and masculinity have been so frequently invoked as universal, supposedly neutral, referents employed to standardize what counts as human at any given time. By these metrics all others are fated to be perpetually out of synch—with deadly consequences. The acquisitive impulse and impositional desire characteristic of white colonial temporalities are messianic in their wish to overdetermine the future through the ordered linearity of the imposed time.[67] Politically, the drive toward temporal *orthodoxy* (literally: straight thinking) sets in motion a decimation of autochthonous rhythms and queer time-signatures, to be replaced with what Walter Benjamin criticized as the empty, homogenous time of modern progress.[68] In the meantime, asynchronous others are to be forcefully kept in line, modulated disciplinarily, or murderously cast out of time altogether. This is a key part of the violence that makes every document of civilization simultaneously a document of barbarism.

I put forward a theoretical account of the interlocution of racial stigma as colluding with imperial expansion through a critical encounter with white subjectivity's investment in possessing space *and* time.[69] To advance a spatiotemporal account beyond racialized topographies alone, I introduce a theory of white time abetted by law and policed by the historically entrenched norms of white supremacy. Drawing from critical race theorist Cheryl I. Harris's influential concept of whiteness as property and Aboriginal anthropologist Aileen Moreton-Robinson's *The White Possessive*, I consider white temporality as a mode of *apprehension*, in the multiple senses connoting perception, objectification, arrest, and anxiety. In short, the time of whiteness is a possessive tense—and a highly imperfect one at that.

I dilate on the temporal dimensions of expectation of future use as inherent in the property value of whiteness. In concert with Du Bois's analysis of whiteness as projected ownership of the earth in perpetuity, white temporality conveys the affective sense of entitlement where time, place, and people are available for the taking. As we shall see, the desire for temporal dominion quickly intersects with the will to exert control over the existing plurality of human differences. In theory, liberalism's unit of analysis is the individual, but whom is apprehended as an individual is temporally inflected and racialized. As Nell Irvin Painter observes, "Whiteness studies hold [the] white race, ordinarily invisible in the black/white dichotomy, up to the light. In them it appears as social, not biological, a powerful social construct letting whites think of themselves first and foremost as individuals."[70] Denial of individuality to people of color is particularly salient in punitive orientations to racial pluralism and pluralization.

In Chapter 2, "Doing Time: Carceral Temporality," I examine carcerality in the United States as a condition of racialized temporal theft and entrapment of those whose time and space are subject to arrest. The chapter considers how segregated carceral temporalities extend well beyond prison spaces and time served. Contemporary mass incarceration is frequently understood to be a reactionary response to people of color moving "too fast" and igniting racial blowback. Complicating and appending such accounts, the chapter explores how race functions as a forward-looking predictive technology, while also registering innovative race-making projects emerging from nonlinear forms of temporal arrest and capture. The weaponization of time and criminalization of racial difference are co-implicated in the regeneration of segregated time, where children of color are apprehended (literally and figuratively) as sites of future dangerousness. The insularity, myopia, and deafness of white temporality spur my reflections on forms of "white noise" and affective economies of pleasure and cruelty that fortify segregated time. The last section of the chapter situates the analysis of carceral temporality in the context of debates over prison abolition by avowing the haunting copresence of slavery *and* colonial dispossession that conjoins the segregated time of prison system to racial capitalism and imperial futurity. There I initiate the kind of time-sensitive theoretical promiscuity the foregoing analysis enjoins by staging an encounter between decolonial theory, Michel Foucault, and Black Panther revolutionary George Jackson.

A brief interlude offers a critical excursion into the work of Jacques Rancière. There I make a case for a temporally attuned "redistribution of the sensible" that registers what he calls the "part that has no part" in terms of the part that has no time.[71] Contemporary capital flows and power relations serve to segregate temporalities to the point that many of the Latinx workers who produce the adornments that typify twenty-first-century progress are often forced to endure nineteenth-century living and working conditions. With this in mind, in Chapter 3, "Killing Time: Imminent Immigrants and the Temporal Borders of Racial Biopolitics," I take up the temporal, as opposed to merely spatial, borders of Latinx immigration and detention, as well as evolving forms of punishment, attrition, and modes of longer-term wasting, such as the indefinite exploitation of temporary labor. Specifically, I explore how race and temporality underlie the discourse of how (im) migrants and refugees should be managed politically through an engagement with Foucauldian discipline and biopolitics.

On the one hand, the historical technique of casting racial/ethnic others in terms of a viral epidemic infestation that must be identified, documented, quarantined, arrested, and even exterminated resonates with what Foucault referred to as the "plague dream." Immigrant suffering, largely normalized, racialized, and concealed from public view, demonstrates the vulnerability and disposability of particular populations that, in his later work on biopolitics, Foucault theorized as *endemic*. In a cross-temporal examination of the relays between that which is *endemic* and *epidemic* we see how the linearity, stability, and reproducibility of white time are reasserted by leveraging the expendable, abbreviated lives of those who fall below the threshold of the human race. Seen through an aperture of race and time—ostensibly opposed political ideologies toward immigration on the left and right betray dangerously corresponding logics. It is a chronobiopolitical alignment that amounts to an unholy alliance around the disposability of immigrant lives and the perpetuation of segregated time.[72] So long as people across the ideological spectrum agree on immigrant expendability to smooth out the uncertainties of white temporality, it really is just a matter of time.[73]

Chapter 4, "Borrowed Time: Life and Debt on Subprime Time," asks how it is that those from whom so much has historically been taken are nevertheless figured as indebted to their oppressors. To do so, I theorize racial stigma as a condition in which one is apprehended as always-already indebted, such as owing a debt to society as criminally deviant, indebted for the "given time" of liberal freedom, and figured as a site of extraction to be "saved" and held in reserve for a later time. I consider debt as a historically entrenched apparatus of capture that redistributes human time and compels racial others to live on borrowed time, segregated from generative, future-looking temporal flows that (in whiter timescapes) afford credit for good behavior and allow one to begin anew. With race and debt as entwined vehicles of neocolonial and Afro-diasporic biopolitics, the politics of debt becomes a core feature of contemporary racialization, dispossession, and epistemology. Yet these elements are often absent from influential contemporary analyses of debt crises. The chapter explores how white time fortifies white supremacy by stigmatizing racial others as time-wasting, uncreditworthy debtors for whom payback comes with the expectation that one expresses servile gratitude for one's own exploitation. Situating politics of debt as a core component of racialization and racial epistemologies invites us to theorize the other side of racial sigma as a mark of indebtedness: namely, whiteness as a form of credit.

Despite the landmark contributions of scholars such as W.E.B. Du Bois and Cedric Robinson, there exists a strong tendency to read the history of capitalism apart from the legacies of colonialism and chattel slavery. A critical encounter with the (supposedly neutral) time value of money reveals colonial financial instruments that were explicitly raced from their inception, but do not appear as such. I consider how mortgages were engineered as a tool to expropriate Indigenous lands in colonial America through foreclosure, and how the liquidity of foreclosure meant that Native land could be securitized and serve as a form of currency available to be alienated like chattel. The inherently predatory, racialized origin of the American mortgage casts the recent foreclosure crisis in new light whereby, in 2009 alone, African American households lost *all* the wealth accumulated since the civil rights movement.[74] More broadly, the concatenation of segregated memory and segregated time with respect to racial capitalism and debt speaks to the disavowal of climate debt, as if the liabilities and assets generated from global warming were equally shared.

Several of the figures in the book display a strange quality as racialized subjects imbued with the power of time travel in white imaginaries. The second interlude is an abbreviated exploration of white apprehension of racial others as vehicles for traversing temporal boundaries. Frederick Jackson Turner's frontier thesis held that settler encounters with Indigenous peoples allowed them to go back in time in order to move forward and form a new (and newly white) American race. In the United States, immigrants are often cast as agents of regressive devolution threatening the polity. Other times, they are (somewhat paradoxically) invested with power to take the country back to its founding though laudable qualities of hard work and conservative religious praxis. Constant throughout is the fixation on racial others as instruments of time travel, betraying psychoaffective attachments endemic to white time. I investigate this curious phenomenon by drawing inspiration from the speculative Afrofuturist fiction of Octavia Butler's *Kindred*. The novel's protagonist, Dana, is an African American female whose touch has the power to transcend linear time and whose body is a vehicle of time travel. Thinking with Butler offers critical perspective on how the trope of racial others as instruments of time travel recurs as a potent fiction in real-life white temporalities.

Chapter 5, "End Times: The Segregated Apocalypse Now," refers to a split temporality where political realists in the center worry about the apocalyptic powers of nuclear warfare, left environmentalists tremble at the global extinction of ecocide, and right-wing racial chauvinists regard threats to white supremacy in world-ending terms. Today, Baldwin's "The Fire Next Time" takes on an intensely prophetic significance, as the *burning house* is the planet, the *fire* is atmospheric, and the *time* is now. I explore how the conflagration of the desire for white temporal sovereignty combined with the production of so-called white trash functions as a politically meaningful accelerant of racial resentment and climate disavowal in segregated time in the United States. The chapter makes an opening move to situate the racial biopolitics of disposability in the context of potentially imminent climate apocalypse.

Amid transnational right-wing, white populist desires to turn back the clock, and a growing apprehension that the credit value of whiteness is under siege, I examine the threat of white disposability under the pejorative "white trash" as a fluid interlocution of race-making and waste-making. The politics of white precarity amid widening inequalities dramatizes racial dynamism as processual and in-the-making, with whiteness a salient site of ongoing racial formation. The chapter sketches the production of anachronistic, liminal whiteness and expendability of the pallid poor as a distinct breed in colonial times, through modern and contemporary productions of white backwardness in US politics, from Locke's "Leet-men" to early agrarian "clay-eaters," to "inbred" country bumpkins, and paleo-conservative "cavemen," all the way to the so-called Trump-tards of today. White attachments to racial status facilitate a preference for policies that actually shorten the lifetimes of the white underclass—a phenomenon physician Jonathan Metzl calls *Dying of Whiteness*.

Is the appropriate response to segregated time a politics and theory oriented toward an integrated time? In the epilogue, I suggest otherwise. Given that a possessive investment in owning time is a key aspect of white temporality, I am skeptical of temporal integration into a shared present as a panacea—particularly when it is the presumed prerogative of white time is to define what it means to be coeval and copresent in the first place. Relatedly, scholarly affirmations of temporal sovereignty as a mode of resisting temporal domination also strike me as misguided. It would be a mistake to map the ownership of control of space associated with territorial sovereignty onto time. The epilogue explores these shortcomings in order to make time for orienting ourselves toward time we do not have, and relational modes of inhabiting time otherwise.

1
White Time
The Race of Segregated Time

The intersection of time and loss has long been an occasion of contemplation, and for good reason. Implying that loss is endemic to the nature of time, Simone Weil remarked that "all tragedies which one can imagine return in the end to the one and only tragedy: the passage of time."[1] The tragedy of time's passage is part of the finality of a mortal life: life is something we are literally born to lose. When we are awake to the fact that a fundamental feature of human temporality is that we all have an expiration date, questions of what we should do with the lives we are fated to lose take on pressing urgency. In some sense, death is a shared destination. We know this life will end, but most of us are uncertain when and how we will take our leave. Yet that uncertainty is not evenly distributed. If it is true that all lives are finite, and all lifetimes precarious, it is equally true that all lives are not equally vulnerable to loss and precarity. As Judith Butler has observed: some lives do not count as lives at all. Only lives that matter in the first place are publicly grievable as lives having been lost.[2] It follows that any meaningful discussion of the inequalities in political death-dealing and morbidity would be derelict without confronting how race serves as an index of such difference, and how the race-based temporal divide is expressed in the rancid instances of lifetimes cut short and cast out of time.

I live in Baltimore, where segregation is primarily regarded as an issue of race and space, only *sometimes* class, but almost *never* in relation to time. Time itself is frequently rendered in spatial terms and discussed using spatial imagery. As the philosopher Henri Bergson puts it, "When we evoke time, it is space that answers our call."[3] Yet in 2013 Johns Hopkins University vice provost Jonathan Bagger made a striking observation: while there is but a six-mile difference separating the Roland Park neighborhood (near the university) from downtown, there is a *twenty-year difference* in life expectancy. Why, he inquired, "aren't we asking more regularly if *they're* OK?"[4] The remarkable statement dramatizes a wider failure to consider issues of race in

Segregated Time. P.J. Brendese, Oxford University Press. © Oxford University Press 2023.
DOI: 10.1093/oso/9780197535745.003.0002

terms of time. Whether *they* are OK means asking about the time of others, and the failure to do so suggests that a racialized, biopolitical ethos of "live and let die" colors not just segregated spaces but also segregated times. How do the foreshortened lives of others and their spectral absences shape the "we" that is the "us" to which he refers? The practice of *not* asking such questions suggests a habituated feature of racialized temporality worthy of further inquiry, particularly if we think that racial identities are performed and subjectivity has a temporal dimension. Simply put, if we can speak meaningfully about white space, we should be able to conceptualize white time.

In this chapter, I make the case for a provisional theory of white time as a temporal force field that exerts regulative, normalizing powers that shape the racial order of things as well as subjective experiences of time, that is, white temporalities. To lay the groundwork, I begin with a very brief review of the philosophical and historical roots of contemporary modes of understanding and inhabiting time. As will become clear, my view is that while physicists have largely moved on from the seductions of Newtonian orientations of time, the same cannot be said for the vast regions and peoples who are heirs to colonial legacies, including much contemporary scholarship. As we shall see, the contingency and multiplicity of time has caused difficulty for the path-dependent attachments of the social sciences and their respective capacities to speak to life-and-death issues of present-day politics. Indeed, one of my working premises is that philosophies of history are political theories in disguise.[5]

I shall situate race within the concatenation of forces that imbue affective experiences of temporality, disciplinary structures, and conventional understandings of time. Since histories of slavery and colonialism are frequently relayed in terms of space, I advance a time-sensitive approach with the view that the "conquest of space is intrinsically tied to a mastery of time."[6] Toward that end, I sketch the temporal entrapments built into the doctrine of discovery and *terra nullius* to render a view of the forced disappearances of nonwhite presence in space and time, effectively amounting to a *tempus nullius*. In an engagement with Frantz Fanon, Aileen Moreton-Robinson, and Cheryl I. Harris, I consider the racial subjectivity required to apprehend time and space as available to be possessed as productive of segregated time generally and white temporality specifically. Frantz Fanon writes, "The white man wants the world for himself alone. He's predestined master of the world. He enslaves it. An acquisitive relation is established between the world and him" (BSWM, 128). Relatedly, W.E.B. Du Bois declares that "whiteness is ownership of earth forever and ever, Amen!"[7] Their insights invite my exploration of the temporal dimension of epistemologies and subjectivities normalized, disciplined, and coded as white. In the spirit of Fanon's imperative that "every human problem must be considered from the standpoint of time," I consider white acquisitiveness as seeking dominion over time—and not just space (BSWM, 12–13).

Time: Standardized and Segregated

Those familiar with the physics of time might plausibly contend that there is no such thing as integrated time, making the phrase "segregated time" a redundancy. Appropriately, the etymological roots of the word "time" can be traced to *division*.[8] And to even the uninitiated reader of theoretical physics, at least one thing becomes quickly apparent: Einstein's theory of special relativity and subsequent developments in quantum mechanics have rendered core aspects of Newtonian time obsolete. Newton's notion of a freestanding, independent, universal Time that operates as the standardized background condition for all of existence now appears just plain wrong. We know that that time is relative, meaning that if we take two people existing at the same time, time will pass differently for one who starts moving than for her friend who remain stationary. The same goes for someone in a valley versus someone else on a peak, or an astronaut hurling through space relative to her earthbound counterpart. In tangible terms, this doesn't just mean there is a difference in those individuals' respective experiences of time's duration, or temporality. It also means that each of their watches will actually display different times, and they will age at different rates. In light of such conditions, the notion that there is a (capital T) Time with an absolute essence or fixed ontological standing appears fantastical. Reading physicists following Einstein's lead in rejecting Newtonian time, one gets a strong sense that all time is segregated time.[9]

It is no revelation that human experiences of time can vary widely, which can be a recipe for abandoning any discussion of the topic before it devolves into renderings of time as irreducibly subjective, aporetical, and apolitical. But to ask why we think of time the way we do, why we measure time in minutes and hours instead of, say, the gestation of flowers, the moons, or texture of snow, presumes that what we call time is a human divination—as opposed to a human revelation of divine ordination.[10] Considering time places us firmly in the realm of contingent social formations. The invention of the clock divorced time from memory, seasonal turns, planetary rhythms, human experience, and even physical change and aging. Time was made available to be quantified, saved, spent, measured in length, and exchanged for money—yet another abstraction with heavy social valence. In a strong sense, clock time initiated its own segregated temporalities since "the machine time of the clock is a time cut loose from the temporality of body, nature and the cosmos, from context around being and spiritual existence."[11] Yet it also opened onto potent modes of synchronicity and discipline.

Around the thirteenth century the first true mechanical clocks appeared, with churches and monasteries among the first to adopt the technology.[12] In medieval towns it became customary for the clergy to watch the clock, call the priests to prayer, and tell the town the time by ringing the church bells. Suffice it to say, the clocks were not merely for keeping track of time for its own sake. They served the disciplinary function of synchronizing human activity—a tool of civilizational pastoral power and "keeping watch" in the dual sense of quasi-panoptical surveillance and technological innovation. As Giordano Nanni has cogently argued, colonial missionaries to Africa were zealous evangelists of clock order and the seven-day work week.[13] The visual symbol of a colonial mission is still a bell—historically the sonic means for establishing temporal control, intended to make natives vassals of the Church and the clock. The mechanized time of the clock became so pervasive that it would be impossible to fully appreciate the Industrial Revolution without accounting for the changes wrought by its ability to quantify time, maximize efficiency and synchronicity, to reorder the rhythms of public and private life according to its intervals, and valorize labor accordingly.[14] The mechanical clock was an innovation that accelerated the sense of human possibility for commanding time and people, a dynamic later catalyzed by John Harrison's ca. 1730 invention of the marine chronometer. The chronometer enabled ships to determine longitude at sea, thereby hastening nautical discovery and colonialism's command over space. Its utility was lauded by Captain Cook after his second circumnavigation of the globe and later used in his establishment of the British Colony of New South Wales.[15] The observation anticipates our inquiry into the tensions and correspondences between temporal and spatial sovereignty, a point to which I shall return.

In and of themselves units of time such as hours and minutes may be devoid of meaning, but the fact that they remain deeply salient is readily apparent. If we consider the clock in relation to the idea of time's independence—something that is measured as if it were external to those doing the measuring, an unruly cast of specters appears. For Plato the earthly world of becoming was tethered to the eternal *Being* in the realm of the forms. *The Republic* is an antidemocratic theory of rule by the enlightened, with a rigid social hierarchy. Plato endorsed slavery as the lot of those incapable of reason and political participation of any sort. This prompted Cedric Robinson's observation on how the regime was "rich in intellectual stratagems *a propos* to the political discourse embedded in the American political order." The American founder's fluency in Platonism, plutocracy, and slavery is part of the descent of white supremacy in the United States. Adapting Nietzsche's take on Jesus of Nazareth, Robinson quips that "Plato survives because if he had not existed, he would have had to be invented."[16]

Plato's ordering of time by way of the eternal anticipated Sir Isaac Newton and God as a cosmic watchmaker. A Newtonian-derived view of time has been perpetuated geopolitically despite its being discredited by physics and either challenged, or simply ignored, by diverse traditions, cosmologies, and lifeways. The physicist Carlo Rovelli gives voice to that suspicion, insisting that Newton's time does not come from our senses but is an intellectual construction, albeit an elegant one.

> If, my dear cultivated reader, the existence of this Newtonian concept of time which is independent of things seems to you simple and natural, it's because you have encountered it at school. Because it has gradually become the way in which we all think about time. It has filtered through school textbooks throughout the world and ended up becoming our common way of understanding time. We have turned it into our common sense. But the existence of a time that is uniform, independent of things and of their movement that today seems so natural to us is not an ancient intuition that is natural to humanity itself. It is an idea of Newton's.[17]

I quote at length because school is hardly the only place where one encounters the idea of time as independent of things. And, with all due respect to Newton's notion that things in motion tend to stay in motion, the notion of universal time has not "filtered through school textbooks" by inertia alone. Furthermore, if "we" have turned Newton's cosmic watchmaker into a form of common sense, we would do well to ask who this "we" is and whether such an understanding of time might be "common sense" in ways closer to the Gramscian formulation—which implies a modality of shared understanding serving the interests of power. In other words, we should ask whether, and how, human interests might be implicated in otherwise taken-for-granted forms of knowing. Asking *whose* interests are served by prevailing orders of time is a core question this study confronts.

Just as I drew modestly on the work of theoretical physicists like Rovelli to illuminate the relations between things like gravity and time, it seems appropriate that the work of a transdisciplinary, experimental political theory should lend a bit of precision to the passive constructions in his formulations. He rightly discounts the idea of Newtonian time as an "intuition natural to humanity itself." Long before Newton, Aristotle understood time as the measurement of change such that if nothing changes, there is, in effect, no time; time ceases to pass.[18] But, one might object, consider those locked in solitary confinement deprived of light or outside stimuli. Do they not experience time passing in the most brutal of ways? Anticipating a debate over mind and motion that would later be taken up by Descartes, among others, Aristotle suggested that if it were dark and our external senses were dull, we would still sense time passing as a result of the internal motions of the mind (*Physics* IV.219b2).[19] Hence, Aristotle would agree that inmates in solitary confinement experience time because the change they perceive is that of their own mind in motion relative to the stasis of their environment.[20] Either way, time remains the measure of movement. Newton acknowledged the existence of such a "common" time that registers days and movements à la Aristotle, but held it apart from a "true" time that passes irrespective of the motions of people, souls, and things.[21] It would be the task of Einstein in particular, and twentieth-century physics in general, to destabilize the presumed unity of time—at least among the scientific community.

Among philosophers, Immanuel Kant adopted a quasi-Newtonian notion of time as absolute—albeit in the sense of a universal apperception. That is, time was subjective but a priori, which is to say that it was "a form of intuition by which experience was ordered; knowledge was grounded in experience, but time was not derived from experience."[22] Humans bring their sense of time to the table of experience, and order that experience accordingly as perceived phenomenon. In making such a move, Kant deftly preserves time as scientifically relevant while divorcing it from the ultimate reality of the noumenal realm, or things in-themselves.[23] Time is a "form of intuition" in the sense that all experiences are consecutive in time, which suggests that time comes from mind. Yet intuition receives input from the world, which suggests time has empirical standing unto itself. When it comes to the question of where time comes from, Kant is effectively trying to have it both ways. On the one hand, we exist in time. On the other, we have to see ourselves outside time to some degree in order to postulate ourselves as moral agents capable of legislating rules that are righteous across time—and not just here and now.[24] With respect to the possibility of a life after death in earthly memory, for example, Kant maintained we have a responsibility to be remembered as acting in the service of history's universal reason.[25]

Despite lofty overtures to "cosmopolitan intent" and "universal history," Kant held parochial inclinations very much befitting his era and station. For all the meaningful differences between Kantian transcendentalism and G.W.F. Hegel's speculative idealism, both were of the mind that where people hailed from in geographical space mapped onto their chronological stage in developmental time. Kant regarded Africans as naturally inferior to Europeans, and Hegel believed that the African continent was without history. In sharp contrast was the triumph of the (European) modern state in Hegel's rendering, which he famously regarded as coincidental with the end of history. Taken together, such formulations entail a linear, progressive temporality, with Europe at the cutting edge of history.[26] This set the stage for modern European males to cast themselves in the role of leading men in history's drama through markers that were at once temporal, gendered, and racial. The consequence was a division between Western history's self-anointed protagonists and those who would serve as raw material in the making, a sharp split between the knowers and the known, the makers and the made. We shall see that the status of time as a universal background condition retains a Newtonian framework with enduring political consequences.

Kairos, Entanglement, and Empire

Drawing upon the Greek distinction between *chronos* and *kairos*, Kimberly Huchings offers a compelling account of how the *chronos* of (European) modernity stems from Newtonian assumptions of timetables, clocks, and calendars as stable means of measurement providing a neutral background condition. The linearity and irreversibility of Newtonian time is also central to causal inference; cause must precede effect diachronically, making patterns identifiable and prediction possible.[27] "The historical and social sciences only emerged as systemic disciplinary fields because of the conceptions of *chronos* bound up with developments of Newtonian and post-Newtonian science."[28] Ostensibly in tension with *chronos* is *kairos*, the interruptive power to superimpose creative, novel, and change-making elements into the otherwise sequential aspects of time. The time of *kairos* is the time of the event. *Kairos* signals periodicity, revolution, and natality. It exists by way of happenings so significant as to divide history into stages. *Kairotic* events can shape memory such that you tell the story of what happened by way of what happened before and what took place after *that* happening.[29]

Pick a theory of history and identify its formulation of *chronotic* time through the sequential chain of cause/effect according to which past, present, and future are divided. Chances are you can spot a conceptual sleight of hand. A driving purpose of theories of history is to instantiate divisions that are anything but natural or uniform. Rather, such partitions exhibit value judgments about marking time by strategically bracketed historical stages identifying progress (e.g., the Renaissance) and decline (e.g., the Dark Ages) as well as transitional engines of change and stasis. Theories of history also gain purchase and allure from the weight they give to the comparative merits and achievements of certain epochs, eons, or eras over others.[30] Furthermore, they frequently do so by presuming to stand apart from their objects of study in the process of differentiation. Think of those that assert that historical progress is driven by exceptional individuals (aka the Great Man theory of history) as opposed to, say, democratic coalitions. Then there are other, more pedestrian, but no less noxious historicisms such as that of *New York Times* columnist Thomas Friedman's assertion that Islam has not yet reached modernity.[31] This study proceeds under the heading that, despite the notion that time operates independently of the human estate, even in those ostensibly neutral machinations of history one finds significant *kairotic* creativity has been smuggled in.

Contemporary politics remains haunted by the lure of time as freestanding, neutral, and universal, as well as the capacity of such standardizations of time to conceal the political interests underlying theories of history and their judgments regarding eras, stages, and periodization. Within political theory, the author who has most prolifically and consistently taken up the subject of time to resist the gravitational pull of linear causality, sociocentric humanisms, and nihilistic temporalities is William E. Connolly. In recent years, Connolly has contested political and intellectual relationships to time by advancing a lexicon of "becoming," "emergent causation," "temporal forking," and "bumpy temporalities," with the latter countering notions of planetary gradualism (basically the idea that the earth is changing too slow for it to matter much) in favor of irruptive processes and temporal multiplicity.[32] Connolly avoids making willful human intervention irrelevant and coalition politics futile by acknowledging causal relations in history while retaining the role of the emergent so as not to evacuate novelty, creativity, and possibility from futurity altogether. Giving ecological and planetary forces their due means, among other things, acting with urgency to confront climate crises without being overly presumptuous about the human capacity to dictate what happens next in the age of the Anthropocene.

Quantum physics teaches us that the nature of reality is unpredictable, but it is not clear that social science has fully learned that lesson.[33] From the fall of the Berlin Wall, to the overthrow of leaders in Egypt, Tunisia, and Libya with the Arab Spring, to the ascent of Donald Trump and the attempted coup on January 6, political science is notoriously bad at prediction.[34] The logos of *chronos* has meant that social science's attachment to path-dependent theories has made it infinitely better at predicting the past than anticipating the future. As Jairus Grove puts it, "Reality is not path dependent."[35]

Relevant to our purposes, I should say, is that the time division of the Anthropocene has itself recently become the site of emergent questions over periodicity. The parts of the world racialized as white are generally better able to temper some of the turbulence of the crisis by leveraging those who pollute less but suffer more, many of whom are in the Global South. This has raised questions of whether the age after the Holocene should be called the Eurocene or the Racial Capitalocene instead of the Anthropocene.[36] To these debates I would briefly add three points that might not be obvious, but which anticipate the discussion of white time. First, implicit in the challenge to *Anthropos* as a modifier signifying an age of human impact on the planet is that not all people, then or now, have historically been considered full members of the human race.[37] So when speaking about human responsibility for climate change, the issue is shadowed by questions of just *who* counts now, and who has been counted, as human. In short, the historical confluence of racism and humanism cannot be left out of the equation. Second, practices of environmental racism among the richest countries mean that the impact of climate change is disproportionately distributed, creating temporal and geographic refugees. Third, the work of parsing human responsibility raises the issue of climate debt specifically, but also the time-sensitive issue of debt more generally. These points resurface soon enough in what follows.

No doubt the projection of a governing, neutral temporal order that presides over a diverse plurality will likely appear as a move suspiciously familiar to race and gender scholars conversant in critiques of whiteness and heteronormative masculinity as objective referents and stable, timeless measures of all things.[38] The personification of the attributes of *chronos* and *kairos* entails a production of backwardness along racial lines to effectuate segregated time. The arc of colonialism has meant that whiteness, despite its historically fluid boundaries, has nevertheless served as a sociohistorical referent through which racial others have been stigmatized in temporal terms. The temporal-discursive markers span from "primitive," "backward," "uncivilized," and "infantile," connoting subjects behind the times, to "alien"—with the latter evocative of monstrous strangers altogether outside of terrestrial spacetime. The racialization of *chronos* is what I take Aimé Césaire to be railing against when he declares that "it is the colonized man who wants to move forward, and the colonizer who holds things back."[39] Césaire mounts an assault on the polarized racialization of civilization and barbarism, arguing that colonization makes barbarians out of the so-called civilized. His inversion famously cast Europe as the creation of the colonies, and not the other way around.

More recently, Achille Mbembe has sharply contested the role of the African continent as symbolic of that which is timeless, resistant to change, traditional, bestial, and chaotic. As I read the implications of Mbembe's work, toggling between *chronos* and *kairos* would not only fail to consider *who* personifies the orderly and the wild in public imaginaries. It would also reproduce the duality of stability and rupture that is so problematic in much social science literature—all while forgetting that chaos is but one of many possible corollaries of unstable dynamic systems.[40] What so frequently goes missing are the temporal complexities that Mbembe refers to as the *time of entanglement* to which we can connect the emergent planetary and ecological conditions. Such crises lead Timothy Mitchell to regard entanglements as "imbroglios of the technical, the natural and the human" and Connolly to theorize *entangled humanism*.[41] In quantum mechanics, entanglement refers to things connected such that they can only be described in relation to each other, irrespective of space—what Einstein calls "spooky action at a distance."

Entanglement seems an appropriate idiom for the relationalities of race and segregated time as well, since whiteness is constituted in relation to people of color, and progress and backwardness are created in tandem. Here it is important to note that entanglement signifies the often messy, dissonant effects of colonialism; there is no absolutely uniform, linear relationship across all peoples and times. This is especially the case because those impacted are not merely acted upon, but cultivate modes of resistance, innovation, and temporal upkeep in asynchronous and asymmetrical ways. That said, one might ask, what about the continuities of racial injustices that stubbornly persist despite these qualifiers? Among them is the collusion between whiteness and colonialism that bequeaths a racist humanism long sanctified in Western theology and theory, and disseminated by dehumanizing practices. Practices of racialized dehumanization exceed the spatial domain of the nation-states that are the staging grounds for much postcolonial thinking about time.[42] Hence, I concur with recent scholarship contending that many postcolonial critics have yet to fully grapple with the impact of interpenetrating temporalities on racial orders.[43] Toward that end, perhaps the time is right to introduce the concepts of white time and temporality.

According to Michael Hanchard's theory of racial time, Afro-diasporic peoples' experiences of temporality shape a non-state-based epistemological community. In what follows, I initiate an inquiry into the forces and tractional pulls exerted by white time and the extent that such temporal vectors can be understood as instruments of power worthy of investigation. While I shall argue in the affirmative, my engagement of the slippery and contested themes of "race" and "time" resists a deterministic view of either in favor of viewing their mutual relation as conditioned by power in flux. In these formulations of segregated time and segregated memory, I neither presume uniform experiences across fluid racial groups nor attempt to encompass the universe of subjective experiences of time.[44] In this sense, my approach to race and time deploys a genealogical sensibility in the Foucauldian and Nietzschean sense of the term, which is to say that it does not pursue an overarching history or invoke particular episodes in search of a universal, but examines white time as part of accessing the power relations surrounding "the birth of universals and their transformation into principles of domination."[45]

White Time

We saw previously that one way political temporalities wield power is by making judgments about historical divisions and time's vector, its direction and speed. Indigenous and decolonial theorists challenge the division and direction of such temporal impositions by arguing that primitive accumulation has never represented a discrete historical stage, as Marx would have it, since colonialism is territorially acquisitive in perpetuity.[46] If I read it as a bygone era and a discrete historical interval, I concur with arguments that the primitive accumulation is vacant and deserves to be rendered obsolete. In fact, the term has its roots in Adam Smith, not Marx, who often refers to it as "so-called primitive accumulation."[47] With respect to time, it's worth recalling some elementary dynamics of imperial capitalism: seizing a people's land deprives them of a means of subsistence; unable to survive upon the proceeds of the land, one has little choice but sell one's time in the form of labor. Yet if we take the phrase "primitive accumulation" wildly out of context, it endures in another sense: colonial innovations of power still function to extract resources from those stigmatized as primitive in, and by, what I shall call white time. We witness its force dispersing and aggregating asynchronous others in places spanning ghettos, reservations, armies, prisons, refugee camps, immigrant detention centers, and morgues. How, and in what ways, does white time serve as a vehicle of spatial and temporal segregation? To anchor the political stakes and elucidate the "whiteness" of time, I turn to the discovery doctrine as a mode of territorial dispossession inhabited by a racialized temporal ordering.

In practice, the doctrine of discovery conferred a superiority of land claims such that title history was only traceable in any legally meaningful way through white landholders. Officially, this meant that the land of First Nations changed hands from one settler colonial power to another, with the primary Indigenous claims to the land, and its original theft, remaining irrelevant.[48] This aspect of the history of Amerindian racialization was achieved by a cleaving of dominion, which was the sole prerogative of European sovereigns, from the lesser right of occupancy that applied to Native populations.[49] As a corrective to segregated memory, one can formulate a legal genealogy charting the legacy of the doctrine of discovery through the Salamanca School and its Anglo resonance in tort law. The doctrine was still operative in the nineteenth-century Cherokee removal via Justice John Marshall's decision in *Johnson v. McIntosh*, and even in the twenty-first-century Indigenous land claims of the Oneida Indians in the northeastern United States.[50] As a prevailing organizational tool for at once making legible time, tradition, and peoples, descent would be leveraged in arguments over slavery and colonialism.[51] On the ultimate implication of the doctrine, Patrick Wolfe is precise: "Property starts where Indianness stops."[52]

Before broadening the scope, let me illustrate one way this disappearance happens juridically through the time-sensitive logic of the discovery doctrine. The assertion of discovery was *instantaneous*, in that it was activated at the moment of a European claim on lands was backed with the violence to ward off other *European* settlers. The distinction is important, since for the claim to be operative it was not necessary for the land itself to actually be settled by the European claimant. In practice, this meant that land claimed by France remained under the dominion of French sovereignty until another European power, such as the British, defeated them in war. If you are wondering where First Nations are in this equation, that's the point. Since all of this took place in the legal realm of "dominion" and the Native peoples were consigned to the lower sphere of mere "occupancy," the process of land acquisition for Indians was "anything but instantaneous" amid the fluid movement of the frontier.[53] In other words, the instantaneity of discovery meant that the Indigenous peoples would have to undertake a long process of trying to legally acquire what had been their own land. In the United States, the result, as we know, was the westward expansion and acquisition of Indian lands by whites.[54] The application of the logic to American affairs was reiterated in the 1823 Monroe Doctrine asserting continental domination and invoked to expropriate the Cherokee in 1830 in Justice Marshall's decision in *Johnson v. McIntosh*. The decision was a vulgar codification of white paternalism toward Indigenous peoples, assigning them the status of wards of the state relegated to the status of requiring the care, protection, and tutelage of "the American President whom they [Indians] call 'Father.'"[55]

The Court's resolution came in the form of the novel formulation of "domestic dependent nations" so as to retroactively assign a version of sovereignty precisely in order to take it away. Lest this appear as the bald-faced theft it clearly was, by infantilizing the Indians as wards of the state and rendering them analogous to orphaned children, the Court could cloak itself in a veneer of paternal responsibility. With a stroke of a pen, the decision simultaneously threw peoples of all chronological ages—indeed entire nations—backward in time. And, for good measure, Marshall notes that the Indians refer to the American president as "their Father"; an implication that, whatever brutal paternal discipline comes next, the misbehaving Indian "children" were asking for it.[56] At this point, the problems of liberal reason presented by the infantile Indigenous should be apparent. By definition, children cannot consent. And the theoretical-political conflagration of race, temporality, reason, and property rights builds further.

As a domestic *dependent* nation, not a foreign entity, Cherokees were prohibited from appealing to the Supreme Court to have their treaties upheld.

When they tried to do so in *Cherokee v. Georgia*, the Court offered a ruling illustrative of the disappearing act that Wolfe aptly terms *corpus nullius*, with Justice Baldwin writing "there is no plaintiff in this case."[57]

Notice how the production of the Cherokees as "nobody," cotemporaneous with the proliferation and disavowal of so many bodies of their dead, speaks to a racial subjectivity that extends beyond the courtroom. Wolfe's *corpus nullius* and the Cherokee as "nobody" anticipate Mark Lamont Hill's contemporary analysis of African Americans marked as "nobody" and made spectral and disposable; simultaneously exposed to officially sanctioned violence and subject to abandonment by the state.[58] The continuous appropriation of colonial acquisitiveness is facilitated by a legacy of white possessive subjectivity seeking ownership over space *and* time.

I examine the time signature of that possessive subjectivity in what follows. To do so, I contend that the colonial doctrine of *terra nullius* (empty space) used to expropriate aboriginal peoples also entails what I term *tempus nullius* (empty time), with both serving as instruments of white time's apparatus of capture. As a fundamental tool of colonial acquisitiveness, the doctrine of *terra nullius* was invoked to declare territory "empty land" ripe for the taking and the instantiation of white sovereignty—both temporal and territorial.[59] Drawing on scholarship documenting Captain Cook's account of Australia's aboriginal peoples, Audra Simpson sharply connects modes of seeing and knowing to the legal doctrine of "empty land," or *terra nullius*, that prevailed in Australia from colonization until 1992. The doctrine supplied the necessary medium to account for the inconvenient existence of the old inhabitants whose "discovery" gave the lie to the "New" in the New World. More precisely, settlers needed mechanisms to literally *dis*count, and thereby dispropriate, the land's original inhabitants. As Simpson suggests, these tensions are not simply about difference, but about establishing presence.[60] Through the empty time of *tempus nullius* Native inhabitants could be emptied of their status as historical beings with human presence. This amounts to a particular spacetime orientation through which the land and the lives of its inhabitants could be subjugated, appropriated, and destroyed in the service of a white *tempus plentitudinous*— or plenitude in the *fullness of time*, as St. Paul would say. In practical terms, *tempus nullius* was effected through settler judgments about Indigenous peoples as without history, as idlers who wasted time, and primitives who oriented their stories according to place, as opposed to Christian eschatology, Newtonian chronosophy, or clock time. For the most part, these "discovered" relationships to time literally did not matter to Europeans. Or, to the extent

Native temporalities mattered, they were proof of Indigenous inferiority. As such, *tempus nullius* represents an expression of a desire for temporal sovereignty that overlaps with territorial sovereignty; with both becoming entwined features of white subjectivity and temporality.

Relatedly, *tempus nullius* served as a condition of possibility for white colonials to set the historical chronometer to zero.[61] Power reserves the right to restart the clock and impose a new temporal order, which (in this case) is conjoined to the ways that the originary violence of the polity is segregated from memory. In the context of colonial invasion, temporal evacuation allows for a creation myth of a polity founded on liberal volitional consensus among equals, among other strategies. Through the phenomenon of writing Indigenous peoples out of existence that Indigenous studies scholar, historian, and White Earth Ojibwe Jean M. O'Brien calls "firsting," the European settlers historicized themselves as the primary people through the myth of Indian extinction.[62] Remarkably, this mythology persisted at the same time Indians still lived in some of the very towns occupied by settlers. By rendering Native peoples as disappeared into the past, settlers could fashion themselves as the modern vanguard of an Anglo-Saxon nation. Per the notions of racial purity settlers came to embrace, present Indians were regarded as not *really* Indian but "mixed." Indians who used the accoutrements their European counterparts associated with white modernity were viewed as no longer present *as Indian*, leaving whiteness as the criteria for "lasting" presence. This is patently a process of making time and making race.

Regarding such racial time-in-the-making, I take the capacity to materially, epistemologically, and politically deprive autochthonous peoples of their presence—in the multiple sense of occupying both time and space—to be elemental to white time. And it is not over yet. Settler strategies of vanishing Native peoples in their very midst by insisting "All the Real Indians Died Off" facilitate the denial of Indigenous land claims, rights, and standing.[63] White fictions of Indians as wasting space intersected with convenient mythologies of Native peoples as wasting time. Indigenous land that was (wrongly) labeled unaltered wilderness was considered "waste" and thus there for the taking.[64] The spatiotemporal evacuation of *terra/tempus nullius* conveys material and political consequences of segregated time, widely discernible across many times and spaces. How many times, for example, have you encountered the dynamic where the aboriginal communities who have inhabited a particular landmass for the *longest* time are among the *least* likely to possess and control significant portions of that territory *now*? In the next section, I mine the acquisitive features undergirding white racial temporality by way of its material and phenomenological apprehensiveness.

White Temporality as a Possessive Tense

The descent of liberalism and contractarian thinking are rife with juridical strategies of disappearing the spatiotemporal presence of others. Tactics of legal erasure are the companion projects of the cultural and political paternalism that Martin Luther King Jr. derided as "temporizing."[65] Recall that temporizing is the means through which people of color are figured as subjects forced to wait for equality and status. In the meantime, nonwhites are available to be disciplined, assimilated, or made expendable. Just as the notion that time can be quantified, claimed, saved, spent, or wasted is a conventional artifice, so too is how one comes to identify others as without history. One must learn to perceive different modes of inhabiting time as wasting time. Whereas the concept of Africa as without history and the belief that Amerindian peoples "waste time" are productions of *white time*, the inculcation that gives way to relating to racial others accordingly is among the ways that white time is experienced—or *white temporality*. Hence I develop the notion that the performative dimensions of whiteness, their roots examined, betray a phenomenology and epistemology capable of reducing myriad forms of otherness as property for the taking. At the core of the dynamic is an ontological reductivity that translates into a politics of infinite acquisitiveness over space and time.[66]

Over the years I have been working on this book, the only sustained treatment of white time of which I am aware is the eponymous article by Charles W. Mills.[67] While there are lines of affinity between them, and I think they can be read as forming a productive alliance, my own formulation of the concept has been developed independently.[68] Mills's theory of white time centers on its role in ideal theory particularly, and the whiteness of the discipline of philosophy more generally. I have advanced the concept in a different direction. Specifically, to extend our aperture between time to temporality, I propose that white time is experienced as an apparatus of capture through which subjects are themselves apprehended, and proceed to capture, while ostensibly free.[69] Stated bluntly, this is white subject formation whereby whites are, in Fanon's parlance, "both the duper and the duped" or, pace James Baldwin, an inculcation though which whites become "the slightly mad victims of their own brainwashing."[70] In Du Bois's idiom, whites are both "imprisoned and enthralled" by what in *The Souls of White Folk* he theorizes as "phantasy" whereby whiteness entails a visceral "passionate" belief among those who see themselves as "world mastering demi-gods."[71] Affectively, whiteness conveys the feeling that one holds a "title to the universe" and wields that belief though a "new imperialism" that seeks ownership of the world for whites by dividing it racially.[72] How, then, to define whiteness? Du Bois's response is scorching. "'But what on earth is whiteness that one should so desire it?' Then always, somehow, some way, silently but clearly, I am given to understand that whiteness is ownership of earth forever and ever, Amen!"[73]

Historically, whiteness has even claimed metaphysical ownership of what it means to own something. In her brilliant theorization of "whiteness as property," critical race theorist Cheryl I. Harris writes that "Possession—the act necessary to lay the basis for rights in property—was defined to include only the cultural practices of whites. That definition laid the foundation for the idea of whiteness—that which whites alone possess—is valuable and is property." Accordingly, possessing whiteness means possessing freedom. "Whiteness was the characteristic, the attribute, the property of free human beings."[74] Performatively, the whiteness of freedom is practiced, imagined, and (re)produced over time as requiring the subordination of racial others in part through a bid for sovereignty over time itself. Following Foucault's thought that any incarnation of freedom is both consumed and produced, one might ask, what is such racialized freedom a production *of*? This, in turn, opens onto a perennial philosophical question of freedom with sharp political teeth: how, as creatures of desire, can humans live as free people?

White modernity's answer to that question is already known. According to the order of white time, humans fated to inhabit bodies that desire can live freely by practices of imperial theft, colonial genocide, chattel slavery, economic inequality, and heteropatriarchal domination. Living freely as a desirous being hinges on subordination, and a core task of liberal philosophy would be to make that dominion legitimate.[75] Politically, this freedom requires the creation of subjects properly disposed to claiming ownership over space and, key to white temporality, time itself.

Just as Martin Luther King Jr. insists that history does not move on the wheels of inevitability, Du Bois also rejects the dominion of white nationalism as inevitable.[76] Rather, at key inflection points in time the white world has actively resisted emancipation, transracial democracy, and the possibility of shared humanity. As Ella Myers observes, "Part of what makes 'whiteness' modern for Du Bois, then, is that it is constructed and asserted in contexts that once seemed headed in a very different, egalitarian direction."[77] Harris stresses that whiteness emerges not from inevitabilities but from a series of "conscious selections regarding the structuring of social relations. In this sense, it is contended that property rights and interests are not 'natural' but 'creation[s] of law.'"[78]

In accord with Césaire's notion that colonization is thingification, the white apprehension of people of color as objects, property, or sites of extraction reflect psychoaffective attachments embedded in white temporality. When Fanon writes, "I am a slave not to an idea, but to an appearance. I am fixed," he speaks of a world in which empirical evidence is supposed to matter. However, irrespective of what Fanon *does* as a psychiatrist, intellectual, and revolutionary, the learned blindness of his white interlocutors leaves them ignorant of the irony they inhabit (BSWM, 116). Fixing people of color comes with its own fixations, namely the widespread refusal to acknowledge motion in time when in the presence of nonwhite dynamism.[79] The acquisitive desire for fixity evokes what anthropologist and Aboriginal elder Aileen Moreton-Robinson refers to as the "white possessive." On my reading, Moreton-Robinson's theorization of the white possessive is distinct from a "possessive investment in whiteness" (George Lipsitz) and whiteness as a "badge" or phenotypical guarantor of privilege (the early Du Bois)—though these are hardly irrelevant.[80] The white possessive is related, if not entirely reducible to, the notion that one could own whiteness—or "whiteness as property" à la Harris.

Moreton-Robinson identifies what she calls "possessive logics" to identify a "mode of rationalization rather than a set of positions that produce an inevitable answer," a mode that "circulate[s] a set of meanings about ownership of the nation, as part of commonsense knowledge, decision making and socially produced conventions."[81] With this in mind, I want to sketch how the relation between property and expectation discloses how white identity penetrates the lower registers of white subject formations. Drawing on Harris, I speak to what Moreton-Robinson suggests is a general lack of attention to the social constructedness of white identity by incorporating a temporal dimension to white identity formation.[82]

Speaking to the temporality of property, Jeremy Bentham holds that "property is nothing but the basis of expectation consist[ing] in the persuasion of being able to draw such and such advantage from the thing possessed."[83]

Underscoring Bentham's point, Harris writes, "The relationship between expectations and property remains highly significant, as 'the law has recognized and protected even the expectation of rights as actual legal property.'"[84] Harris is clear that the theory does not imply that all value or expectations translate into property. Rather, the point is that valued expectations (in the form of things tangible or intangible) which the law protects, are property. Building on Joseph Sax's assertion that respect for "reasonable" expectations is at the essence of property law, Harris deftly ties whiteness as "the quintessential property for personhood" to expectations of white superiority whose entrenchment over time makes those expectations reasonable. This, in turn, allows her to configure whiteness and expectations—and, of course, white expectations—as property recognized by the law intended to reify racial hierarchy.

In the law whiteness is constructed as an objective fact whose reification means that the "relation between people takes on the character of a thing and thus acquires a 'phantom objectivity,' an autonomy that seems so strictly rational and all-embracing as to conceal its fundamental nature: the relation between people."[85] For Harris, this manufactured "phantom objectivity" makes whiteness a legally recognized object of continued and expected control. While I do not disagree, notice how (with the projected expectation of rights conceived as property) futurity also becomes implicated in the domain of sovereignty. In addition to whiteness, time increasingly appears as a propertied domain. Returning to expectations, Harris connects legally protected expectations of white privilege as property by drawing on Margaret Radin:

> If an object you now control is bound up in your future plans, or in anticipation of your future self, and it is partly these plans for your own continuity that make you a person, then your personhood depends on the realization of these expectations.[86]

The statement rings true, but I want to read it with a slightly different inflection by momentarily de-emphasizing the realization of expectations. If plans for continuity are part of what makes you a person, then it is not just your future realization of expectations that is at issue. Also at stake is your personal power to plan and expect in the present, with your control over what happens next tethered to the "object you now control." The dynamic also speaks to the relays between white time and white temporality.

White time connotes the chronotic, linear (re)ordering that resets the clock and imposes rhythms, intervals, notions of progress and backwardness, and so forth. Accordingly, the right to expect the ongoing continuity of those impositions as a taken-for-granted way of experiencing the present is a feature of white temporality. The latter concept does not, however, imply that all so-called white people experience time the same way, nor is it reducible to the variety of experiences of time across peoples identified or identifying as white. White temporality connotes the normalizing temporal forces, flows, affective attachments, and rhythms birthed and sustained by the institution of white supremacy. Included among these is the expectation of future control, or control of the future, as a racialized orientation to time coded as white.

Radin's reference to present control of "objects" in relation to planning for a future is especially evocative in the context of a legacy of regarding humans as property—or as able to be dispossessed of property—on the basis of race. Harris references whiteness as property in terms of the expected rights of future enjoyment, the ability to exclude, and the reputation value of whiteness. By my lights, time is also interpolated into the discourse of ownership, command, and coming enjoyments that only *some* can count on. These expectations of privilege imbue one's sense of present personhood and speak directly to how time is racialized as white in the cases Harris adumbrates. The expectations of white time are such that the prevailing temporal structure itself becomes reified to the point that the order of time takes on the character of an ownable "thing." As I discuss in the next chapter, expectation also speaks to race as a *predictive technology* whereby whiteness has a "social and cultural purchase, and its possession enhances one's life chances as configured through the logic of capital."[87] In the grip of the apprehension and uncertainty of unexpected events, it is the times (and, by definition, the lives) of racial others that white supremacist structures seize upon in order to smooth out the irruptions in white time—and they do so through temporal segregation.[88]

I have chosen apprehension for its obvious possessive connotation, but also because it traverses time, temporality, and affect to "imply marking, registering, acknowledging without full cognition. It is a form of knowing, it is bound up with sensing and perceiving, but in ways that are not always—or not yet—conceptual forms of knowledge."[89] Colloquially, we say that a nervous person is apprehensive in the face of an uncertain future. The apprehensiveness of white temporality might be understood as seeking possession of time—namely though the desire for, and belief in, ownership over what happens next. In the face of insecure apprehension comes a seduction by a will to control others who might derail that future.

Apprehension also takes the form of affixing nonwhites in a creditor-debtor relation that, through something of a phenomenological-political magic trick, reverses linear time by stigmatizing nonwhites as indebted to their oppressors. Branded as deviants owing a debt to society, people of color are deserving of punishment and required to exhibit good behavior while "doing time" in a carceral society, often expected to express gratitude for their own exploitation and the "privilege" of living on borrowed time. This opens onto myriad forms of political and economic predation associated with life on what, in Chapter 4, I consider "subprime time."

With every uptick in the pastoral power of the carceral state that polices white time by brutally disciplining people of color, the property value of whiteness increases.[90] Extending the idiom of whiteness as a form of equity, and noting the property value of reputation, one can acknowledge the value added to whiteness as a form of credit. As an investable asset and subject to depreciation and appreciation over time, I shall contend, whiteness persists as a form of credit through which it remains a deeply meaningful currency of power. The apprehensiveness of the white possessive, vectored in space and time, is part of ongoing race-making projects. It bears repeating that race as race-making is not description, but a process of bringing political subjects into existence. The various time signatures affixed to certain racial populations suggest as much.

When it suited the interests of power, Native Americans were conveniently viewed as the walking dead headed to inevitable extinction, while Africans were destined for slavery. Such variance illuminates the possessive logic of white time. The racial timestamp is itself a projection of Euro-colonial desire, a stigma and remainder of what whites desired to extort from the population in question *at the time*. In the context of chattel slavery, temporal control is tantamount to the dominion over bodies and space in the name of productivity. At the same time, the forces of temporal imposition also occasion complex forms of resistance, time appropriation, and innovations exceeding white time signatures.

The temporal sabotage of work-slowdowns and foot-dragging found those who cracked the whip (the white "crackers") accusing the enslaved of working on "Black time." On another level, fugitives and maroon communities upended the myth of enslaved life as irreversible and fated—what Barrington Moore called the "conquest of inevitability."[91] Creative practices of making time birthed rich sonic modes of survivance and "keeping time." These ranged from communities of shared pleasure and empowerment convened by the cadence and beauty of the Black prophetic tradition, to the call-and-response work songs that shaped the blues and the quintessentially American art form that would become the metaphor for temporal improvisation itself: jazz.[92]

Lest we get ahead of ourselves, let us briefly register what happens when we take up the temporal aspects of racial subjectivity, while focusing on the relays between segregated white time and possessive white temporality.[93] While this is by no means an exhaustive list, whiteness functions as a *mode of apprehension* in the following senses of the phrase that I shall develop in the coming pages:

- Apprehension as a dynamic of possessive appropriation of supposedly inert space, territory, and nature—or the notion that "in time, all this can be yours" (Moreton-Robinson, Harris), or "in the beginning all the world was America" (Locke).[94]
- Apprehension as a default position whereby racial others are regarded as disposable resources exploited to shore up contingency and uncertainty for the dominant populations—or the biopolitical logic of "live and let die" (Foucault), where anachronistic others are expendable, such as the commonplace that "immigrants do the jobs Americans can't do, or won't do."
- Apprehension as an ontological rendering of otherness through which difference is arrested temporally and effectively frozen in time as fixed—as in "All the real Indians died off" (Dunbar-Ortiz and Gilio-Whitaker), or "Look! A Negro" (Fanon).
- Apprehension as the will to make known definitively through linear descent, such as Native American DNA (Tall Bear) and the dynamic whereby "Man, the chosen one, knows himself and knows the world, not because he is part of it, but because he establishes a sequence and measures it according to his own time scale, which is determined by his *affiliation*." (Glissant).[95]
- Apprehension as a temporal posture of entitlement—or the white privilege to "walk in like you own the place" and people will treat you accordingly (Sullivan, Du Bois).[96]
- Apprehension as a posture through which white subjectivities anticipate and interpolate otherness as objects of desire waiting to be

assimilated into hegemonic chrononormative timescapes—or "In time, everyone becomes white"/ "whiteness as destiny" (Fanon); the notion of racial others as those who need to "catch up" (Hanchard, Chakrabarty, Said).

We shall see that apprehension is likewise operative in the disposition to regard the end of white supremacy as the *real* end of times that happens amid the disavowal of the apocalypse of ecological catastrophe. Apprehension conjoins the political projects of keeping people in their place and keeping them in time, in the manifold sense of perceiving criminals as such and capturing fugitives from (white) justice. As the next chapter attests, fugitives from white time are subject to temporal arrest and contemporary racialized modes of policing time redolent of carceral temporality.

2
Doing Time
Carceral Temporality

"A prison is a trap for catching time," writes Adam Gopnik.[1] The blunt truth of the statement makes those who do time an obvious point of entry for a discussion of segregated time. By now, the statistics are familiar. The United States makes up only 5 percent of the world's population, yet interns 25 percent of the world's prisoners; the highest rate of incarceration in the world—exceeding that of repressive regimes such as Russia, Iran, and China.[2] Despite having crime levels below the international mean, there are more people under correctional supervision now than were in Stalin's Gulag at its height.[3] Speaking to the complexion of incarceration, sociologist Loïc Wacquant contends that the imprisonment of African American men "has escalated to heights experienced by no other group in history, even under the repressive authoritarian regimes and in Soviet-style societies."[4] W.E.B. Du Bois wrote powerfully of being asked by a white man, "How does it feel to be a problem?"[5] The contemporary carceral condition is white supremacy's answer to the perceived "problem" of racial others in white spacetime.

Scholar and prison abolitionist Angela Davis observes that "The prison sentence, which is always computed in terms of time, is related to abstract quantification, evoking the rise of science and what is often referred to as the Age of Reason . . . precisely the historical period when the value of labor began to be calculated in terms of time and therefore compensated in another quantifiable way, by money."[6] Time served in prison is clearly time spent spatially segregated, yet the ambit of the system extends well beyond the space of the prison and the duration of the sentence. For those whose racial difference is criminalized, the constant threat of carceral contact can shadow one's "free" time with profound consequences for everyday life, experiences of citizenship, and future possibilities.[7] Simply put, the imposition of carceral temporality encompasses a massive apparatus of policing time.

Racialized mass incarceration is an enduring injustice whose roots scholars typically trace to Jim Crow and chattel slavery. Notably, Davis sounds

Segregated Time. P.J. Brendese, Oxford University Press. © Oxford University Press 2023.
DOI: 10.1093/oso/9780197535745.003.0003

its depths in the scientific rationality of the Enlightenment—and implicitly, racial capitalism and colonialism. Indeed, before there was the school-to-prison pipeline, or petrol pipelines across Indian reservations, there were human pipelines from reservations to residential schools where whites trafficked in the stolen futures embodied by Native children. And before *that*, there was imperial invasion, warfare, capture, theft, and resettlement. What I am calling carceral temporality has long been part of the colonial politics of fixing racial others in time, what anthropologist Johannes Fabian critiqued as a denial of coevalness.[8] The stigma of nonwhites as incapable of copresence undergirds implicit biases whereby people of color are apprehended as "behind the times," primitive, uncivilized, libidinous, infantile, and deviant. In timescapes coded as white, populations raced as asynchronous are subjected to having their time *and* space apprehended, redistributed, and even annihilated as a normalized matter of course. As we shall see, subjection to carceral temporality entails asymmetrical exposure to disciplinary interruptions of time whereby one can be cast outside of the dominant temporal flows of resources and privilege.

In this chapter I theorize carcerality in the United States as a condition of segregated time and racialized temporal theft. In so doing, the chapter elucidates contemporary carceral temporality as a weapon of white time. The acceleration of racialized mass incarceration since the 1970s is frequently understood as a reactionary response to people of color moving "too fast." According to the contradictory (il)logics of white time, those same populations supposedly regarded as backward, idle time-wasters can alternately be perceived as moving too fast—igniting a temporal politics of racial blowback. While white resistance to racial progress is indeed a potent force, I explore how race also functions as a forward-looking probabilistic, predictive technology that perpetuates segregated time. Innovative race-making projects also emerge from nonlinear, improvisational forms of temporal policing. Thus I investigate the evolving mechanisms of power that conceal and mediate racialized suffering and fortify the relative invisibility of segregated carceral temporalities in white time.

White temporality names experiences of time in which the institutional forces of white supremacy have "come to seem like somatic facts."[9] The somatic facts at issue in this chapter include the habituated expectations of who is liable to do time, who is assumed to have a record, who is coded as criminally threatening future dangerousness by algorithms and predictive policing strategies, and whose suffering can be leveraged as part of someone else's "good time." These are things that, to borrow from Pierre Bourdieu, "go without saying because they come without saying."[10] What frequently goes without saying in segregated time today is that police serve as the primary point of contact between people of color and the state—and white people wield the police as a cudgel against racial others. Put simply, white temporality cannot be understood outside the pecaritization and enforced absences of nonwhites. Police are militarized and professionalized such that the transnational connections to empire and colonial counterinsurgency tactics can no longer be ignored. My analysis is premised on an acknowledgment that North American carcerality has rhizomatic roots stretching back to slavery *and* colonialism; spacetimes spanning the plantation and the reservation, as well as futuristic imperial ambitions with nodal points conjoined to racial capitalism.

Scenes of family separation of Latinx migrants and refugees at the border and their children in cages (some of whom later go euphemistically "missing") evoke harrowing travails of Native families whose children were kidnapped and/or sent to Indian schools.[11] The US prison system houses a disproportionately Black and Brown population, and police executions of African Americans are simultaneously omnipresent and understated. At the same time, Native Americans are most likely to be killed by police.[12] Yet I want to insist that none of these evocations are vestigial—at least not in any ontological sense that they belong essentially to the past and then irrupt anachronistically down the line.[13] Take police killings of people of color. Too many are features of everyday suffering in racial timescapes that, from the chromosphere of white time, seem like relics of the past emerging as insurgent ghosts. The constant threat of carceral contact—from slave patrols to lynching and police executions as public, disciplinary spectacles—partakes of a long history of racial terrorism employed to maintain white supremacy initiated before the nation's founding.[14] Strangely, in white temporalities racial violence can be simultaneously apprehended as a vestiges of lynching from a bygone era *and* as current events made new and newsworthy for their stunning novelty. To disclose segregated temporality, one might ask: *for whom* does the present racialized injustice and precarity appear as shockingly interruptive or as a vestigial relic of another time?[15]

My intention in the account of segregated time and carceral temporality presented here is not to choose a singular causal narrative from competing points of emphasis among historiographical explanations for present-day crises. In part, this is because my view is that one can discern multiple ghosts.

For instance, Angela Davis hears troubling echoes of slavery and convict leasing in the prison industrial complex, Michelle Alexander views mass incarceration as a new Jim Crow, and those working at the intersection of race and technologies of predictive policing today discern what Ruha Benjamin calls the New Jim Code.[16] Ruth Wilson Gilmore places more emphasis on incapacitation of prisoners than labor extraction, though she also maintains a steady focus on the growth of carcerality in relation to the broader political economy. Against the logic of rehabilitation that is largely obsolete, Gilmore argues that "incapacitation doesn't pretend to change anything about people except where they are."[17] Yet incarceration—and the imminent threat thereof—shapes experiences of present spacetimes within and beyond prison walls.

In newsworthy moments when people of color become hypervisible in the white world, the correspondences between segregated time and segregated space surfaces in public analogies likening cities like Ferguson, Baltimore, and New Orleans to other countries. And not just *any* countries, but so-called *underdeveloped*, *Third World* countries.[18] In a word, occupied territory.[19] Case in point, the hallmarks of colonial urban spaces Fanon referred to as Manichaean divisions are flagrant here in Baltimore, where the divide is known as "The Black Butterfly" for its shape.[20] It is also a symbol of segregated time: the vast differences of life expectancy mean that the distance of two miles is roughly equivalent to twenty years.[21] Likewise, the butterfly is representative of the spatial boundedness of racial segregation of peoples overpoliced and underprotected—so even one's free time is not entirely free. At the same time, the insidious workings of carceral temporality are not bounded by segregated space. The reach of incursions such as Immigration and Customs Enforcement raids, no-knock warrants, hypersurveillance, and police stops fortifies the view that people of color are mobile states of exception.

This chapter is divided into five sections. After complicating and appending the relatively familiar account of contemporary carcerality's acceleration as a reactionary response to people of color moving "too fast," I explore how the weaponization of time represents a racialized form of temporal theft that extends carceral temporality beyond prison spaces and sentences. I do so in part by addressing how the criminalization of racial difference functions as a mode of racialized social and biopolitical reproduction implicated in the generation of segregated time. Because children of color embody a future that threatens particular aspects of white time, they are especially subject to being *apprehended* as criminals in both the corporeal and perceptual sense of the phrase. The insularity, myopia, and deafness of white temporality spurs my reflections on forms of "white noise" that fortify segregated time, cotemporaneous with entrenched affective racial economies of pleasure and cruelty. In the closing section entitled "Fugitive Justice," I situate the analysis of carceral temporality in the context of prison abolition. By staging a brief encounter between decolonial theory, Foucault, and Black Panther revolutionary George Jackson, I initiate the kind of time-sensitive theoretical promiscuity the chapter enjoins.

Doing Time in "Our" Time

> Neither slavery nor involuntary servitude, *except as a punishment for crime whereof the party shall have been duly convicted*, shall exist within the United States, or any place subject to their jurisdiction.
> —Thirteenth Amendment of the Constitution of the United States of America, Section 1 (emphasis added)

Speaking to the darker side of American exceptionalism, Michelle Alexander's words resonate still: "No other country in the world imprisons so many of its ethnic and racial minorities. *The United States imprisons a larger percentage of its black population than South Africa did at the height of apartheid.*"[22] For decades, Black men have been five to seven times more likely to be in prison than white men, are much more likely to receive decades-long sentences or life without parole, and are much more likely to be on death row.[23] A historical comparison puts these points in stark terms: today there are more Black men under the control of the criminal justice system than were enslaved in 1850.[24]

Looking through the prism of segregated time, one prominent explanatory narrative for how the contemporary carceral state became engorged can be gathered under the temporal politics of racial blowback. Such narratives emphasize the fearful perception that African Americans were moving forward too fast and threatening to escape their status as subordinate and anachronistic.[25] Indeed, when it comes to policing white time, there is no shortfall of historical incursions of racialized social control in response to the gains of people of color perceived as moving "too fast." White supremacist backlash spans Indian removal, slave revolts, Reconstruction-era suffrage, the civil rights movement, and the proliferation of hate groups in reaction to the first African American president.[26] Against this backdrop, scholars have understandably given white backlash a significant role in explaining the recent intensifications of carceral power as a means of racialized social control.[27] Apprehensive in the face of accelerating bids for equality, the nostalgic politics of white temporality seeking to arrest time, and to own time, offers an ominous reboot of Hannah Arendt's formulation: "It is, contrary to what one might expect, the future that drives us back into the past."[28] Hence I want to acknowledge reactive white resentments that generate backlash to racial progress as ongoing continuities, but without obscuring changes in racial-temporal strategies. Proactive and nonlinear, even spasmatic, innovations in how time is weaponized also play key roles in race-making episodes and dynamic processes of racialization.[29]

As an overdue corrective to political science's ahistorical tendencies, the nascent field of American political development has begun to productively contest and complicate unilinear accounts of temporal politics. As part of what is now known as the "southern strategy," conservatives capitalized on an opportunity to conjoin civil rights with crime, thereby reframing racial issues as criminal ones—a maneuver facilitated by the historically entrenched stigma of Black deviance.[30] The shift in framing allowed overt references to race to be replaced with coded language advocating an opposition to crime. It was part of an innovation that Vesla Weaver describes as *frontlash*, which she defines as "the process by which formerly defeated groups may become dominant issue entrepreneurs in light of the development of a new issue campaign."[31] In this context, the formerly defeated were the white opponents of civil rights who creatively shifted the debate from social reform to punishment. In so doing, these proactive political entrepreneurs leveraged race to effect a distinctive shift in policy.

> First conservatives attached civil rights to lawlessness by arguing that civil disobedience flouted laws and would inevitably lead to lawless behavior. Thus, nonviolent protest was connected to riots. But then, through a reverse claim, they disconnected the relationship they had just sewn, by arguing that the riots were not connected to legitimate grievances but to "crime in the streets." . . . The strategy relied on two mutually reinforcing elements: (1) depoliticization and criminalization of racial struggle and (2) racialization of crime.[32]

Weaver's approach highlights the political and theoretical stakes of racial-temporal politics by acknowledging prevailing white resentment, while also resisting reactionary backlash as a generalized catch-all explanation. A time-sensitive approach allows her to make a case for why crime policy changed—and when. Despite the forward-facing connotations of "frontlash," the analysis is that the novel crime policy represents neither innovation entirely outside of history nor mere repetition. Rather, it is a kind of political opportunism where entrenched biases and norms were strategically leveraged by seizing the moment to augur a dramatic shift in the scale and velocity of imprisonment. Part of the explanatory upshot is that racial struggle becomes visible as the groundwork for crime policy, as opposed to being the outcome of a crime wave, as more conventional explanations would have it. As I understand the theory, where backlash would be limited to a path-dependence that happens the way a coiled spring snaps back, frontlash leaves room for improvisational tactics that are "preemptive, innovative, proactive, and above all, strategic."[33]

One of Weaver's analogies for frontlash is a weed that, poisoned by chemicals, mutates and regrows. The point is that at stake politically and theoretically is a particular (if contestable) understanding of time. Even those who are not fluent in Deleuze's rhizomes can appreciate how mutating weeds are distinctive from those that are transplanted, even if the thing they morph into is still a weed. By contrast, the politics contesting affirmative action was not, according to Weaver, frontlash. The existing rhetoric of color-blind equality was redeployed against "racial preferences" and "reverse racism."[34]

Indeed, many whites resented redistributive policies on the grounds that "reverse discrimination" provided an advantage to the undeserving (Black) "welfare queens" Reagan infamously derided as having "80 names, 30 addresses, 12 Social Security cards" with a "tax free income" over "$150,000."[35] And while I suspect there might be more novelty in that race-making episode than Weaver allows, particularly around Reagan's weaponization of racially coded language,[36] I shall be concerned with the innovations on legacies of race as a probabilistic and ultimately even predictive technology. For obvious reasons, "probabilistic technology" evokes the accelerating cybernetic, algorithmic, and electronic innovations used as tools to anticipate *the* future—as opposed to uncertain, plural future*s*. These kinds of rapidly changing technologies can undoubtedly function as instrumental tools of frontlash. Race as a probabilistic technology connotes the ways racial differences convey divergent levels of insecurity, degrees of future uncertainty that can accelerate, or temper, the desire to manage certain political subjects as risk.[37]

What does this have to do with carceral temporality? Here it is helpful to recall Ruth Wilson Gilmore's oft-cited definition of racism as "state-sanctioned and/or extralegal production and exploitation of group differentiated vulnerability to premature death."[38] Police do not just act in response to past offenses, they act in advance. There is a history of the use of policing to transform the insecurity wrought by racial difference into risk to be managed. And continuities and innovations in proactive policing blur the line between probability and prediction—or, if you prefer, between subjects deemed wildcards and subjects that are irredeemable. The dynamic of race-making underway and in motion between race as a probabilistic technology and a predictive one is part and parcel of what we might think of as the concurrent race-ing of race. I regard this as a different inflection and contextualization of Foucault's directive to analyze insidious mechanisms of power and control from the viewpoint of the technologies themselves.[39] That is, he was concerned with wider disciplinary logics as productive (and not just restrictive) powers; what might be generally stated as a focus on subject formation in the context of the modern carceral society.[40] Stuart Schrader lucidly conjoins the continuities of racial subject formation to policing: "Race is not racism's predetermined object; it is what racism produces. The occlusion of this fact is intrinsic to race's autonomization. Racism produces the benefit from state projects of race-making, including police discretion, which has been called whiteness."[41]

Over the arc of the twentieth century, European immigrants were largely shedding their deviant stigma, while the criminalization of blackness endured. As Khalil Gibran Muhammad illustrates in his rich study *The Condemnation of Blackness*, the federal government and social scientists played key roles in this change and continuity.[42] With the help of statistics passed off as objective and race-neutral, the struggles of Euro-Americans would come to be fashioned as issues of class, while Black inequality remained tethered to race and criminality. Consequently, today documented racial biases exist at every level of the criminal justice system, with Black people bearing an outsized burden. On the street, police with special "qualified" legal immunity exploit their power to act as judge, jury, and executioner. In the courtroom, prosecutors have awesome amounts of discretion to decide whom to charge with a crime, the degree of severity of the criminal offense, or whether to pursue charges at all.[43] It bears repeating that research shows that disparities in policing and punishing across different populations have more to do with racial identity than actions like violent crime.[44]

Scholars, in turn, have placed heavy emphasis on the drug war as a mechanism of racialized social control mechanized by such tactics as flagrant disparities in enforcement of Black spaces, asymmetrical sentences between powder and crack cocaine, mandatory minimum sentences, three-strikes laws, and the lack of adequate legal representation—particularly among the racial underclass.[45] Nor can racial disparities in drug-sentencing and arrests be dismissed on the grounds that people of color simply use and sell drugs with greater frequency than whites. The use and the sale of illegal drugs are "remarkably similar" across people of all colors.[46] In fact, criminologist Michael Tonry has found that whites use drugs *more* often and sell them no less than Blacks.[47] While I stress that the problems of segregated time and carcerality exceed the more glaring temporal appropriations of actual sentences handed down and time served, lived time behind bars or in "administrative segregation"—the euphemism for solitary confinement—remains *incredibly* important.

To state the obvious: race and class matter with respect to who languishes behind bars waiting to be processed or sentenced and who can post bail. As Equal Justice Initiative director Brian Stevenson frequently observes, the United States has a system where it is better to be rich and guilty than poor and innocent.[48] Race is especially material in the length of sentence terms and susceptibility to "enhancements," such as allegations of gang membership—which carries an additional one to five years.[49] By blatantly criminalizing *identity*, and not just criminal *action*, the system cannot conceal the fact that its capacity to seize one's body and one's time are tied to group membership. There exist crimes that are only criminal, and actionable, if perpetrated by those within particular age range—crimes that fall within a category revealingly called "status offenses."[50] And the work of creating temporal outcasts by creating new crimes impacting people of color has frequently been a bipartisan affair—as was the case in the legislation tellingly named the Street Terrorism Enforcement and Prevention Act of 1988.[51]

Anglo-liberal jurisprudence wields the prerogative to selectively dispense with treating individuals as self-possessed, rights-bearing citizens equal under the law. Allen Feldman has said that "arrest is the political art of individualizing disorder," yet when it comes to whose time and body are subject to criminal apprehension, much is still determined by societal desire to "impute crime to color," as Frederick Douglass put it.[52] The conflation of color and criminality in public rhetoric and political imagination persists. Today, it would be silly to think that the "get tough on crime" policies advocated by politicians of every stripe will actually result in the mass arrest, prosecution, and imprisonment of larcenous white Wall Street bankers or other elite corporate criminals.

Punitive orientations to diversity continue to be sustained by what Desmond King and Rogers Smith term racialized policy alliances.[53] In terms of who is inclined to favor more punitive policies today, Lawrence D. Bobo and Victor Thompson find that race is the single most decisive factor, with rural whites the most likely to endorse punishment, despite being the least vulnerable to violent crime.[54] As an added political incentive for more punitive policies, inmates can be counted as residents where they are incarcerated, thus increasing the region's political representation.[55] The overlap between segregated space and segregated time is glaring. Penitentiaries disproportionately intern people of color, with a significant number located in rural white areas far from inmates' communities. Inmates are denied the right to vote in all states except Maine and Vermont, the two whitest states in the nation.[56] It hardly takes a leap of imagination to draw lines between present-day prison gerrymandering and antebellum white southerners' insistence that the bodies of the enslaved be counted in the census. From this brief sketch, one can discern racialized means of keeping time in the present day as the contemporary face of segregated temporality.

Keeping Watch: The (Re)generation of Segregated Time

Incarcerated people of color are disproportionately compelled to "serve time" in ways that perpetuate the legacy of white supremacy through time.[57] Yet carceral temporality is not delimited to the duration of the sentence handed down. Time served in prison does not account for divergent experiences of time or segregated temporality. On its own, the quantifiable time of the sentence does not tell us much about the temporal experiences of youth born disproportionately vulnerable to carceral contact and the militarized policing and surveillance. For children of color raised with family and friends behind bars, punishment and incarceration can take on an air of inevitability. Bryan Stevenson tells of African Americans expressing an urgency to compress all of their life experiences in the near term, because they expect to be incarcerated before reaching adulthood.[58] Among those in communities where prison time seems like shared fate, the problem is not what Lauren Berlant calls "cruel optimism," or an unhealthy attachment to an unavailable future.[59] To the contrary, racialized impositions of carceral temporality have made it difficult for some to even imagine a future not captured by segregated time. Let us explore some of the ways that the contemporary carceral condition functions as a mechanism of racial subordination and temporal theft while also coloring temporality outside the prison.

It remains perfectly legal for states to disenfranchise ex-felons for life, making people of color especially likely to be denied the vote.[60] Bruce Western has argued "we can read the story of mass incarceration as part of the evolution of African American citizenship."[61] True enough. In fact, we can also read the story of the American practice of popular sovereignty as inextricably tethered to the ability of white people to police people of color—up to and including the power over life and death.[62] The disenfranchisement of racial minorities in the context of segregated temporality continually evolves to reinforce the conflation of US citizenship with whiteness. The fractured nature of contemporary times is such that the citizenship status of racially dominant groups cannot be properly registered without accounting for the relative deprivation endured by those who, in the meantime, are condemned to an existence doing time as virtually voiceless political ghosts—even beyond the prison walls. The legalized discrimination against ex-felons in matters of employment, public housing, and social services, and wider social opportunity, means that those released from prison continue to do time as lifelong members of a permanent "racial undercaste."[63] The use of the word *caste*—as opposed to *class*—is deliberate. Caste signifies the incapacity for future upward mobility that shadows a segregated present (often in the context of white publics that regard caste and segregation as vestiges of the past). The temporality of the racial undercaste is divorced from timely employment opportunities and capital flows available to nonstigmatized populations. It is conjoined, however, to whites whose time is enriched by the subordinate status of racial others as (among other things) expendable.

For inmates and their families, ongoing spatiotemporal segregation is often reinforced by shame and social marginalization. Future relationship prospects and associational possibilities are further restricted, as ex-felons can be prohibited by law from interacting with other felons, barred from certain occupations and licenses, made ineligible for student loans and public assistance—effectively subjected to civil and social death. Austerity policies favored by political elites work as accelerants that evacuate resources from social services in favor of engorging the penal system at the behest of law enforcement unions and lobbyists.[64] Suffice it to say, as multiple social ills ranging from homelessness to mental illness are outsourced to the police, carceral temporality becomes an ever more entrenched somatic fact of life.

In an unsettling disclosure of the segregated perception of white temporality, studies have found that white police officers encountering Black minors frequently see them as older than their chronological age.[65] Failing to recognize children as minors, they are *apprehended* by police as adults in both the material and psychic senses of the term. Being denied their status as children phenomenologically makes Black minors prone to being violently robbed of their youth—and their lives.[66] In 2014, twelve-year-old Tamir Rice was doubly robbed when he was (allegedly) perceived as an adult with a real gun by police, who without pause killed a child with a toy pistol. Prior to the deadly encounter, however, dispatchers told the police in route that Rice likely had a toy gun. They shot him anyway. Ella Baker's words ring as true now as they did in her own time: "Until the killing of black men, black mothers' sons, becomes as important to the rest of the country as the killing of a white mother's son, we who believe in freedom cannot rest until this happens."[67]

Segregated space and segregated time collude in myriad iterations of structural racism woven into everyday rhythms. There is the school-to-prison pipeline of segregated American education whereby children of color are arrested for offenses as subjective as backtalk and juvenile insubordination. And, irrespective of chronological age, African American children are disproportionately likely to be charged criminally as adults. The trauma that endures long after arrest is its own time trap. The United States is the only country in the world that condemns its children to die in prison. Targeting youth of color, the generation of segregated time is implicated in the gender of segregated time and the production of female carceral citizenship—with some incarcerated mothers shackled while giving birth.[68] It would take at least another manuscript to parse the gender of segregated time as it relates to race and carcerality, but the intersecting themes merit acknowledgment nonetheless. As Marie Gottschalk points out, the children of the incarcerated (along with residents of high-incarceration neighborhoods who have never been arrested or done time in prison) are subjected to heightened surveillance and the threat of carceral contact wrought by intensified monitoring.[69]

Young people of color are in the crosshairs of predictive technologies deployed in the service of white time.[70] Using algorithms and machine learning to supposedly anticipate and prevent crime ahead of time, law enforcement is torquing its temporal horizons to encompass predictive policing. Employing tools like the algorithm called COMPAS, parole boards and criminal courts calculate the risk of future recidivism with data and techniques professing objectivity and impartiality. Yet (entirely predictably!) algorithms have been found to have significant racial biases.[71] A developing field in criminology, the use of data analytics to assess one's likelihood of offending *even before birth* represents a present-day incarnation of a problematic *chronotic* logic surveyed in the previous chapter.[72] These mechanisms influence present police practices, the times, places, and subjects of surveillance, the infamous school-to-prison pipeline, and so forth. Jackie Wang takes exception to the drive and techniques of pre-fixing human subjects through technology, contending, "This is why law-and-order politicians often focus on juveniles: they embody collective anxieties about the future of society. Thus, predictions do much more than present us with a probable outcome, they enact the future."[73]

Driven by what mathematician and data scientist Cathy O'Neil calls "weapons of math destruction," predictive metrics figure in sentencing disparities while also being more broadly meaningful insofar as they hubristically presume to see into a future time.[74] As vehicles of segregated temporality, the chronologics of predictive policing reflect the apprehensiveness of white time and the conduits connecting its capacities of corporeal-chromatic capture. The somatic facticity of racialized deviance in the past and present is encoded into computer programs that function as virtual time-machines with quasi-oracular powers. The specifications of the technology may be new, but the predictive political strategy has a complex history. Prior to the most recent explosion of algorithms and artificial intelligence, Bernard Harcourt rightly contended that predictive policing and actuarial analysis tell us more about those doing the policing than the policed. The fact that we are predisposed to believing in profiling and predictions of criminality "tells us something about our desire to believe, our desire to predict, our desire to know the criminal. We are predisposed to wanting the actuarial model to be right—regardless of the empirical evidence."[75]

This time it is not *just* the myth that the numbers supposedly speak for themselves, as Gibral Muhammad persuasively argued, but also an algorithmic rationalism that is marketed as hovering indifferently above the fray of human fallibility. People may have racial biases, so the logic goes, but computers do not. I shall leave it to those with expertise in cybernetics to detail the problematic mechanics of those technologies. The issue is relevant here because it amplifies and accelerates how race functions as a technology of power. Specifically, the encoding of people of color as risk betrays how race functions as a probabilistic technology of segregated time. "Predictions are . . . about constructing the future through the present management of subjects categorized as threats or risks . . . in marking subjects as potential risks, they are actually produced as such."[76] When racial otherness is apprehended as a liability, difference is figured as a contingency to be shored up in order to securitize the future and to reassure (white) presence.

As a prerogative of white power, this predictive politics of vision is deadly. As recently as 2017 it was deemed permissible to use the so-called future dangerousness of Black defendants as justification for sentencing in death penalty cases.[77] Compounding the chronobiopolitical outrage, power preemptively protects white time from "future dangerousness" by preventing generational reproduction in the first place. (Ask yourself: does it seem anachronistic that between 2006 and 2010 nearly 150 incarcerated women were sterilized in California alone?) Critics say the practice targets inmates viewed at higher risk of serving a jail term in the future. It cost the state $147,460, which Valley State Prison's former ob-gyn, Dr. James Heinrich, defensively called "reasonable" for a ten-year period, "compared to what you save in welfare paying for these unwanted children—as they procreated more."[78] Not only does Heinrich's paternalism convey the infantilization of Black women, he (seemingly reflexively) restages the painful history of eugenics and forced medical experimentation on women of color in the name of scientific advancement and social progress. Likewise, the sterilization program is disturbingly contiguous with Nietzsche's genealogy of punishment as historically employed to safeguard "the purity of the race or maintain[ing] a social type."[79]

Like time itself, statistics, computers, actuarial modes, and race have all wrongly passed as objective, neutral, and even residing outside the morass of politics. The conflagration of these elements elucidates how the forces of carcerality inside and outside the prison facilitate the (re)generation of segregated time. Again, these are only *some* of the temporal dynamics at work. When youth of color are treated as risks threatening present and future security—regarded as "superpredators" in practice (even when the quiet part is not said out loud), questions should arise about the nature of the society and the expected future in need of defending. That, to so many people of color, the transgenerational quality of the ongoing temporal theft of youth is *not* news speaks to the poignancy of registering the whiteness of particular temporalities.

This not to imply, however, that these dynamics are fixed in perpetuity or that they go uncontested. A number of organizations headed by women of color devote time they do not have to confronting the machinations of white supremacy. Mothers Reclaiming Our Children, the prison abolitionist group Critical Resistance, Idle No More, and Black Lives Matter are all fluent in the politics of time as "a politics which takes the temporal structures of social practices as the specific objects of its transformative (or preservationist) intent."[80] And it is hard not to be at once humbled and emboldened by the incredible tenacity of women like civil rights icon Fannie Lou Hamer, who endured unspeakable depravity of torture and overcame imprisonment and sterilization in order to give birth to a new politics.[81] In the next section, I discuss the affective economy of racial pleasure, political invisibility, and segregated time. The fact that such issues of segregated time are themselves largely segregated out of mainstream discursive space beckons us to theorize how their present absence is maintained.[82]

White Noise

Valerie Rohy speaks to the mutually constituted nature of divergent, racialized time zones, writing: "White, public, linear, historical time is not separate from but informed by anachronism, whose vertiginous temporal loops it declines to acknowledge."[83] Rohy does not develop a detailed concept of white time, but her suggestion that its linearity disappears alternate timescapes is a useful point of departure. Dominant temporalities are easily taken for granted as given in the context of historically conditioned denials of alternate time zones and divergent experiences of time. The painful exclusions of cross-temporal social death function such that asynchronous others can often see how prosperous times are subsidized by their subordination, but cannot fully partake of their bounty. The tantalizing effect of a temporal glass wall functions something like a two-way mirror. Those whose presence remains spectral to so many whites can see into the very time zones from which they remain disproportionately excluded. It suggests that social death is not far removed from Berlant's notion of "slow death," which "refers to the physical wearing out of a population and the deterioration of a people in that population."[84]

Berlant's formulation is useful for conceptualizing the biopolitical expenditure of lives of outsourced prison labor, incapacitation, and the relative political invisibility of carceral temporality in white timescapes. If we read her syncretically, alongside and against Angela Davis's work, Berlant's account of ordinary time is instructive: "In an ordinary environment, most of what we call events are not of the scale of memorable impact but rather are *episodes*, that is occasions that frame experience without changing much of anything."[85] In the contemporary context, Berlant's discussion of episodes calls to mind episodes of television shows like *Lockup*. Since episodes of these shows reveal at least some of the miserable conditions of US prisons, it would be mistaken to say that mass incarceration is *entirely* invisible from mainstream life. One might argue that, after all, prison shows are literally prime time infotainment. Yet the televised prison genre does not provoke anything approaching widespread outrage, indignation, or social mobilization. Angela Davis contextualizes the problem by drawing on cultural critic Gina Dent to draw attention to a long-standing media-saturated landscape where prisons are ubiquitous features of film and television.[86] Stretching all the way back to Thomas Edison's first films, such as the 1901 *Execution of Czolgosz with Panorama of Auburn Prison*, Dent observes that the prison has been "wedded to our experience of visuality, creating also a sense of its permanence as an institution."[87] The normalization of prisons as a genre of visual media serves to naturalize their presence as a taken-for-granted feature of the social landscape. Contemplating Davis's portrayal of prisons as "one of the most important features of our image environment," one implication is that these are sites of affective pleasure, and ironically, even escape—at least for the viewer.[88]

In view of how episodes displaying on-screen suffering and violence can get absorbed as a routine pastime and dissolve into the ambient white noise of everyday life, I concur with Berlant that:

> Often when scholars and activists apprehend the phenomenon of slow death in long-term conditions of privation, they choose to misrepresent the duration and scale of the situation by calling a *crisis* that which is a fact of life and has been a defining fact of life for a given population that lives in that crisis in ordinary time.[89]

The passage begins to articulate one of the modalities through which racial deafness is reinforced through what I take to be the *racialized* crisis-ordinariness of white temporalities. The sinister sides of segregated temporality are more easily disappeared by way of their spectrality—how they are simultaneously present and absent in important ways. The virtuality of racial crises points us toward why there is reason to be skeptical that spectacular scenes of nonwhite suffering would necessarily be transformative. We have seen how white temporality's dissolution of Black suffering into its ordinary time is sustained in part by its disavowal of crises that are ordinary aspects of many nonwhite timescapes. But for the disavowal of segregated temporality to maintain its ordinariness, it must be continually reinforced. "White noise" is among the obstructions that help to maintain a collective deafness to other experiences of time.[90]

Peter Euben draws on Don DeLillo's eponymous work to theorize white noise as "an entropic blanket of information in a media saturated society" that accrues to a "random mix of frequencies that renders signals unintelligible."[91] It is the threatening symptom of a media culture that "reifies the present" with a machine-gun fire of "successive images" that "dissociate definitions of reality from the past" helping to engender white American political amnesia.[92] When contemporary innovation collides with racial amnesia, white noise is the pollution emitted from the resulting combustion. This is abetted by twenty-four-hour cable news cycles spinning out stories of desperation with maximum concision and minimal depth. The flow of sights and sounds proceeds ahistorically with an urgent tone and titillating speed, resisting any pause that would allow the viewer time for critical reflection. The rapid pace of information without memory can make current events appear to emerge from nowhere and teeter on the verge of meaninglessness—virtually enveloping the audience in a theater of the absurd. Not incidentally, such time is alternately absorbed by the commentary of talking heads and paid advertisements that break in with amplified volume.

Within the durational structure of white time whereby the past and its presence are disavowed by segregated memory, the grievances and aspirations of people of color are available to be dismissed, muted, or misperceived. That is, they are often dissolved into what Stephen Best and Saidiya Hartmann aptly call "Black noise": "the kinds of political aspirations that are inaudible or illegible within the prevailing formulas of political rationality."[93] It is little wonder, then, that at the same time when Chuck D declared that rap was "Black America's CNN," many whites simply dismissed the nascent art of hip-hop as noise, just as they had once dismissed jazz as "race music."[94] The everyday crises experienced by African Americans, expressed so acutely by groups like Public Enemy and NWA, were untranslatable amid white noise because it amounts to "the past demanding its due against the present and future."[95] White noise is a sign of the times. It is also a signifier of how white time is racialized and segregated in strange and opaque ways that remain overlooked and understudied. It is the riotous propulsion of suffering screened in movies and television episodes whose slick production entertains audiences by providing a "neutral packaging" for violence, a normalization of human cruelty that desensitizes viewers to the racial violence that subsidizes many of the comforts of digital capitalism enjoyed by viewers. "The hum of white noise [is] a distraction from the politics of race and imperialism."[96] The politics of race and imperialism are, of course, often explicitly featured in the innovative expressions of racial others many whites perceive as "Black noise"; from W.E.B. Du Bois's assertion that, in Philadelphia, "the police were our government," to NWA's epic "Fuck the Police" and Public Enemy 1998 track "Bring the Noise."[97]

Of course, there are many ways that political aspirations can be inaudible or illegible. Consider the extent to which the subversive elements jazz and hip-hop have been subsumed into a commercialized "good time."[98] Frederick Douglass lamented that whites perceived even the saddest of slave songs as expressions of happiness, irrespective of their content.[99] As Hartman writes, "The fixation on the slave's 'good times' conceals the affiliations of white enjoyment and Black subjection and the affective dimensions of master and servitude."[100] Beyond the lost-cause absurdity of slavery as a good time, the fixation on slavery's benevolence was accompanied by the racial coding of Afro-diasporic peoples as more musical and rhythmic. Such racial distinctions served to separate Black and Indigenous subjects, with the former destined for perpetual labor and the latter for inevitable extinction. Roughly a century after Douglass, James Baldwin opened "Many Thousands Gone," writing, "It is only in his music, which Americans are able to admire because a protective sentimentality limits their understanding of it, that the Negro in America has been able to tell his story."[101] White sentimentality is a psychoaffective attachment that distorts and diminishes the content, complexity, and humanity of African American musicians across time. When visceral emoting takes the place of meaningful action, that which is heard as Black noise is met with a politics of quiescence and "a dangerous and reverberating silence" that is "the inevitable result of things unsaid."[102]

When insulated by a protective sentimentality, the challenging incomprehensibility of Black noise can, over time, become white noise—at least to some. Sonic norms of racial sentimentalism encourage Black artistic expressions to be ignored, or apprehended as ahistorical soundtrack-backbeats of white pleasure. Received as fungible raw material, the music is available to be neutered of its potential to interrupt the "regularization" of racialized mass death—along with the uniqueness of the time signatures borne by the content and its creators.[103] But assuming that subversion or even storytelling is the only purpose of the music risks a reductive, instrumental telos that swiftly becomes problematic. For her part, Hartman takes pains to acknowledge the complexity and even opacity of the politics of the slave song.[104] In his classic *Invisible Man*, Ralph Ellison uses the "Sambo" figure of the happy Black entertainer to satirize racialized forms of *non*seeing normalized in white phenomenology. The novel discloses how African Americans are apprehended and objectified by the white gaze and also disappeared through a theft of personhood. Like blackface minstrelsy, Sambo is evocative of the slave who must be "made to appear to be born to dance in chains," reveling happily in servitude and reinforcing white notions that s/he deserved to be in bondage.[105] It is against this legacy that Zora Neal Hurston memorably warned, "If you're silent about your pain, they'll kill you and say you enjoyed it."[106]

Today, the attention-gathering qualities of white noise contribute to liberal modernity's production of apolitical subjects whose shared addiction to technology, "trivial excitation," and nostalgia is the closest they come to a "sense of engagement in common enterprises."[107] The very experience of the common is largely virtual. White temporalities are inundated with an endless barrage of amorphous information devoid of historical background, "alternative facts" stand in for truth, and are buttressed by segregated internet ecologies of (white) network spacetimes steadily convening virtual online publics. The reality that would anchor the virtual has been all but reduced to a mere adjective used to describe a form of the entertainment itself: reality TV. Among its most noxious and iconic productions is a racist reality-TV president who expertly cannibalized time by commanding attention. To the extent that the realities of slow death, social death, and the various modes of being out of time outlined here are registered in white timescapes, they are absorbed *in part* through racialized crisis ordinariness.

I say in part because the disavowal that conceals segregated temporality is made both continuous and innovative by the inconvenient truth that, to varying degrees, whites experience contemporary time as beneficiaries of the continued suffering and the ongoing political marginalization of racial others. Amnesiac publics refuse to acknowledge the long-standing role of race in the creation of disposable populations, the very expendability on which white supremacy depends. Acknowledgment is also impaired by forms of willful white deafness and myopia to those who are "out of time"—a disavowal incentivized, normalized, and sustained by a mediated world.[108] Consequently, all the mediated ways that contemporary temporality is saturated or accelerated do not complete the list of obstacles to acknowledging segregated time.

White noise can be a pleasure filter that provides a soothing baseline sense of affective calm and stability.[109] Think of viewers participating in economies of enjoyment by consuming the suffering of others as a normalized feature of everyday life. The fact that race is a compositional element of these violent scenes necessitates confronting their historical embeddedness in what imbues experiences of time with whiteness. While there is a need to critically examine forms of learned deafness, myopia, and desensitization, I want to be careful to acknowledge white noise in the context of other entrenched affective frequencies. Namely, white pleasure in the suffering of racial others persists as a historically embedded habituated form of enjoyment and sinister undercurrent of white temporalities. As Hartman powerfully elucidates in *Scenes of Subjection*, and Ida B. Wells writes of with respect to public lynching, this is not desensitization. Far from it. Rather, at issue is the grotesque indulgence in spectacular pain—the racialization of what Nietzsche calls "festivals of cruelty."[110]

A sustained treatment of the role of media in white time is beyond the scope of this study, and the brief foregoing discussion can only broach the topic.[111] I hasten to add that there are important distinctions between whites' psychoaffective attachments to differently raced peoples—which themselves are subject to change over time.[112] One can, I think, appreciate these distinctions while also noting they are part of a broader perceptual violence whereby forms of racialized apprehension serve to instrumentalize nonwhite peoples as expected sites of extraction and enjoyment in and through time. That the modes of objectification are plural, multiple, and even contradictory testifies to the fungibility imputed to the bodies and times apprehended for what perversely counts as a "good time" from the perspective of white temporal norms.

Ill-attuned to the complex rhythms and tonalities of unique experiences of segregated times apart from its own, the whiteness of temporality renders incomprehensible and irrational the ways and means by which the resistance of outcast groups is so often figured in terms of time. Just as racial inequalities are experienced as impositions on human time, it is also the case that resistance to those incursions, and the corresponding desires they provoke, are often conceived in temporal terms that many do not have ears to hear.[113] King's multiple rearticulations in *Why We Can't Wait* and "Negroes Are Not Moving Too Fast" were decried or dismissed as extremism by white moderates. More than half a century later, Rev. Al Sharpton called "time out" at the funeral of George Floyd, who was murdered by Derek Chauvin, a white policeman who kneeled on his neck for eight minutes and forty-six seconds—a grotesque instantiation of necropolitics, visuality, and segregated time. The US government responded to the subsequent protests of Black Lives Matter against police violence with even *more* militarized violence, underscoring the settler state's will to ensure that the benefits of whiteness as property remain contiguous and uninterrupted through time. Such intensification of violence is legible as the policing of white time to ensure the flows of goods, services, and privilege remain smooth and relatively seamless. As I shall argue in the coming chapters, the policing of racial time as insurance against threat and contingency is consonant with whiteness as property. Present moments imbued with the expectation of future enjoyment of the privileges whiteness conveys are elemental to white temporality.[114]

Fugitive Justice

The rhythms of the modern telos of whiteness as destiny have failed to make the same all those whom liberalism says should be equal. The resounding political response has been an ongoing "criminalization of residual difference."[115] Native studies, decolonial thought, and the Black radical tradition register a plurality of ghosts haunting carceral time, reframing Foucault's assertion that the failure of the prison is the success of the prison.[116] "Prison is a recruitment center for the army of crime. That is what it achieves. For 200 years everybody has been saying, 'Prisons are failing; all they do is produce new criminals.' I could say on the other hand, 'They are a success, since that is what has been asked of them.'"[117] Amid the specters of slavery and colonialism interpenetrating racial capitalism today, prisons are not failing because they produce new criminals. The production of criminals is exactly what was required of a carceral system designed to create a "criminal milieu that the ruling classes can control," making it "pure illusion" to believe the criminal justice system is geared toward engendering universal obedience to the law.[118] The limits (or failures) of prison as localizable, finite, institutional space translate into the successes of societal carcerality replete with racialized regulative temporalities aspiring to extend indefinitely over time.[119]

Some brief reflections on the spectral presence of colonialism, slavery, and empire in the relays between incarceration and civilizational education are helpful in contextualizing the role of carceral time in a "recruitment center for an army of criminals."[120] The school-to-prison pipeline of today makes calls to defund the police in favor of education sound incomplete at best. This all the more so now that schools are hotly contested sites where prohibitions against "critical race theory" aim to ensure the entangled racial legacies at issue here are not studied. For starters, the US reservation system originated as its own kind of open-air prison and disciplinary laboratory, where settlers paternalistically labeled First Nations dependents on their own land. Many adults confined to the reserve refused to surrender their lifeways altogether, so Indian schools were constructed to target children in a civilizational process that blurred the line between cultural and forensic genocide.[121]

Originating with the Puritan John Elliot's "praying towns," established in the seventeenth century, the schools evolved and were later formalized under Grant's Peace Policy in 1869. In 1879 Richard Pratt of Pennsylvania established the Carlisle Indian School, the first off-reservation school designed to make it more difficult for children to run away and return to their parents.[122] In the interest of facilitating assimilation, children were forcibly taken from their families for most of the year, with parents who refused to give up their children subject to imprisonment. Some were incarcerated at Alcatraz, which (not incidentally) the American Indian Movement would occupy from 1969 to 1971. To draw the connection to the prison even closer, the Carlisle school was modeled after the Fort Marion Prison in Florida, which Pratt had also developed. As Indigenous studies scholars have demonstrated, these schools were sites of extreme sexual violence, torture, medical experimentation, forced sterilization, clandestine burials, and their own kind of convict leasing where children were forced to labor in white homes rather than returning to their families.[123] The stated purpose of the policy that would eventually force over one hundred thousand Native children to attend these schools was to "kill the Indian to save the man."[124]

The enduring injustices of the Indian school system have led many to rightly argue that public apologies for these institutions are not just woefully insufficient. They can actually exacerbate injury by hermetically sealing the transgressions in the past, and severing them from present-day politics.[125] From outside the privileged chromosphere of segregated white time, apologies can sound less like historical redress than an imperative to quit complaining and get over it. By making the injustice anachronistic and in the past tense, the settler state makes present grievances illegitimate. Reflecting segregated time more broadly, these political contests also reveal the relation between white time, conceived as linear with discrete tripartite divisions between tenses, and white temporality as the habituated experience-cum-expectation of the prerogative to render racial atrocities as past in order to control the future.

White noise makes the grievances, aspirations, and contributions of people of color misinterpolated or illegible to the point that possibilities for justice become fugitive. By attuning to the frequency of carceral temporality, we find but one channel among many broadcasting a wider concern: a defining feature of white temporalities is their recurrent capacity to strand asynchronous others in an abysmal meantime, cast out of Time. The carceral underside of liberalism's segregated temporality functions to confine modernity's untimely others to a suspended time, caught between the ruptured traditions of the past and the unrealized promises of future democratic prosperity. The interval between the "bygone" and the "not yet" is key, as it marks a time lag between injury and repair. In this meantime the possibility of just deserts evanesces into what Steven Best and Saidiya Hartmann call "fugitive justice."[126]

Fugitive justice does not simply signal the impossibility of bringing the dead back to life and returning to them the time they are owed. Nor does it simply denote our inability to travel back in time and make repair coeval with injury. It also marks how liberal justice appears dubious, dissonant, and fantastical to those repeatedly denied even the imperfect measures of fairness and equality that the abolition of racialized mass incarceration and carceral temporality would represent. In this way, theorizing segregated temporalities is a necessary, if incomplete, step toward acknowledging time as a vector of power deeply implicated in the racial subordination that continually makes justice fugitive.

I have been advancing a time-sensitive diagnostic with the hope that it might be a modest step toward carceral temporality's abolition. Carceral temporality understandably invites questions around how to theorize and enact abolitionist temporalities. On the subject of abolition times and temporalities, my remarks will be necessarily preliminary.[127] This is not least because resisting the forces making justice perennially fugitive means not presuming that every criticism of justice deferred-as-justice-denied comes tethered to a desire for future justice that is knowable in advance. What counts as justice here and now is significantly already prefigured by impositions of Anglo-liberalism that many of its asynchronous others do not recognize as legitimate in the first place. I take this to be an animating spirit of the riposte, "We don't want a bigger slice of the pie. We want a different pie."[128]

Put differently, not all those told to wait are of the view that the only political goods worth working for are already preordained by the prevailing order. White noise can make it seem that way by dissolving alternate futurities into inchoate Black noise. Politically, this means that not presuming to know the future too well does not amount to a cop-out, or a waste of time. It is arguably elemental to subverting the vectors of settler colonial temporal sovereignty imbricated in white time. As I will discuss, many opponents of carceral reform who favor abolition express a resonant sentiment. There is well-founded suspicion among abolitionists that reform is what gives the penal order the time and space it needs to innovate and thrive. Relatedly, activists who draw sustenance and imagination from a range of aesthetic, sonic, and literary sources adopt an improvisational ethos as better equipped to counter the innovations of forces like frontlash without being trapped in prevailing rhythms and flows.

My position is that the temporizing strategy of incrementalism embedded in reform is a companion project to the imperative that people of color "catch up" to white time. Civilizational discourse tells political subjects it racializes as backward what they need to do to be contemporaneous with the powerful. Essentially, this amounts to promising those supposedly trapped in the past time-travel to the present. Reform that does not address historically entrenched racial legacies does much of the same, all the while concealing how it leaves in place carceral temporality as a race-making structure of time. From this vantage, calls for reform read as demands for stasis thinly shrouded in temporizing incrementalism. Prison and police reform mean more of the same. As Foucault put it, "One should recall that the movement for reforming the prisons, for controlling their functioning, is not a recent phenomenon. It does not even seem to have originated in a recognition of failure. Prison 'reform' is virtually contemporary with the prison itself: it constitutes, as it were, its programme" (DP, 234).

I return to the topic shortly. For now, it cannot be overstated that cultivating receptivity to these features of segregated temporality cannot be subsumed into figuring others' time as a simple, derivative byproduct of hegemonic temporalities. In very different ways, Michael Hanchard, Richard Iton, Neil Roberts, Homi Bhabha, Dipesh Chakrabarty, and Elizabeth Grosz all rightly caution against resolving problems wrought by Euro-modernity into a dynamic where heterogeneous "others" merely wish to "catch up" through processes of mimesis.[129] In this most obviously colonized apprehension of racial timescapes, what counts as political progress is a symmetrical, dialectical process with Euro-modernity as the prime mover and everyone else fated to be perpetually out of synch.[130] It is an instantiation of a politics of temporal inevitability whereby, pace Fanon, whiteness is destiny. It is a familiar truism that one cannot catch up to someone who had a head start. Less familiar in accounts where progress looks like a racial game of catch-up is how various kinds of white noise distort myriad expressions of desired futures, diverse time signatures, and cosmologies invented and embodied by putative temporal castaways.

Toward that end, Robert Nichols has productively drawn what he takes to be otherwise neglected connections between the prison and colonialism.[131] Referencing the permanent crisis of the workfare-welfare state that has been displaced to rural areas, he notes that Gilmore expresses the need to "figure out how the ground the prisons stand on becomes available for such a purpose." Nichols follows suit to recast Gilmore's imperative by taking it quite literally, reminding readers that where the land comes from "has a deeper and longer history" and that colonial "territorialized sovereignty ... aspires to impose an exclusivity and singularity of command and control that obliterates alternative normative orders beneath and beyond its aegis."[132] He concurs with Gilmore's emphasis on prisons as sites of spatial segregation, providing what she terms a "geographic solution that purports to solve social problems."[133] With affinities to Gilmore and Davis, Nichols registers the distinctive normative foundations of prison abolition rooted in Indigenous peoples' rejection of settler colonial sovereignty. That rejection is grounded in the alternate lifeways and cosmologies of Native peoples whose aspirations are, stated in terms of this study, irreducible to desires to synchronize with white time. To the contrary, much Indigenous scholarship denies there is any sustainable future in the current dispensation.[134]

Not only does the so-called future tense look different, but also what counts as the not yet past in the form of the prison as an instrument of war, and ongoing territorial expropriation. In keeping with the enduring truth that colonialism is a structure, not an event, the blurred lines between the military and police are not new to Indigenous peoples or their politics.[135] The resonance between empire as a global police force and the police as an instrument of domestic social control has long been apparent to Native populations whose existence in what Kevin Bruyneel calls the "third space of sovereignty" unravels the foreign/domestic distinction.[136] Although not stated in these terms, Nichols's argument also strikes me as providing strong evidence of racialized crisis ordinariness insofar as what is dramatized by some as a new event is an ongoing feature of life for Indigenous peoples. In addition to challenging the biopolitics of racial populations, he maintains that Indigenous critique distinctively "challenges the ideological distinction between the logic of war and the logic of pacification upon which carceral expansion depends" and positions critical prison studies within the wider ambit of settler colonialism and territorialized sovereignty.[137]

I am genuinely sympathetic with Nichols's affirmation of the distinctive normative grounding of Indigenous intervention. It is in solidarity that I worry the muscularity of his position allows the untimely bridgework of the Black Panthers, the Black Liberation Army, and revolutionary voices within and beyond the Black radical tradition to go missing. Their insights draw important connections between territorial dispossession, empire, and carcerality while interrogating the logics of race and war—and race war. The Black Panther leader and prison revolutionary George Jackson is exemplary in his ability to speak to these overlapping themes in untimely ways. The chapter closes with a brief vignette on Jackson and Foucault to modestly suggest the kind of analysis enjoined by the time-sensitive approach advanced in these pages.

Jackson vehemently called out the prison system in terms of "war" perpetrated on contemporary "slaves" in prisons "that have always borne a certain resemblance to Dachau and Buchenwald, places for the bad niggers, Mexicans and poor whites."[138] When he writes of parole officers sending men back to prison for selling Black Panther newspapers as "Failure to Maintain Gainful Employment," it recalls the arrest and re-enslavement of newly emancipated freedmen for offenses like "indolence," vagrancy, and unemployment. (This is essentially the racialized crime of wasting time, where time not spent enriching whites is defined as unproductive.) The connection to empire is unmistakable in Jackson's reference to the turn to "revolutionary antiestablishment position that Huey P. Newton, Eldridge Cleaver, and Bobby Seale projected as a solution to Amerika's black colonies."[139] He refers to himself as "a slave" for whom "the social phenomenon that engages my conscience is, of course, revolution," as one "born to a premature death, a menial, subsistence-wage worker, odd-job man, the cleaner, the caught, the man under hatches, without bail—that's me the colonial victim."[140] His commitment to revolution, as opposed to reform, was inextricably tied to his opposition to racial capitalism. "Revolution within the modern capitalist society can only mean the overthrow of all existing property relations.... Anything less than that is reform."[141]

Jackson's antipathy for reform was, in turn, driven by his temporal politics. "If revolution is tied to dependance on the inscrutabilities of 'long-range politics' and 'the process,' it cannot be made relevant to the person who expects to die tomorrow. There can be no rigid time controls attached to 'the process' that offers itself as relief, not if those for whom it is principally intended are under attack *now*."[142] A voracious reader, Jackson studied Mao Tse-tung, Karl Marx, Kwame Nkrumah, and Che Guevara (among others), but his sense of time made him bristle against dogmatism. Speaking to the capacity of oppressive power to innovate, he references Lenin's *Guerrilla Warfare* to make the case that unforeseeable, emergent forms of struggle are part and parcel of the coming crisis. It follows that "the old guard must not fail to understand that circumstances change in time and space that there can be nothing dogmatic about revolutionary theory."[143]

My intention is neither to elide the experiences of Indigenous and Afrodiasporic peoples nor to conflate George Jackson's politics with the diverse range of abolitionist visionaries today. Rather, it is to gesture to how the political work of desegregating time draws on these entanglements to contest and creatively exceed their entrapments in untimely ways. Like Fanon, Jackson placed a strong emphasis on motion—particularly the kinetic interplay of theory, experience, and politics. Quoting John Gerassi, he affirms theory "rooted in experience, broadened by historical knowledge, tested by combat, and fortified by reflection."[144] Jackson regarded "Amerikan sociopolitical and economic life in general" as fascist, reasoning that "the definition of fascism is a police state wherein the political ascendancy is tied into and protects the interests of the upper class—characterized by militarism, racism, and imperialism."[145] He openly declared the situation a state of war.

After Jackson was murdered by prison guards in 1971, Michel Foucault coauthored a piece in French arguing that his assassination was an "act of war," premeditated in response to the alliance formed by Black and Brown prisoners. However blinkered or unlikely, Foucault's alignment with Jackson is untimely in another way; he and the other members of the GIP (Prison Information Group) presciently predicted that US courts would never prosecute Jackson's killing.[146] Foucault's relative inattention to race, colonialism, and slavery are well-documented shortcomings for theorizing the carceral dimensions of segregated time.[147] Yet a somewhat different corrective is called for when European luminaries like Foucault engage antiracist struggles and thinkers (even imperfectly) and those political and theoretical debts are dismissed as if undeserving of acknowledgment.[148]

Today, the racial political economy of time is directly connected to political economy writ large; inmates' bodies are sites of detention (lost time, time in the hold, or time out) and extraction ("time served" and apprehended) that serve the interests of power. State-sponsored carcerality persists in concert with a lucrative, expansionist, private prison industrial complex. The fact that the two are not mutually exclusive is indicative that the blurring of boundaries between private interests and those of the state is an emblematic quality of racial capitalism—though it is often attributed to what is "new" in neoliberalism.[149] Powerful lobbies on behalf of for-profit prisons and police ensure that the features of mass incarceration described here remain in place, while outsourcing inmate labor. Prisoners are tasked with making everything ranging from eyeglasses to processed foods, furniture, and more. The "more" includes defense equipment used by the US military that is subsequently made available to outfit the very domestic police who target communities of color for punishment and profit.[150] It is not by accident that prison abolitionists adapted the moniker "prison industrial complex" from President Dwight D. Eisenhower's warning about the "military industrial complex"—ever more proof that colonialism always comes home. As we look forward, the broader aperture of segregated time also helps torque the analysis of contemporary policing and race as exceeding the spatiotemporal boundaries of the nation-state.

As Stuart Schrader argues in his superb study *Badges without Borders*, the globality of policing as a project has contributed mightily to the continual expansion of police power domestically.[151] The hellscape on the home front is the product of a global national security apparatus geared to quash colonial insurrections.[152] Tracing a long history of developing strategies of imperial governance from the Indian Wars, Schrader illustrates how technical reformism and developmentalism in policing did not obviate racism so much as reformat it domestically and abroad. The resulting strategies might be shorthanded as overlapping agendas of "empires without imperialists" and "racism without racists."[153]

On the ground, this meant employing practices such as racial and ethnic diversification of police ranks, with an emphasis on those with military service. "With reliance on delegated police assistance, the United States implemented an approach to pacification that looked back toward earlier lessons from frontier and colonial campaigns and looked forward toward new international settlement characterized by discretionary empire."[154] Colonial strategies of enlisting Indigenous proxies for police purposes were, in turn, applied at home, with counterinsurgency forming the connective tissue. As Schrader puts it, "In counterinsurgency, the necropolitics of violent containment and liquidation have been yoked to the pastoral politics of social improvement."[155] Particularly in the context of a threadbare welfare state, policing takes on a productive role in human development and subject formation. Wielding instruments of violence and pacification, counterinsurgency aims to produce a particular kind of political subject and temporal order. It does so not only by protecting the material property of some while dispossessing others, but also by policing the rhythms of a capitalism whose aims and flows also exceed the nation-state.[156]

With respect to the "normative orders beneath and beyond" the aegis of colonial sovereignty, the temporal ordering of liberal justice presented as the best and only available option worthy of aspiration is an elemental component of the prescriptive structure of colonial incursions. Imperialism's conquest of inevitability is a conquest of time. The rights-based, procedural orientation of Anglo-liberalism—with its present-centered focus and aversion to collective debt obligation, its history of using the (white, male) individual as the unit of analysis, comes freighted with its own time signatures. Liberal forms of timekeeping make Indigenous critiques of the politics of recognition all the more relevant to ensure that the response to the denial of the right to be coeval does not become code for a politics of catching up. Nor should we be deceived by a politics of copresence as a solution if what counts as being present is once again defined by the logics of white time. Liberal modes of counterfeit acknowledgment can take the form of eviscerating tribal governance, paternalistically "elevating" Indigenous people as worthy of liberalism's promises of temporizing universalism that says, "Yes, but not yet" to aboriginal humanity, the outright seizure of Native lands in the name of national or economic progress, or employing the market-leveraged depredations of First Nations—desperation historically produced by the settler state—to compel the ceding of lands through sale, parceling, debts secured by land, or leases permitting extraction.[157]

With prosperity and progress always to come, the liberal order can exist simultaneously alongside deeply illiberal policing practices always available to be called upon and excused as part of a broader developmental strategy. As a supplemental sleight of hand, those who resist the overwhelming force of the police and get beaten down can then be said to have acted irrationally by poorly choosing their own grim destiny.[158] On the level of pedestrian rhythms, we witness the criminalization of "furtive movements" (presumably moving too fast while not being white) or loitering (the updated version of vagrancy; wasting time, not moving fast enough, or at all). On a broader scale, there is the well-worn white colonial tactic of publicly apprehending those who resist as proof of an inherently violent, savage preference for war among racial others. By insisting that the carceral system amounts to state-sponsored warfare waged on the racially and economically subordinate, Jackson and the Panthers inverted the liberal formulation of criminals as those who make war on the state. We shall see in the next chapter that war is among the bumpy contingencies in white time that get stabilized and smoothed out by apprehending the time of people of color.

Interlude 1: The Part That Has No Time

For political theorists whose vocation calls them to "travel in order to see," what does it mean to hear "Black noise"? The dissonance of Black noise and the deafening power of white noise discussed in the preceding chapter call into question the visual imagery of the sighted traveler frequently invoked in political theory. It raises the need to productively embolden our lexicon with an idiom and sensibility better equipped to register temporality. Optical metaphors add spatial depth to our conceptions of politics, but the static nature of spatial representations of time ultimately fails to capture the very dynamism and flow that characterize human experiences of temporality. As Elizabeth Grosz writes, "The reality of time is not reducible to the reality of space and of objects, though it can only be seen in its effects on them. It is most directly understood and experienced outside of images, models and representations as a force, an impulse forward."[1] Spatial representations that miss the fluidity of temporal forces risk perpetuating a brand of theory anesthetized to time as a vector of power. Still worse is the risk of employing modes of theory that inadvertently reproduce discursive maneuvers complicit in using time as a means of perpetuating spatial distance. Congruent with the last chapter's discussion of policing time, Jacques Rancière has written insightfully about the legacy of politics as policing. A brief encounter with the space-time relays in his work will help bring the political and theoretical correspondence into sharper focus.[2]

Rancière cautions that "it is not merely a matter of stressing time over space. Disciplinary thinking uses time itself as a principle of spatialization. It replays, as a methodological principle, the Platonic assertion that 'work does not wait,' which amounts to locking up workers in the space of their absence of time."[3] As an alternative, Rancière affirms a "method of equality" that must simultaneously implement what he calls a "principle of historicization and a principle of untimeliness, a principle of contextualization and decontextualization."[4] Contextualization allows for communication across lines of difference through words that "resound in their concrete place and time of enunciation," where the untimely move of decontextualization permits an opening in order to

> draw the line of escape, the line of universalization on which the poor romantic floor-layer meets the aristocratic philosopher of antiquity and verifies that they have something in common, that they speak about the same thing: the capacities of *having* or *not having* time. The untimely method of equality implies another way of thinking the Universal. The Universal is not the law ruling over the multiple and the particular. It is the principle at work in the operation which calls into question the distribution of the sensible separating universal matters from particular matters. Accordingly, untimeliness is a way of thinking the event in terms of multitemporality, in terms of intertwining plots.[5]

Rancière acknowledges the mutually constituted dyads of the timely/untimely, the universal/particular, along with the various modes of inequality that shadow equality. His insightful analysis in *Dis-agreement* updated and sharpened the (Aristotelean) lesson that a polity becomes legible precisely by way of that which it excludes—what he calls "the part that has no part."[6] Yet I shall argue that it is precisely in his rendering of this fugitive part where Rancière's analysis lacks the untimely sensibility he endorses in the preceding passage.

For Rancière, politics happens when the excluded part interrupts the "natural order of domination"[7] and refigures the "dividing of a society"[8] by becoming articulate.[9] Through speech, the part that has no part performs a kind of embarrassing equality that disrupts the (arch-political) designations that police the line intended to separate out those who "naturally" count from those who remain uncounted, uncountable, and virtually invisible. One site of politics happens when those whose presence is spectral demonstrate "speech that does not simply express want, suffering or rage, but intelligence" and reveals how "the speech that causes politics to exist is the same that gauges the very gap between speech and the account of it."[10] To put the matter more succinctly, when a subordinate draws a superior in an argument, s/he proves they are equals—at least insofar as there is a mutual capacity for understanding the terms of the discussion that can only occur between rational beings. By demonstrating the "equality of any speaking being with any other speaking being," it "makes visible what had no business being seen, and makes heard as discourse where once there was only place for noise."[11]

The aesthetic imagery of the "part that has no part" is, of course, spatial. The limits of its utility become apparent insofar as it fails to fully register the temporal dynamic through which politics transfigures "a place for noise" into discursive space. Missing from the account is how noise becomes a resonant discourse in time, not just space. Otherwise put, it is not simply that the speaking other demonstrates equality through speech. S/he/them also demonstrates, and indeed insists upon, a measure of contemporality. The very resonance of that speech *as speech* hinges upon the other's status as a coeval party heard *now*. Still the demand for receptivity is also a demand to reinvent the form and content of "the now" as presence—respecting the present as connoting a position in space (here) and in time (now). It follows that theorizing a politics that does not disavow the part that has no part requires more than a "redistribution of the sensible" that is more inclusive of those who make claims from the margins. The distribution of the sensible requires a temporal register so that the marginal claims (or "Black noise") of those forced out of time can "make sense" in the first place.[12]

While by no means the last word, the shift at least begins to grapple with the modalities of power through which the excluded part is repeatedly relegated to what we might call a "time out of Time." Apart from Time, the part is a part that has no Time (or a part whose time is foreshortened), and a part for whom the whole has no time to spare. Just as the excluded part gives the whole its integrity, the segregated time of that excluded part contributes to fashioning the "time of the whole" as a cohesive epoch. Disrupting that cohesion through politics calls for interrupting the temporal flows that normalize practices of rendering others anachronistic. As we saw previously, anachronistic others are exposed to strategic temporizing that postpones equality and freedom to reinforce segregation in time, while solidifying inequalities in political space.

Strategies of temporizing universalism are themselves fashioned in particular epochs and mobilized against temporal outcasts, simultaneously affirming their right to have rights in principle while postponing their conferral in practice. The correspondence between time and space appears as a contemporary investment in "temperance," or *sophrosyne*: the Greek virtue of knowing one's place, which reverberates with its own kind of Platonic white noise from his taxonomy of political order.[13]

With the help of Cedric Robinson, we can rejoin Rancière, who lucidly acknowledges the connection between segregated time and segregated space with his assertion that "the *sôphrosunê* of the artisans is identical to their 'lack of time.' It is their way of living the interiority of the city as radical exteriority."[14] Nevertheless, as long as time and space are collapsed conceptually, Rancière's deep worry that politics gets collapsed into a mechanism for policing who does what is unlikely to be assuaged politically. An untimely engagement with Rancière is generative precisely because segregated temporality is endemic to the very "inegalitarian partition of the perceptible" that he decries.[15] This excursion may seem esoteric to some. To better appreciate the political relevance, it is helpful to acknowledge that the perilous overlap between knowing one's place and knowing one's time that persists in contemporary white time has historical grounding and racial reverberations in Platonic political policing. As Cedric Robinson suggests, perhaps the times of ancient Greece and colonial America aren't so segregated after all.

Robinson reflects on the American founders' fluency in Plato, plutocracy, and slavery, noting his *Republic* was "rich in intellectual stratagems *a propos* to the political discourse embedded in the American political order."[16] This is not just because Plato famously endorsed slavery as the lot of those incapable of reason and political participation of any sort—though that certainly was the case. The American founders were steeped in the more broadly antidemocratic ethos of Plato's political philosophy. After democratic Athens executed Socrates, the most just man Plato knew, *The Republic* reads as a mournful turning away from faith in the demos.[17] Synonymous with the ephemeral, democracy threatens insecurity by way of accelerating injustice at the hands of the supposedly mindless masses, necessitating the fixity of *The Laws*, earning Sheldon S. Wolin's retort that *The Laws* was "Plato's revenge on Athens."[18] The antidemocratic theory of *The Republic* featured rigidly structured hierarchical rule of a supposedly wise ruling class, a courageous warrior class, and a temperate citizenry. This meant that everyone needed to know their place in terms of formal politics, but it also entailed a more penetrating policing of the order of one's internal being. For Plato, statecraft was soulcraft.

Such an ethos lends itself nicely to partisans of white supremacy, particularly to settlers given to fits of paranoia over Indigenous insurrection and slave revolts. As Robinson writes:

> Plato's political theory thus repressed the history of popular rebellion and with it the recognition that social agency might have its genesis from the general populace. Even his "treatment" of the degeneracy of democracy to tyranny, the *demos* is denied true agency through the selection of a

demagogue. In his philosophy, "justice" (permanent order) is opposed to liberty and equality.[19]

Through a strategic application of segregated memory, Plato's denial of agency to the demos offers comfort to the ruling class. We know this reassured ethos actually persisted historically through the shock sent through Europe and the colonies in the wake of the Haitian Revolution.

So riveting was the hysteria in the face of Black agency that Europeans variously attributed the slave revolt to a communicable disease or magic. In the final analysis, what was the depth of the Platonic imprint on the American founders? In a reworking of Nietzsche's take on Jesus's existence, Robinson avers that "Plato survives because if he had not existed, he would have had to be invented."[20]

3
Killing Time

Imminent Immigrants and the Temporal Borders of Racial Biopolitics

Oscar J. Martínez writes that "In the American mind the border came to represent a divide between progress and backwardness, between good and evil."[1] In this chapter I explore how contemporary US immigration politics is inhabited by a curious, and even seemingly contradictory, mix of sociotemporal impulses. On the one hand, Latinx immigration has been cast as an epidemic threat and depicted as a degenerative assault on development, progress, prosperity, and morality. Calls to fortify the border today align with the rhetoric of immigrants as a viral infestation to be exterminated. At the same time, the country's economic and biopolitical health are leveraged on time stolen from immigrant workers needed to perform dangerous, exploitative labor. Disproportionately racialized as nonwhite, Latinx workers are exposed to plural morbidities in the form of social death and forensic death that comes fast, slow, and sporadic. Latinx immigrants also experience and embody segregated temporality by working to produce the accoutrements of twenty-first-century digital capitalism while being forced to endure conditions typical of centuries past—well below the median contemporary standards of living and working enjoyed by the racially dominant group. They often toil to make the goods of late modernity that their meager wages often do not permit them to own. Taking the problematic, historically entrenched invocations of Latinx (im)migrants as epidemiological threats as my point of departure, I examine immigration politics in terms of segregated time, not just segregated space.[2] As Martínez asserts, the border should be considered a temporal, and not merely spatial, boundary.

Consonant with the analysis advanced in the previous chapter, I explore how the expendable lives of Latinx immigrants criminalized by the border and consigned to temporary, dangerous work are utilized to shore up the linearity, stability, and continuity of segregated white time—especially in times of perceived crisis and contingency. Until fairly recently, the prevailing scholarly consensus was that biological racism had fallen out of fashion and given way to "racially coded" language and "dog whistle politics,"[3] requiring sharper interpretive tools to address more subtle forms of "cultural" or "ethical" racism.[4] The need for acute analysis undoubtedly remains as pressing as ever, but it is hardly the case that anti-immigrant racism has gone undercover or that previous racisms have been rendered obsolete. In the United States today, political leaders at the highest levels openly declare immigrants outside the human race, insisting these "aren't people—these are animals."[5] Nativists use alarming epidemiological rhetoric to cast nonwhite migrants as vectors of disease and *as* disease, simultaneously the infected and the infestation itself. These alarms of immigrant invasion and contagion signal dangers to the security of the body politic to be fought, arrested, detained, quarantined, inoculated against, deported, expelled, or exterminated.[6]

A range of scholars have acknowledged there are serious political stakes when immigrants are cast in terms of natural disasters such as "a brown tide rising" carrying criminal delinquency, intrusive barbarism, and viral epidemics capable of spreading with rapacious fertility.[7] These evocations of biological racism are not merely vestigial flashbacks to the past; they are part of a present-day iterations of what Leo R. Chavez calls "the Latino threat narrative."[8] By now, there is substantial historical evidence of what can happen when human populations are coded as vermin, pestilence, and infectants. And advances in science long ago disproved notions of polygenesis, speciation, and breeding practices of animal husbandry as applicable to humans.[9] Nevertheless, from the heights of power there has been a resurgence of eugenicist notions that "there are superior people" who, when coupled with other elites, produce superior offspring.[10] The apparition of past racisms suggests that they were never entirely gone, but spectral.[11] Grappling with the temporal politics of racial spectrality entails acknowledging how racial formations believed to be bygone can still haunt present and future moments. Never entirely absent, antecedent racisms do not necessarily return to any "here and now" fully reincarnated in their prior form. Rather, race is improvisational, iterative, and processual in ways that recall Malcolm X's quip that "racism is like a Cadillac, each year they introduce a new model."[12]

The mixture of continuity and change that I take up here involves the curious dynamic by which Latinx immigrants are able to be racialized as both disease and cure, infectant and inoculant—depending on the times.

The ongoing technique of casting racial/ethnic others as an infestation that must be walled off, quarantined, and even exterminated resonates with what Foucault referred to as the "plague dream," the desire of the powerful for a perpetual state of emergency, engendering the fearful obedience of the governed. Yet the precarious, rightless Latinx immigrant as the ideal laborer resonates with his later work, where disposable racial others are useful for shoring up *endemic* threats. These threats are contingencies, eventualities, and random events that recur over extended periods and thus need to be managed, such as labor and food shortages.[13]

By modestly placing Foucault's works on discipline and biopolitics into contestation and dialogue with migration studies, as well as Latinx politics and scholarship, I explore how discipline and biopower coexist simultaneously in white time.[14] The endemic and epidemic political logics are pernicious examples of what I have been calling the apprehensiveness of white time, a spatiotemporal disposition that seeks to dominate time and facilitates the accelerated disposability of nonwhite peoples—the polyvalence of the "race" of segregated time. As we shall see, racialized temporal theft is especially visible when the hegemonic racial timescape comes under perceived threat by way of Latinx others moving "too fast" in terms of gaining rights, status, and even demographic presence. Likewise, the proliferation of disposable peoples accelerates during times of labor shortage, economic scarcity, military conflict, and so forth. For Foucault, the movement from epidemic to endemic happens sequentially over historical time, with race entering the picture belatedly as a key biopolitical index separating who lives and who dies. By treating discipline and biopolitics as episodically synchronic, rather than diachronic, I disturb the temporal stages he assigns to each while also illuminating nonlinear, innovative, and dynamic race-making processes that go missing when migration is addressed with respect to territoriality alone. The immunity paradigm provides interpretive insight into the simultaneity of disciplinary and biopolitical power, while also illuminating the apparent contradiction in American politics whereby immigrants are alternately regarded as both a cure and a disease.

Viewed through the prism of segregated time and US immigration politics, ostensibly opposing political attitudes evince dangerously corresponding logics regarding the disposability of immigrant lives. When progressives argue that immigrants "do the jobs Americans can't do, or *won't*, do," they partake of a disciplinary separation of the good versus bad migrant, furthering a biopolitical agenda insofar as migrant jobs are undesirable precisely because they often entail dangerous, withering, exploitative, life-risking labor. Whether as infestations or inoculants, disposable populations regarded as outside of the human race securitize the rhythmic continuity of white time against uncertainty.

The chapter proceeds by first considering the theoretical and political stakes of the border as a temporal, and not just spatial, boundary of immigration politics. I then take up Foucault's analysis of the plague dream for insight into contemporary immigrants cast as epidemic infestations used to justify present-day states of emergency. The discussion of epidemic threats is followed by an analysis of how Latinx immigrants are employed to shore up endemic contingencies and random events for the benefit of white time. This, in turn, allows us to see how discipline and biopolitics function simultaneously for racialized ends. Accordingly, in the closing section resistance figured in temporal terms dramatizes how immigrant presence sustains the prevailing temporal order.

Immigration across Spacetime Borderlines

In the age of reactionary pseudo-populism in the United States and abroad, right-wing politicians expressing anything short of a "zero tolerance" brand of anti-immigrant policy do so at their own political peril. From other corners come frequent assertions that the United States is a nation of immigrants—a country that welcomes immigrant others. Yet this commonplace view reveals a peculiar kind forgetting of both Native Americans and American nativism; a disavowal of historical precedent when it comes to matters of settler colonialism and race-based immigration practices.[15] On the left, opponents of xenophobia frequently contend that nativism is the *exception* to the seductive myth of an immigrant America, not the norm. Hence the familiar incantation that "this is not who we are." Yet the history of American nativism has been concealed by way of a curious kind of national amnesia that takes the form of disavowal: a willful denial of what one knows, at least on some level. The cost of this historical disavowal includes a widespread inability to intuit the ways in which nativism and imperial history not only shape immigration policy, but have also defined national identity and citizenship in exclusionary and normalizing ways.[16]

Segregated memory conditions our sense of the present time, and thus the context within which immigration disputes take place—or go missing. As

Gloria Anzaldúa recalls, the status of Mexicans and Chicanos as "illegals" with no claim to the land that they allegedly trespass upon is rooted in a disremembered colonial past. "The Gringo, locked into the fiction of white superiority, seized complete political power, stripping Indians and Mexicans of their land while their feet were still rooted in it."[17] Remarking that, with the capture of Santa Anna in 1836, "*Tejanos* lost their land and became foreigners overnight," Anzaldúa points to the contested relation between temporal periodization and territorial sovereignty.[18] The power to expropriate Tejanos came with the capacity to reset the clock and remake political subjects into noncitizens by reordering both space and time. Since the 1930s, activists and intellectuals have employed a politics of mnemonic resistance by resurrecting the historical claims of Mexican Americans in order to contest such borderlines.[19] In view of how disavowed history is tethered to their disavowed presence, it follows that Latinx peoples would stage resistance in temporal terms. Protestors counter the politics of invisibility by echoing Anzaldúa's insurgent countermemory with placards that read: "We didn't cross the border, the border crossed us."

I shall return to the point. For now, I want to underscore how what is at issue is not only marginalized memory, but the particular ways in which segregated time has racialized experiences of time and rendered the presence of immigrant temporalities largely spectral in the public imaginary. Just as the institution of chattel slavery stigmatized blackness, the entwined legacies of colonialism and empire are inscribed in the stigma of Latinx identity and persist as historical remainders with enduring political significance. Lina Newton speaks directly to the influx of Mexican émigrés in the context of stigma, arguing that "'the border,' along with the various meanings and imagery that the region carries, is a mark that the Mexican-origin population must bear—and one that European immigrants and their grandchildren do not."[20] With respect to the correspondence between stigma and temporality, the "mark of the border" is deeply implicated in the racialized components of who is forced to wait for goods, services, and status. A sizable portion of Latinx immigrants wait decades without being able to enjoy the same advantages of their counterparts who have been in the United States for the same amount of time.

In *Generations of Exclusion* Edward E. Telles and Vilma Ortiz examine four generations of Mexican immigrants and make the case that these émigrés continue to be disbarred from the privileges conferred upon Euro-Americans well after undergoing the typical rites of passage for immigrants entering into the United States, such as learning English. "[A] large part of the Mexican American population has not been allowed the same opportunities that have been given to mainstream America and these disadvantages tend to get reproduced over generations."[21] The authors' distinction between Mexican Americans and mainstream America can be read as different experiences of the flow of time indexed by race.[22] For Mexicans, economic integration stalls after the second generation even though political, cultural, and social assimilation continues after the first generation of immigration.

> Although European immigrants were often racialized as nonwhite, they were largely accepted by the second or third generation, which allowed them to fully or nearly fully assimilate. For Mexican Americans, though, we find racialization especially in education well into the fourth generation, even though cultural and other forms of assimilation may occur.[23]

Notice how the entwined issues of time and temporality, and not just space and territoriality, are important features of racialization. It bears mention that this racialization does not take place in a vacuum, but is conditioned by a variety of historically contingent factors—notably the hotly contested status of undocumented peoples.

Speaking to the complex political work of the border, Alicia Schmidt Camacho writes that the border is "both fixed and shifting line, one that paces the dance, back and forth, among the undocumented, the refugee, the labor contractor and the police."[24] I shall leave the granular historiography to others, but it is important to note that the shifting ways that the borderline cuts across space and time—and implicates the police and labor contractor—should be understood in relation to how the racialized carcerality discussed in the previous chapter articulates with the criminalization of immigrant bodies discussed here. As Martha Escobar argues, this includes complex relations between the criminalization of welfare, the effects of the increased abilities of African Americans to make citizenship claims on the state in the wake of the civil rights movement, and how these dynamics throttle the (re)production of the criminalized immigrant as the ideal laborer.[25] Akin to their Afro-diasporic counterparts, Latinx peoples are racialized as wasting time and lazy, while also ironically valorized as those from whom productive time can be stolen in the name of progress.

When I first became aware of migration politics years ago, I wondered whether Latinx immigrants were expected to toil in the shadow economy for some imagined length of time in order to mirror the perceived sacrifices in the memories of European émigrés and their descendants—all as a condition of achieving the rights of citizenship. After all, I reasoned, resentment that undocumented migrants are failing to wait their turn and jumping the queue speaks to the racial order assuming the prerogative to set the timetable for admission in the first place.

In the time that has passed since those early musings, the United States has witnessed a historical shift away from the notion that immigrants are American "citizens in waiting," as suggested by Hiroshi Motomoro's eponymous book title.[26] Mainstream nativists assert that illegal aliens should never expect to become citizens, and US citizens should not harbor that expectation for them either. Those once understood as forced to wait are no longer even viewed as waiting, but increasingly criminalized, living "in detention" off the grid, or toiling clandestinely as *permanent temporary* labor. The familiar dynamics of white time imposing a waiting period has shifted toward a politics of segregating Latinx immigrants into a particular kind of indefinitely suspended spacetime. Along with the segregated time of immigrant detention, there are the anxious times of undocumented workers living in a form of carceral temporality at once related, and yet distinct, from that of the last chapter.[27]

What Paul Apostolidis aptly calls *la vida encerrada* "means not only being shut inside a closed area but additionally carries connotations of being imprisoned or trapped and is also used to describe the caging or fencing in of animals such as livestock."[28] To cross the border illegally is to enter *la vida encerrada*; it is to penetrate a temporal condition where one's invisibility is maintained in the suspended meantime of various kinds of enclosed, clandestine hiding spaces, and beneath adopted facades. Apostolidis's interviewees recounted harrowing stories of being locked up while in the charge of human smugglers, or coyotes. They told of being held captive in border way stations, detained in the suffocating confinement of the backs of trucks, and locked within abandoned houses. Tragically, the need to remain hidden only reinforces the relative invisibility of these particular experiences of time and the unequal power relationships that benefit those so deeply invested in their concealment. The fear of deportation functions as a sharp disincentive to collective organizing, to put it mildly. The peculiar kind of unfreedom experienced by undocumented workers is one where mobility is typically confined by a fear that immigration officials (*la migra*) might descend at any moment. The restrictions on movement, and even the conditioning of one's rhythms and bodily functions, are shaped by a heightened awareness of the need to remain hidden. Here is Ramon Díaz:

> The biggest difference is that here you spend all your time shut in [*encerrado*]. . . . It's not like in your own country. Because in your own country . . . you spend all your time outside. And not here. Here you do everything shut up inside [*encerrado*]. . . . You come home from work tired and you have to do things at home . . . and then when a person comes who doesn't have papers, who is afraid that *la migra* might come—it's even worse![29]

Lurid testimonies portray experiences of being *encerrada* as a simultaneous compression of space that is matched with an extension of time's duration. As a result, the "obrera [female worker] may mark time by how long her body can endure the routine and may measure space by the confinement of the industrial plant."[30]

At the same time as the life *encerrada* ("shut in," "enclosed," or "locked up") persists for imminently deportable undocumented workers, more traditional forms of being locked up or acutely disposed of and laid to waste are hardly obsolete amid the proliferation of immigrant detention. To the contrary, these spacetimes are segregated and mutually implicated in ways that serve the interests of white power. For insight into how these weaponized temporalities interact, I critically revisit Foucault and the politics of exploiting racial others to deal with ailments endemic to the polity (like the need for laborers to do dangerous work) while simultaneously casting those same populations in terms of epidemic plagues in need of capture and extermination. We begin with the political "plague dream," so strongly resonant in the United States and abroad whereby migration politics is figured in terms of epidemic threat.[31] Punitive measures taken on behalf of contemporary security have been especially intrusive for racial others who are so frequently surveilled, apprehended, deported, violated, and indefinitely incarcerated. Immigrant "plagues" are deployed as crises in need of humanitarian intervention through a discourse that accelerates the militaristic border politics, policing, suffering, and death-dealing that the stated emergency supposedly aims to contest.

The Plague Dream

In his landmark work *Discipline and Punish*, Michel Foucault indicted the abstractions of political philosophy as serving as the virtual accomplices of modern subjugation. While the esoteric philosophers and jurists of the Enlightenment era imagined the model of society in terms of a contract that would deliver humans from their natural state, Foucault argued that those who actually knew something about how power functioned on the ground had a very different model of society. He contended that the "soldiers and with them the technicians of discipline" had as their model of society not a contract based on individual consent, but the image of society as a well-trained army that could march in uniform synchronicity and precision (DP, 169). Here is Foucault:

> Historians of ideas usually attribute the dream of a perfect society to the philosophers and jurists of the eighteenth century; but there was also a military dream of society; its fundamental reference was not to the state of nature, but to the meticulously subordinated cogs of a machine, not to the primal social contract, but to permanent coercions, not to fundamental rights, but to indefinitely progressive forms of training, not to the general will but to automatic docility. (DP, 169)

Foucault follows this model of society as a collective of "docile bodies" with panoptical images and textual depictions of what he calls the "means of correct training" (DP, 170–194).

Less remarked upon, if no less remarkable today, is Foucault's subsequent account of the ideal governable society. After introducing the dream of society as operating under the discipline of a well-trained army, Foucault argues that, for the architects of power who operated at eye level, there was a separate—but not unrelated—aspiration that has received comparatively less attention. It is "the political dream of the plague" (DP, 197–198). Contesting the imaginary realms that anchored social contract theory, Foucault writes: "In order to make rights and laws function according to pure theory, the jurists place themselves in imagination in the state of nature; in order to see perfect disciplines functioning, rulers dreamt of the state of plague" (DP, 198–199). The political plague-dream both aligns and departs from Foucault's antecedent discussion of carceral space and disciplinary timetables. The threat of the plague came freighted with intense pressures to identify, stigmatize, and quarantine those infected—and to do so on a mass scale in order to protect the healthy. Under siege by a mysterious ailment, the populace is ever more willing to succumb to increased panoptic surveillance and governmental scrutiny. Public health demanded that infected individuals be visibly stigmatized so that they could be segregated from mainstream society for the sake of the common good.

To avoid widespread extermination, everyone has to accept increased intrusion and heightened visibility at the pleasure of the state. Citizens are enlisted as the eyes and ears of the government in order to spot symptoms of infection in their neighbors—and then "rat out" anyone symptomatic by rendering them to the police for quarantine. As a result of the elevated risk, the timetable for the public consent to be surveilled would, by necessity, have to be accelerated—assuming, of course, that we can call such a move consent. Either way, the threat of impending death incites a frenetic compression of time that demands an immediate segregation of space. In contemporary parlance, collectivities threatened by the plague are all the more willing to surrender privacy and freedom for the sake of security.

It is important to note that the plague dream is distinct from the experience of an actual plague, particularly with respect to how states of emergency necessitate spatial segregation. As Foucault puts it, the "utopia of a perfectly governed city" is one where the plague is "envisioned as a possibility at least" (DP, 198). The government capitalizes on widespread apprehension in order to move closer to the ideal exercise of disciplinary power in the name of public health. The "idealization" Foucault depicts is a scenario where the fear of a future plague enervates a fear of an incessantly plagued future. The potential of future plague becomes so normalized that even the possibility that collective life could, or should, be different virtually disappears beneath the horizon of conscious awareness. It is the dream of a continuing state of emergency and state of exception that goes on through time until it is neither emergent nor exceptional.

With contemporary states of emergency in mind, we can ask: what is the relationship between the mechanism that identifies, stigmatizes, and quarantines infected persons and the processes that suspend ordinary time in the name of public health and security? Foucault argues:

> The exile of the leper and the arrest of the plague do not bring with them the same political dream. The first is that of a pure community, the second that of a disciplined society. Two ways of exercising power over men, of

controlling their relations, of separating out their dangerous mixtures. (DP, 198)

With the leper as a metaphor of exclusion, the nightmare of the plague is an analogue for "all forms of confusion and disorder" that accelerate disciplinary projects (DP, 199). They are "different projects, then, but not incompatible ones" (DP, 199)[32]—especially, one might add, when it comes to matters of race. In the relays between "plague" and "purity" Foucault collocates two aspirational modes (or "dreams") the modern state has aimed to achieve through models that are not contractual, but military and medicinal. These models, and his exposition of panopticism in general, were provocations challenging the assumptions of anyone with a vested interest in understanding society in strictly contractarian terms.[33] For those uncritical of liberalism and Enlightenment rationality, to trace the implications of Foucault's argument was to follow a lit fuse.[34] After all, if there is no secure border between consent and coercion, then it takes but a few logical steps until the legitimacy of governmental power authorized by social contract theory implodes entirely.

In the transition from the spectacle of punishment to disciplinary surveillance, Foucault charts a course that marks a shift between the "enclosed" tactics of power of the plague-dream that result in a "sort of social 'quarantine' to an indefinitely generalizable mechanism of 'panopticism'" (DP, 216). The term stems from Foucault's adaptation of Jeremy Bentham's panoptical prison, where inmates' cells encircle a blinding light broadcasting from a central tower such that prisoners are always subject to surveillance, allowing the guards to see without being seen (DP, 214). With the blaring light of the prison tower representing a form of power that is visible yet unverifiable, those incarcerated will self-police (DP, 201). Importantly, the image of the panopticon extends beyond a technique of control that maximizes efficiency in the context of the prison; it becomes a feature of modern subjectivity (DP, 205). That is, just as prisoners regulate their behavior by internalizing the possibility they might be under surveillance, so too do ostensibly free people self-police to conform to prevailing regulations and social norms. Disciplinary power is insidious in part because self-surveillance becomes so routine that it can remain unacknowledged as a form of power in the first place.

The politics of panic at work in the plague dream radiates through ongoing states of emergency today. Anxieties over security are driven by insurgent threats also cast in epidemic terms: such as the possibility that the country is infected with hidden terrorist "sleeper cells" that secretly feed off the body politic and then erupt unexpectedly to violently attack their host. Citizens are directed to keep watch and serve as informants so as to improve the odds that the vectors of contagion can be arrested and killed lest they spread further—whether in the form of Islamic terrorism or immigrant gangs lurking in sanctuary cities. Underscoring the role of race, it is telling that, despite the well-documented clear and present dangers posed by florid, prolific expansion of white supremacist terrorist groups, the state has only belatedly begun to recognize them under the heading of "domestic terrorism." Meanwhile, political entrepreneurs continually exploit racial chauvinisms to produce political subjects as plague-level terrorist threats; from the social movement dissidents of Black Lives Matter to Indigenous water protectors and their allies opposing invasive oil pipelines. We now turn to the biopolitics of the *endemic* to gain a better sense of how the segregated time of quarantine, detainment, and incarceration articulates with the fugitive temporalities of undocumented immigrant laborers who toil in the attenuated, precarious, and taxing spacetimes of *la vida encerrada*.

Racial Biopolitics and the Endemic

Almost immediately after writing *Discipline and Punish* Foucault gave a series of lectures at the Collège de France that showed how the thorny issues he posed in the book anticipated an even more ambitious investigation into what he called biopolitics. Biopolitics involves the regulation of births, deaths, and public health—all of which flow through an evolving web of economic and political interstices. The form, if not the content, of Foucault's introduction to biopolitical circuitry echoes that of his genealogy in *Discipline and Punish*. After hammering the prevailing philosophical and methodological norms until his audience hears them ring hollow with self-contradiction, Foucault carves a doorway opening onto what he takes to be at stake politically. He indicts the common analytic whereby the impulse for self-preservation results in individuals who contract to authorize a sovereign with absolute power over their lives—the very lives whose protection drove them to consent to the contract in the first place. Foucault asks: "Mustn't life remain outside the contract to the extent that it was the first, initial, and foundational reason for the contract itself?" (SMBD, 241).

How can it follow logically that the desire for self-preservation could ever license the sovereign's power over life? The consent that was supposedly foundational leads toward a desperate situation where the sovereign—not the subject—gets to decide matters of life and death (SMBD, 240). There is something deeply problematic when the principled protection of the individual's right to life somehow gives way to an abdication of that very right in the name of its protection. At first glance, the attention Foucault draws to the paradox of sovereignty might seem to be leading us back to an earlier set of worries, namely John Locke's objection to Hobbes's almighty Leviathan.[35] But Foucault's explicit concern is not to resolve the paradox of sovereignty through the people's so-called right of revolution. Such a project would be deeply troubled by his destabilization of liberal consent. And, at any rate, his focus is elsewhere. Specifically, Foucault shifts direction away from an analytic exposition of the philosophical conundrum of the contract in order to illuminate how its ambiguity became symptomatic of a biopolitical relationship between the regulation of life and death.

According to his abbreviated genealogy, the key paradox involves a nineteenth-century transition that saw the sovereign's power to "take life or let live" "complemented" by the power to "make" life or "let" die (SMBD, 241). Rather than train his sights on overzealous sovereigns that authorize mass death under the pretense of shielding life from *epidemic* maladies, Foucault's interest is captured by the kinds of creeping attrition and demise that was *endemic* to the polity. "At the end of the eighteenth century, it was not epidemics that were the issue—but something else—what might be called endemics" (SMBD, 241). That which is endemic represents "serial phenomena" with a particular temporal dimension, meaning that it "must be studied over a period of time" (SMBD, 246). Whereas epidemics are episodic carriers of death that "swoop down on life" from above in a particular historical moment, endemics are "permanent factors . . . which sapped the population's strength, shortened the working week, wasted energy and cost money" (SMBD, 244). As endemic features of society, forms of withering morbidity and its debilitating features were contemporaneous with an uptick in public hygiene and "institutions to coordinate medical care, centralize information and coordinate knowledge" (SMBD, 244). Ultimately, the struggle to manage that which is endemic to a population is a struggle to manage the very contingency of life itself, an uncertainty that gets amplified by the repetition of "aleatory events" (SMBD, 246). It is the contingency of human life that dramatizes the issue of race. Why?

Racial others are made disposable in the prevailing temporal order for the purpose of fortifying the lives and times of the dominant population—the same population that wields the power to define itself as human. Those not fully human are used to shore up endemic risks for the population accorded human status within the polity. Thus racial difference becomes instrumental in the differential distribution of vulnerability, contingency, and precarity associated with modern existence by making those outside the human race expendable. Asking about the political consequences of the distinction between the human and the nonhuman leads us to how Foucault defines racism. His definition is uncharacteristically concise: "it is primarily a way of introducing a break into a domain of life that is under power's control: the break between what must live and what must die" (SMBD, 254). The distinction between what must live and what must die is plainly operative in warfare, but in the context of race it functions in novel ways beyond the logic of kill or be killed. The historical rationale undergirding the distinction, as Foucault sees it, is one of speciation. It presumes that the increased death among an inferior subset of a population will increase the vigor, purity, and proliferation of the racially superior group (SMBD, 255). In other words, the decimation of an inferior race means that "life in general" will become healthier and purer (SMBD, 255). Foucault's invocation of "life in general" in the context of race compels us to acknowledge that he is referring to the *human* race as the primary referent, which also conjures the history of liberal humanism and its constitutive outsides. Either tacitly or explicitly, subhuman populations are available to vaccinate the fully human lives of the racially dominant against death by virtue of the disposability of the subordinate population (SMBD, 249).

If we reflect momentarily on the title of the published lectures, *Society Must Be Defended*, it stands to reason that any invocation of threats to the security of society and human life stems from the values used to measure of what counts as the society in need of defense, and that which poses a threat to its integrity. Human values and valuations—especially what counts as *human* and *value*—are historically contingent formations, subject to variation over time and place. The particular power constellations in any given space or time cohere to form a grid of intelligibility that makes "the human" legible while simultaneously giving structure and meaning to human degeneracy as a danger. Since the human race and its others are always coconstituted and subject to variation across time and space, examining the contours of these variations relative to contemporary racisms is a good point of intervention—especially at a time when the "society that must be defended" is riven with white supremacy.

Foucault is viewing race through the lens of various biological and evolutionary developments in the eighteenth and nineteenth centuries, including Darwinism and the later emergence of social Darwinism. Claiming to be aware that modern racism is a function of colonialism, he writes that it is "by using the themes of evolutionism, by appealing to racism" one can arrive at a justification for "colonizing genocide" (SMBD, 257). Still, Foucault's reflections on these implications, here and elsewhere, are incomplete and ultimately unsatisfactory. As others have noted, his writings can be ambiguous with respect to the cross-temporal (dis)continuities of biopolitics.[36] And despite his references to "local knowledge," his reference points are largely Eurocentric, and criticism of his impressionistic historiography abounds.[37] Furthermore, immigration politics troubles the historical shift he identifies away from traditional forms of sovereignty and toward novel forms of "making live and letting die." Border politics is a site where the top-down death-dealing of old-school state-sponsored sovereignty is alive and well; migrants are still jailed, raped, and shot. Notwithstanding these limitations, I want to revisit and reconfigure his reflections on how the utilization of racial others as leverage against endemic death is neither exhausted nor typified by the acute extermination so brutally exemplified by the Nazi regime.

Biopolitics functions to expose certain populations to prolonged attrition, wearing down and exposed to innovative forms of longer-term wasting. Importantly, that exposure also encompasses the psychological depletion of ostracism, segregation, internal exile, or "social death."[38] Hence Foucault's remark: "When I say 'killing,' I obviously do not mean simply murder as such, but also every form of indirect murder: the fact of exposing someone to death, increasing the risk of death for some people, or quite simply, political death, expulsion, rejection and so on" (SMBD, 256). Proverbial "marks of the border" contributing to racially ascribed criminal deviance and social death are not limited to phenotype. They also include performative aspects of racial identity, including linguistic and kinetic-behavioral traits required to "act white" and become coeval and synchronous with white time at any given historical moment.[39] To the extent that Latinx populations are racialized by an association with inferior, dysgenic, or asynchronous spaces and times, they represent a threat of backward regression of the progressive culture coded as white.[40] Racial-temporal stigmas are demonstrative of a cotemporaneous overlap of the political dreams of a pure community and a disciplined society (DP, 198), with the stigmatized vulnerable to a disciplinarily politics with biopolitical ends. It is to this simultaneous overlap of discipline and biopolitics that we now turn.

Live and Let Die

Racial others have long been cast in terms of an infectious virus that contaminates the body politic. Historically, the maneuver is all too familiar: when a certain group of people is identified as a viral spread that should be avoided *like* the plague because they *are* the plague, it is often a prelude to war and even genocide.[41] The history of people labeling others as biological contagions arguably exemplifies a fusion of disciplinary, discursive, and biopolitical powers. The contemporaneity of disciplinary power and biopower at work in the preceding formulation might invite the charge that I am taking unfair liberties with Foucault. Even careful readers of Foucault carve a divide between disciplinary power as operating on the level of individuals, and biopower as operating on masses/populations.[42] Nevertheless, I find the distinction too sharp. So rather than map a crevasse at the interface of discipline and biopower, I want to take Foucault seriously when he writes:

> This technology of power [biopower] does not exclude the former [discipline], does not exclude disciplinary technology, but it does dovetail into it, integrate it, modify it to some extent, and above all, use it by sort of infiltrating it, embedding itself in existing disciplinary techniques. (SMBD 242)

In the US context, where phenotype is a key, if not the only, racial signifier, the correspondence between race, visibility, and disciplinary surveillance should not escape our notice. Nor should we ignore the biopolitical "regulatory technology" geared toward "protecting the security of the whole from internal dangers" in an effort to "try to control the series of random events that can occur in a living mass" (SMBD, 249).

Reading Foucault's account of disciplinary power today, I find it hard *not* to think of racialization, considering his contention that a key classificatory feature of the panoptic gaze is its capacity to identify individuals and group them accordingly—a process he describes explicitly in terms of speciation. Surveilling visage must be able to "see, to isolate features, to recognize those that are identical and those that are different, to regroup them, to classify them by species or family" (DP, 89). Arizona's notorious 2010 "papers please" or "show me your papers" law (SB1070) afforded local municipalities increased authority to take up the duties of immigration enforcement that had previously been under the auspices of the federal government.[43] Subsequently adopted by five other states, the legislation allowed police to demand proof of citizenship status from whomever they deemed suspect of criminal activity—including possible immigration violations.[44] In a move disturbingly reminiscent of the Fugitive Slave Act of 1850, Alabama's law (HB 56) demanded employers check the immigration status of anyone they hire, and deputized the police to investigate the status of anyone they stopped whom they suspected of being in the country without proper documentation. Of course, this is state-sanctioned racial profiling; those most likely to have their status questioned by police are not likely to be white. Anyone unable to produce the relevant documents is subject to incarceration (the euphemistic "detention") and potential deportation.[45] Importantly, the law also makes it a crime to harbor, transport, or assist an undocumented immigrant—thereby producing another category of criminal deviance.[46]

Whereas *Discipline and Punish* charted the course of punishment moving from public spectacle to internalized discipline via panopticism, immigration politics features sites of disciplinary spectacle.[47] With respect to how that appears now, Leo Chavez challenges Foucault's shift from spectacle to surveillance, arguing that the vigilante anti-immigrant Minutemen Project "used surveillance to produce a spectacle on the Arizona-Mexico border."[48] To put the point in terms of the foregoing argument, their goal was to ratchet up public fears to plague level as part of a disciplinary strategy that would ultimately mobilize boots on the ground, punishment, detentions, and deportations. Key to their purpose was to discipline citizens to be the eyes and ears of a much broader surveillance apparatus, a point exemplified by the group's slogan that they were "Americans doing the job that government won't do" in an effort to get the state to do it.[49] The discipline at work in the Minutemen's "border theater" is not unidirectional, nor aimed only at the undocumented. Rather, it reinforced a boundary between immigrant Others and citizens under siege through "an act of symbolic power and violence that defined their own citizen-subject status."[50] This reinforcement is part of a continued racialization of the American citizen-subject as white that allows the divide between citizen and alien to supersede any number of available identities—such as that of fellow human. For instance, to the limited extent that immigration politics contains a public conversation about excessive cruelty, it is often framed in terms of whether this or that policy represents an appropriate way to treat foreigners. It is rare to hear public figures ask whether it is appropriate to treat *any human being* with such cruelty.

To consider the enduring utility of spectacle as a disciplinary political strategy, consider the much-dramatized threat posed by the migrant caravan moving toward the US-Mexican border in advance of the 2018 midterm elections. This reboot of the plague dream featured a migrant infestation where Central American children were allegedly placed strategically out front to conceal the "unknown Middle Easterners" embedded within.[51] The US government sent National Guard troops to the border in defense of what the administration overtly called a national emergency. The work performed by this disciplinary spectacle was part of a wider, ongoing racialization of immigrants as deviant that included ICE raids, the vilification of so-called sanctuary cities, and daily outbursts of racist invectives and demands that minority politicians "go home" to foreign countries—even as the elected representatives of US districts. While the caravan was especially timely as a distraction, its status as spectacle should be understood as part of a broader convergence of discipline and biopower with respect to race. As political leaders openly avow that the separation of migrant families and the spectacular cruelty of caging of children in "tender age facilities" are intended to deter future migration and the spread of "anchor babies," it should be apparent that this is a mobilization of a disciplinary project toward biopolitical ends.[52] Strategies designed to discourage immigration through a militaristic "border surge" and to encourage "self-deportation" are but thinly veiled euphemisms. They barely conceal the human costs of driving migrants into more dangerous territories, exposing them to precisely what Foucault means when he speaks of a regularization of mass death.

In effect, claiming that the spectacle of immigrant suffering is a deterrent amounts to a political sleight of hand. By implying that televised cruelty is intended to make an example of individuals in the service of deterrence, the stated disciplinary agenda distracts attention from the broader biopolitical structure that systemically targets populations raced as less than human. To date, thousands of migrant skeletons and human remains have been discovered in desert regions; many of them are unidentified and attributed to the US militarization of border regions where it was comparatively safer to cross.[53] Focusing on the remote regions of southern Arizona he calls the "land of open graves," anthropologist Jason De Leon contends that the horrific suffering experienced by migrant travelers "is neither random nor senseless, but rather part of a strategic federal plan that has rarely been illuminated and exposed for what it is: a killing machine that simultaneously uses and hides behind the viciousness of the Sonoran Desert."[54] Taken together, the militarism of sending soldiers to the border, the jailing of children who literally embody futurity, the separation of families, the incarceration euphemized as "immigrant detention," and the executive authorization of troops firing on refugees function at once as high-tech disciplinary media spectacles as well as pungent displays of old-fashioned sovereignty. In concert, they represent a contemporary concatenation of temporal forces marshaled in the service of reproducing racial hierarchies through a neocolonial order of segregated time.

The preceding scenes illustrate how a threatened white population marks Latinx immigrants for surveillance, detention, and deportation. Yet our view of discipline, biopolitics, and race remains incomplete without an account of how arguments on behalf of immigration often hinge on foreigners' perceived capacity to serve as useful vaccines against endemic threats to the polity. Nativists utilize disciplinary spectacles to dramatize immigrant threats, but do so in the service of biopolitical, race-making projects capable of also maintaining an exploitable domestic reserve population of laborers, soldiers, and subjects for the settler-state draw upon over the long term—particularly during times of crisis and instability. With this in mind, in what follows I focus my inquiry on the particular "aleatory," yet "serial" phenomena endemic to the historical trajectory of US immigration and the logics of power that facilitate the indispensability of Latinx immigrant disposability. The phenomena Foucault labels as aleatory are "unpredictable when taken in themselves or individually, but which, at the collective level, display constants that are easy, or at least possible, to establish" (SMBD, 246).

The serial phenomena we encounter today could encompass a range of recurrent, yet disruptive, events. Such contingencies might include exogenous or endogenous economic shocks that result in shortages in the labor market, natural disasters, or even less dramatic episodic natural happenings—like cold or warm spells that demand newly ripened crops to be picked quickly lest they go to waste.[55] And, as I discuss later, in the food supply chain there is a visible metabolic connection between the laborers whose energy and time provide relatively low-cost nutritional sustenance that disproportionately benefits the racially dominant population. At bottom, calories are a metric of energy. It follows that consuming energy leveraged on the foreshortened lives of others is one step removed from consuming the time of their lives. Accordingly, Ella

Baker contested this kind of temporal cannibalism with her wisdom that "if you share your food with people, you share your lives with people."[56]

Indispensable Disposability

The preceding examples attest that race figures importantly in how the endemic contingency of life is negotiated by the racially dominant group by way of the heightened disposability of racial subordinates. Those racialized as Hispanic are at once useful in the negotiation of endemic death, yet also available to be cast in epidemic terms—when the time comes. In the present-day context, the ambiguous status of Latinx immigrants makes the population available to be cast in terms of what is endemic and epidemic to the polity—relative to political necessity. Immigrants raced as anachronistic can be cast as threatening regression and cultural degeneracy on the one hand, while in prior times, their ascribed powers of racial time travel were occasionally seen as useful to a polity nostalgic for a less corrupt past. Bonnie Honig adds insightful texture to the picture with her analysis of how the foreigner is also invoked as a "supercitizen" whose work ethic, patriotism, and traditional values are exactly what is needed to bring America back to its founding.[57] Queer theorists and gender scholars have also made important observations with respect to how immigrants (such as Latinx Catholics) are often seen as embodying family values, heteronormativity, and conservative religious beliefs.[58] Cast in a different light by the Right, at different times Latinx procreation is forgivable since at least it happens between a heterosexual man and a woman. In short, all these ascribed traits hold the promise of *purifying* a polity that has been corrupted by its departure from its founding principles—the opposite of infecting it. And as the apt title of "supercitizen" suggests, ascribing fantastic powers like time travel and national rebirth to racial others also casts stigmatized populations outside the bounds of humanity.

Whether as an epidemic threat or insurance against endemic liabilities, the stability of white time is securitized by the expendability of racial others. In different times, nonwhite immigrants are alternately excoriated as an ominous danger that must be expelled and guarded against and also extolled for their utility as laborers, soldiers, domestic caregivers, and so on. It hardly takes fluency in Kantian ethics to see how this framework fails to acknowledge the intrinsic worth (as opposed to the instrumental value) of others. At bottom, biopolitics is at work in a dynamic that behaves as if the more a racially subordinate population dies, the more the dominant population may live. Too many mainstream voices in the immigration debate are in agreement about the indispensable disposability of immigrant labor, and thus immigrant lives. For progressives who argue for liberal border policies justified by the utility of immigrant labor, it bears repeating that these jobs often require dangerous, low-paying work that risks exposure to death and maiming that can come fast, slowly, or intermittently. In practical terms, the valorization of immigrant labor hinges on a political economy of time appropriation that spans the acute morbidity associated with military service, mining, logging, fighting forest fires, and so on, as well as various forms of long-term exploitation, wasting, maiming, and attrition inherent in grueling farm, factory, and slaughterhouse work.[59]

With respect to military service, citizenship is not a requirement to serve in the armed forces and risk death on behalf of the security interests or imperial ambitions of the United States. To the contrary, military service has long been used as an incentive to prove one deserves status, dignity, and even humanity—as was the case of African Americans who served in the Civil War. Quarantined Japanese concentration camp internees were among those who served with distinction and died in World War II. And after September 11, 2001, the Bush administration allowed service in the military as grounds upon which undocumented immigrants could expedite the citizenship process, though the subsequent administration pushed back against this trend.[60] Sociologist Amy Lutz notes that while hailing from a lower economic class is the most significant predictor of who is most likely to serve in the military, "research by the Pew Hispanic Center indicates that Latinos tend to be overrepresented in personnel who 'most directly handle weapons' and underrepresented in 'technical occupations such as electronics and communications.'"[61] In one of the most stark expressions of how biopolitics utilizes the death of internal "others" as a means of strengthening the polity, 111 formerly undocumented immigrants who died during US military service have been awarded "posthumous citizenship."[62]

The obvious tension we confront is that of a political apparatus alternately willing to kill off lives of those whom it was ostensibly sworn to protect. The ambiguity brings us back to how the contemporary condition articulates a form of biopolitics wherein race figures prominently. Here again is Foucault:

> A biopower that wished to wage war had to articulate the will to destroy the adversary with the risk that it might kill those whose lives it had, by

definition, to protect, manage, and multiply. The same could be said of criminality. Once the mechanism of biopower was called upon to make it possible to execute or isolate criminals, criminality was conceptualized in racist terms. (SMBD, 258)

Read as a warning about a kind of political autoimmunity, the passage helps us grapple with how it can be simultaneously the case that Black and Latinx peoples make up such a significant portion of not only the armed forces but also the prison population, which is itself a site of punishment and extraction. It illuminates how asynchronous peoples can be alternately vilified and praised, disposed of yet regarded as indispensable—a dynamic that anticipates the discussion of surplus populations and reserve populations taken up in the next chapter. Meanwhile, the multiracial complexion of the armed forces is even employed as an argument against decolonial critics of American empire who draw connections between past and present imperialism.[63] One reason these logics are so deeply disturbing is because they are undergirded by instrumental rationality and attendant dehumanization that masquerades as beneficence in the form of public policy.

To be clear, my purpose is not to draw a false equivalence between the xenophobic white nationalists' positions on the right and proimmigration advocates on the left. Yet, in view of the foregoing analysis of border biopolitics, there is reason to be troubled by the valorization of immigrant labor, which falls back on a disciplinary posture parsing "good immigrants" from "bad immigrants," with the latter condemned to segregation in space and time. From the perspective of biopolitics and segregated time, ostensibly opposing constituencies on the left and the right risk forming an unholy alliance around the indispensable disposability of immigrant lives. Recall that President Obama backed muscular efforts to militarize the border despite promises of immigration reform, hitting a then-record of two million deportations. Immigrant detention became the fastest growing form of mass incarceration in the country. Obama frequently sold his argument for immigration reform by contending that immigrants do the work that "Americans can't do or won't do." We can stipulate that Americans *won't* do work that requires them to risk their lives doing jobs that are dangerous, dirty, and unrewarding. Set that aside for the moment and turn your attention to the first part of the locution to consider the following: What work is it that Americans *cannot* do?

For a president who trafficked so effusively in the discourse of American exceptionalism and citizens' ability to overcome seemingly insurmountable obstacles, the suggestion that there is anything Americans *cannot* achieve would sound dissonant, if not treasonous. The statement only makes sense if citizenship is understood in terms of status—and even as coextensive with humanity itself. Americans *can't* do certain jobs *because they are Americans*. Simply put, to be an American citizen is to enjoy the benefits of being above non-American others who, not incidentally, bear the burden of dangerous work that risks a living death, slow death, social death, biological death, or all of the above. To test whether the biopolitical logic of "live and let die" is operative today, ask yourself: would US immigration policy be different if it was intentionally crafted with the guiding rationale that "the very fact that you let more [immigrants] die will allow you to live more"? (SMBD, 255).

Postscript: Radical Presence and Temporal Resistance

Drawing on Abdelmalek Sayad, Kitty Calavita writes, "It is often observed that immigration acts as a mirror that 'clarifies that which is latent ... in the functioning of the social order, it unmasks that which is masked to reveal what many prefer to ignore.'"[64] In this chapter I have endeavored to modestly contest the politics of invisibility attaching to segregated time by exposing the relationship between racialized temporal spheres. The foregoing does not pretend to be an exhaustive portrayal of all the possible entwinements of segregated time as it pertains to immigration, nor can it hope to comprehensively map the flux and contingency of ongoing race-making projects. What count as aleatory, random potentialities are subject to change over time, and colonial legacies are imprinted on the racialized ascription of certain populations as embodying randomness, chaos, and dangerous figures of excess.[65] And while it would take at least another manuscript to begin to do justice to myriad forms of resistance figured in temporal terms, I want to close by briefly reflecting on forms of political counterconduct and improvisation that contest white time.

Long after Sojourner Truth asked, "Ain't I a woman?" and before Black Lives Matter, an infuriated W.E.B. Du Bois asked whether he *still* had to argue his humanity. In 1968, pictures from the sanitation strike in Memphis, where Martin Luther King Jr. was assassinated, show protestors wearing placards reading "I am a man." Recent immigrant protesters have invoked the same exact verbiage. It is telling that so many Latinx activists who risk visibility and its dire consequences do not merely state their claims in the language of rights-based liberalism, but feel compelled to argue their very humanity. As Apostolidis points out in *Breaks in the Chain*, the workers at Tyson meatpacking plant resisted the normal flows of anemic resistance offered by the official union in favor of a more democratic form of organizing. Those who mounted a wildcat strike at a Tyson protested their status as nonhuman "animals," "slaves," and disposable "trash" by fomenting resistance on their own "rather than turning to the state's law to rescue them."[66] Looking forward, their methods of engagement included public expressions of human creativity as modes of "arguing" their human presence within the contested borders of "now."

The capacity to interrupt the normal flow of goods and services is a potent tool of demonstrating how the habituated rhythms of the present political ecology depend upon segregated time. Strikes often disrupt the usual hierarchy of who gets to tell whom to wait for goods and services, and can even short-circuit the metabolic connection that sustains everyday life in the food supply. The work stoppages and slowdowns are some of the interruptive "breaks" referenced in the title of Apostolidis's book. In Chapter 1, I suggested that experiences of white time are frequently imbued with a sense of entitlement that seeks an outsized command over what happens next. By contesting their own disposability, the workers (at least temporarily) contravened prevailing expectations of relatively cheap, readily available food. In practical-temporal terms, immigrant laborers slowed down to the point of letting the meat fall off the belt rather than assent to the speed of the "disassembly line"; they insisted on not waiting for human necessities (whether in the form of medical treatment or bathroom breaks), and they contested the company's practice of counting illness against them as time off. Interestingly, they strategically narrated these actions by intuiting the prevailing time signatures and expectations and reinterpolating their activities accordingly. More precisely, they defended their slowdowns by connecting them to the consumers' right to safe meat—appealing to self-interested expectations, rather than presuming humanitarian interests or human decency.

The dynamics at play are not reducible to workers merely keeping time with the (dis)assembly line, nor are they marshaling a reclamation of stolen time that happens all the time. The modulation is a time signature of its own. In my view, some of the most intriguing facets of temporal innovation occur as people employ a politics of using *time they do not have*. Indeed, in his recent book on day laborers, *The Fight for Time*, Apostolidis provides a textured account of the temporalities of workers who both endure and contest their dehumanizing precaritization.[67] With laudable courage, undocumented peoples demand, and exercise, their right to appear by refusing to remain hidden in *la vida encerrada* by way of strikes, slowdowns, and evolving strategies for reclaiming stolen time. Among these modes of temporal reorganization are solidaristic times in worker centers where day laborers engage in "anticapitalist sociality" that runs counter to the tedium of seemingly endless waiting for work—or the sped-up labor "time scape of bodily endangerment" when they are intermittently hired.[68] The work discloses the spectral presence of those in the shadows of white time, but who nevertheless share in the cocreation of what counts as "this" time. Their presence frequently goes missing, but if they were to vanish for good, they would surely be missed.

The 2006 immigration protests evinced another kind of radical presence contesting the politics of the endemic that goes missing in white time. However briefly, they disrupted the routinized, monochromatic, business-as-usual syncopation of white temporalities—and were almost immediately segregated from public memory. Cristina Beltrán lucidly accents the natality and a creativity of insurrectionist radical immigrant presence, while also sounding cautionary note around valorizing immigrant labor.[69] Statements that "I'm a worker not a criminal," "We build your homes," and "Got Food? Thank a Farmworker" risks reducing immigrants to their labor value.[70] At the same time, such assertions can be politically strategic since they accurately confront the white racial amnesia that disavows a collective debt to Latinx peoples and renders them perpetual debtors. The issue of how racial stigma conveys irreparable debt and compels nonwhites to live on borrowed time is the subject to which we now turn.

4
Borrowed Time
Life and Debt on Subprime Time

In theory and in practice, liberal freedom has often been a shorthand for freedom from the past. For the beneficiaries of white supremacy, it is convenient that it has also meant freedom from registering debts to liberalism's Others. In segregated time, it always too soon for transracial freedom and equality and too late for reparations. Liberalism's aversion to collective debt obligations to the past does not bode well for polities haunted by genocidal colonialism, ecocide, and the diminution of enslaved subjects to the status of property. In an especially asinine inversion, it is those from whom so much has been taken in land, labor, and lifetimes who are racially stigmatized as always already indebted. In various ways, bearers of racial stigma are branded as perpetually owing their time, labor, and gratitude—in effect their lives—to their oppressors and the forces that bind them. Refugees, immigrants, and Native residents of occupied lands are paternalistically told to be grateful for the "gift" of liberal freedom and civilizational progress coded as white.[1] Those racialized as idle, lazy, and chronically prone to wasting time are subsequently subject to having their time colonized and made "productive" as defined by the labor rhythms and agendas of white power. It is a cruel irony that, in order for their labor exploited in the service of white wealth, so many of those racially coded as slothful, backward, and social parasites are preemptively criminalized as owing a "debt to society."

The theme of this chapter is debt as it relates to segregated time. At the same time, there is a prevailing sentiment that present-day debt crises gather virtually everyone into a quasi-universal global precariat. The dream of an ownership society has itself been rendered largely anachronistic, outshined by a sprawling, variegated crises of indebtedness. With debt operating at the levels of the individual, the national, and even the atmospheric, the panic is not delusional. Debt seemingly cripples virtually everyone, from young people with credit cards and student loans in arrears, to middle-aged homeowners facing foreclosure, to an aging senior population staring down

Segregated Time. P.J. Brendese, Oxford University Press. © Oxford University Press 2023.
DOI: 10.1093/oso/9780197535745.003.0006

insolvent pension accounts. Austerity measures, bank bailouts, and tax breaks for the wealthy serve up socialism for the rich and capitalism for the proliferating poor. And all this is happening amid a withering social safety net that was never sufficient in the first place. In the academy, luminaries like Gilles Deleuze have diagnosed a distinctive entrapment of late modernity as a time when "man is no longer man enclosed, man is in debt."[2] More recently, Maurizio Lazzarato proclaims that today we are "all guilty before capital."[3]

One can appreciate the consolidating forces of capital, its incessant displacement of local rhythms, and its ongoing production of disposable populations. But it is not at all clear to me that our respective times are all leveraged in the same ways—especially in matters of race. Simply put, race plays a potent role in how debt is politically (re)inscribed, experienced, and ostensibly repaid. So when neoliberal capitalism is excoriated for having made us all into a "race of debtors," it strikes me as too fast a move.[4] As we shall see, the dynamics of racialized debt and credit often go undertheorized, though recent scholarship on racial capitalism has made important contributions in this respect—particularly in the fallout of the subprime mortgage crisis.[5] Here is Fred Moten:

> Blackness is the site of absolute dereliction at the level of the Imaginary, for "whoever says 'rape' says Black" (Fanon), whoever says "prison" says black (Sexton), and whoever says "AIDS" says black—the negro is a "phobogenic object" (Wilderson).[6] In the United States whoever says "subprime debtor" says black as well.[7]

Moten suggests that racial stigma signifies subprime creditworthiness. This is true of financial and social capital and—as I shall contend—time as well. Predatory subprime lending clearly functions as an apparatus of financial capture and material dispossession in space. In the context of imposed racial debt, political subjects rated "subprime" are also made vulnerable to a redistribution of time. In addition to myriad forms of stealing time and forced punitive payback taken up in what follows, segregated time is eminently legible in the ways that racialized creditworthiness allows only *some* to part company with the past and dispense with debt. In societies riven with white supremacy—and white time—the ability to start over and begin the future anew is a temporal form of racial privilege. Bearing this in mind, I explore how debt does not just neutralize time, as some have suggested (MIM, 49). Racial indebtedness weaponizes time.

The everyday phrase "living on borrowed time" connotes temporal scarcity; a condition of apprehensive precarity. This might be a feature of the temporalities of those disproportionately branded as irredeemable, perpetually indebted, and chronically out of time. Of course, borrowed time also signifies debt. This beckons us to take up the issue of *whose* futures are leveraged in order to secure the present racial order of time and from whom (or what) time is ostensibly borrowed. In this chapter I examine how racial stigma functions an as accelerant of what I shall call subprime time; a time zone that promises to synch up with the dominant flows of progress and prosperity, but ultimately "races" its subjects toward ever-imminent expropriation, arrest, and foreclosure. Subprime time might be thought of as a temporal forcefield that initially appears vectored toward future wealth and status that comes with catching up to civilizational/colonial powers coded as white. But like the ballooning interest payments on a subprime loan, subprime time increasingly compounds its subjects' enchainment to the past until they are left with far less than they started with—and ultimately out of time altogether. I develop this line of inquiry by reflecting on the experiences of Native Americans predated upon, and dispossessed by, the early settlers' use of a then-novel innovation: the foreclosable mortgage.

The Anglo-colonial invention of the foreclosable mortgage helps illuminate how credit debt has served as an enduring vehicle of predatory racial accumulation. The failure of Euro-centric scholarship to consider it as a tool of Indigenous dispossession exemplifies segregated memory in the service of segregated time. Part of the difficulty in theorizing the temporal segregation forcing some to live on borrowed time today stems from the long-standing disavowal of segregated memory whereby racism has been divorced from capitalism—as if one could be adequately historicized and understood independent of the other. Scholars' growing invocation of the phrase "racial capitalism"—with deep debts to figures such as Cedric Robinson, W.E.B. Du Bois, C.L.R. James, and Eric Williams—challenges the artificial divide between the two terms.[8] The segregated memory separating capitalism from race makes racial capitalism a novelty when it should be a redundancy. As Jodi Melamed writes, "The term 'racial capitalism' requires its users to recognize that capitalism *is* racial capitalism."[9] It follows that the contemporary condition of indebtedness cannot be divorced from the racialized legacy of capitalist accumulation bequeathed by colonialism, indentured servitude, and slavery. Rather, such a conceptual break partitioning discrete tenses itself exemplifies a temporal imposition racialized as white.

A brief genealogy of mortgage foreclosure reveals a racial time-trap beneath contemporary arguments to undo past injustice by "democratizing credit" through expanded subprime lending practices that are supposedly color-blind. More broadly, we see how race is employed as a predictive technology, with creditworthiness aligning with whiteness. I shall examine how those apprehended as nonwhite are targeted for future dispossession by debt by theorizing whiteness as a form of credit. Credit, from the Latin *credere*, "is indistinguishable from one's personal reputation or status as worthy of being believed."[10] Building on Cheryl I. Harris's formulation of whiteness as property, it follows that whiteness is meaningful store of value over time. For Harris, whiteness is constructed as a species of property "by recognizing the reputational interest in being regarded as white as a thing of significant value."[11] Future expectations are protected "property," with whiteness as something one puts stock in and a sociopolitical currency available to be leveraged, securitized, and—as I shall argue—negotiated as a form of credit.

Let me state at the outset that my purpose is not to adjudicate neoliberalism as a philosophy of history, nor do I attempt to resolve debates over its geographic boundaries and start date.[12] Instead, I want to dilate upon select features that recur in many (if not all) accounts of the contemporary moment called neoliberal. In addition to being pilloried for making everyone a debtor, neoliberalism is portrayed as a mode of governmentality whereby each individual is taken to be an entrepreneur of their self, as Foucault would have it. He maintains that if neoliberalism had a motto, it would be "Live dangerously."[13] I am inclined to think that if the entrepreneurial self had a motto, it might be "To each their own brand." Today, one's brand is stamped by things like professional credentials, an expansive online presence, recognizable signs of value and dependability (read: predictability), ideally alongside other florid displays of creditworthiness. Selves properly branded as worthy sites of outside investment and speculation garner loans and credit, and present as viable candidates for employment, intimate partnerships, and myriad sociopolitical goods. It follows that the role of racial stigma in this branding, and the kinds of dangerous living on borrowed time it conveys, is the subject before us now. I am deliberately employing the meaning of the verb "to brand" as connoting market value and commodity identity, as well as a signifying status marker: of chattel, property, spoiled identity, social deviance, and subject of social death.[14]

Brands are not fashioned outside of history, so part of the goal is to better understand searing conditions through which the racial stigma bequeathed by the enduring legacies of colonialism and chattel slavery brands nonwhites as always already in debt—and thus consigned to live on borrowed time. By extension of this logic, whiteness has credit value whose proverbial branding I shall also investigate.[15] Toward that end, this chapter deliberately proceeds asynchronously. Rather than provide a linear, chronological rendition, I disturb familiar time-signatures by taking the contemporary failure to grapple with predatory lending as an invitation to explore strategies of racial dispossession that haunt instruments of credit and wealth accumulation marketed as future-oriented. I begin by introducing the entwinements of race, debt, and time that often go missing from contemporary analyses of debt crises through a critical encounter with Maurizio Lazzarato's influential *The Making of the Indebted Man*. To underscore the role of race in the relays of debt and segregated time, I then revisit the 2008 mortgage crisis as a form of present-day African American property dispossession through debt. This is followed by a turn to the colonial roots of the foreclosable mortgage as an instrument of Native American expropriation.

Where Fanon and Césaire remind us that colonialism always comes home, the contemporary scenes of foreclosure depict present-day incarnations of colonialism coming for *your* home. This dread is especially, if not uniquely, palpable if you are a person of color. By modestly, and no doubt imperfectly, bringing Indigenous studies into contact with post, decolonial, and Afro-diasporic scholarship, I sketch borrowed time as a temporality of the subprime in the context of the Americas. Race functions as a predictive technology; an index of predatory capture marking stigmatized subjects as persons of *interest* in white time and vulnerable to subprime time.[16] White paternalist colonization of time conveys a logic of "given time" and "saving time" deployed against those branded primitive and in need of salvation through the supposed gift of white time. From this analysis emerges a temporal trajectory whereby human disposability happens fast and slow. One is not always killed outright in white time. Sometimes it saves you for later. The interval is life on borrowed time.

A Race of Debtors?

In Lazzarato's *The Making of the Indebted Man*, the debtor–creditor relation has so intensified the machinations of exploitation and domination as to dissolve the very distinction between workers and nonworkers, retirees and welfare recipients, even consumers and producers. By his lights, "Everyone is a 'debtor,' accountable and guilty before capital" (MIM, 7). Drawing on Deleuze's assertion that there was never any pure liberalism—rather there was always state capitalism—Lazzarato holds that "just as there has never been liberalism, capital has never had a progressive or modernizing side" (MIM, 173–174). There is hardly anything approaching uniformity with respect to the temporal markers between liberalism and neoliberalism.[17] Rather than attempt to adjudicate the contested periodicity between liberalisms, my purpose in this section is more particular. I take up Lazzarato's influential analysis of indebtedness in our time to dilate upon what it portends for racial others. We shall see that the particularities of indebted racial subjectivities tend to either go missing from the analysis or get subsumed under the broader forces he theorizes. Yet rather than simply identifying this absence, I wish to pursue a more generative mode of intervention by grappling with how the inequalities I have prefaced are racialized.

In view of the declaration that "everyone is a debtor, accountable and guilty before capital," we begin by asking: what does it mean to be guilty before capital? Lazzarato's most immediate answer is consumption, the vehicle through which "we maintain an unwitting relationship with the debt economy" (MIM, 20). Credit cards are highly symbolic in this respect, since plastic digitally automates our consumption, lubricates the creditor/debtor bond, and facilitates an easy slide into permanent indebtedness. As I read him, even paying one's credit cards off on time and in full would not provide an escape from the relationship, since creditworthiness is itself a precondition of consumption. Consumers need to be creditworthy in order to consume, which effectively underwrites their participation in the broader system of credit and debt. And the roots of the problem run deep. Grounding his analysis in Nietzsche's landmark critique of the creditor/debtor relation in the second essay of his *Genealogy of Morals*, Lazzarato contends that the indebtedness conveyed by Christianity's notion of original sin and the perpetual indebtedness to Christ's sacrifice anticipated the moral framework for the contemporary social formation of indebtedness in perpetuity. "If in times past we were indebted to the community, to the gods, to our ancestors. We are henceforth indebted to the 'god' Capital" (MIM, 32).

Just as, for Nietzsche, the modern state was not born from a social contract but through violence, so too was the indebted condition we inhabit not derived from voluntary agreement but through force and coercion. The condition of being thrown into a structure of debt abides irrespective of the fact that individuals are born into a socioeconomic world not of their own making, and are likely the subjects of governments that have taken on debt on behalf of a citizenry who will bear its burden across generational time. "If it is not individual debt, it is the public debt that weighs, literally, on every individual's life, since every individual must take responsibility for it" (MIM, 38). Pace Nietzsche, the archetype of social organization is not exchange but credit. Lazzarato is careful to qualify his position, noting that exchange is not altogether abolished today but functions through asymmetries of power (MIM, 33). More insidious still is how the moral infrastructure of indebtedness exists in part because the neoliberal subject is not simply a laborer or wage earner but an "entrepreneur of the self." Since he is supposedly his own boss, he can freely choose whether to rent himself out. As human capital, he could always be working on his brand around the clock, well beyond the prolonged time of the laborer's working day that Karl Marx theorized as "absolute surplus value" in volume 1 of *Capital*.[18] In short, the entrepreneurial self is infinitely responsible for his own position in the socioeconomic food chain. From there, of course, it is but a short step from infinite responsibility to infinite guilt.[19]

The response to the Greek debt crisis is emblematic of how the preceding dynamic is politically visible to Lazzarato. Economists, pundits, and politicians speak in one voice to denounce the Greeks, saying: "'You are at fault.' 'You are guilty.' The Greeks laze about in the sun while German Protestants slave away under gloomy skies for the good of Europe and humanity" (MIM, 31). The problem has taken on such magnitude that being guilty before capital encompasses much more than financial debts; it is deeply imbricated with ongoing subject formation, subjectivation, and ultimately the reproduction of the subjection of self and others. Exceeding the terrain of finance, the logic of debt penetrates the psychosocial-corporeal dimensions of human life that Foucault theorized as the soul (MIM, 23–25, 29–36). By acceding to the existing order, we not only fail to challenge the assumption that capitalists have a moral right to the surplus value of workers' labor à la Marx. We also partake of a morality of custom that employs guilty indebtedness to make us predictable, calculable, and dependably static (MIM, 41–44, 104).[20]

Temporality is thus a key aspect of Lazzarato's argument, not least because the demands of capital surpass the theft of "labor time" on the job. The incessant work of, and on, the self-as-indebted "preempts non-chronological time, each person's future as well as the future of society as a whole" (MIM, 46–48).

When every self is a firm, one's entrepreneurial work on that self is never done. The consequence is that debt has become the "principal explanation" for the "strange sensation of living in a society without time, without possibility, without foreseeable rupture" (MIM, 47). "With the debt economy, it is no longer possible to distinguish labor from action, as Hannah Arendt was still able to do" (MIM, 65). It follows that those born in times of ubiquitous indebtedness experience time as vacant of the natality that Arendt understood as the ability to begin anew. The distinctly human capacity for miraculous action is what is foreclosed upon, the condition in which one is capable of breaks in repetition that give way to acts of creation. Amid the prevailing debt economy, "both chronological labor time and *action*, non-chronological time, time as choice, decision and wager on what will happen" are estranged (MIM, 55). Drawing on Marx, Lazzarato argues that this withering of possibility is a result of a creditor-debtor relation that cements an adversarial relationship between people that cannibalizes the trust in self and other that is required to "take a chance on the unknown, the unforeseeable, the uncertain," resulting in a complete alienation wherein the "ethical work constitutive of the self and the community" is shattered (MIM, 57). Perhaps it was this sensibility that moved Occupy Wall Street demonstrators to contest the indebted subject as isolated by displaying placards reading "You are not a loan."

Taking the place of innovative expression, original self-creation, and natality is a kind of freedom that remains tethered to the leash of indebted consumption (MIM, 31). This indebted freedom is conjoined to a Foucauldian pastoral control, a disciplinary apparatus through which it becomes possible to "individualize the government of behavior and totalize the regulation of the population" (MIM, 125–126). Through this core component of neoliberal governmentality, beneficiaries of social programs become debtors; the unemployed are beholden to insurance regimes, and welfare recipients are wards of the state (MIM, 104). An important aspect of repayment comes in the form of conduct. Accordingly, debtors' behavior is the subject of intense surveillance, recursive inspection, and hypervigilant chaperoning on the part of the state—not to mention an (un)healthy dose of public shame (MIM, 132–137).[21] To add more injury to insult, these same populations are also subjected to the biopolitical impact of debt that institutionalizes precarity and diminishes lifetimes by disappearing healthcare and truncating retirement years. This happens by extending the duration spent toiling in the workforce—presuming, of course, the worker is fortunate enough to live that long. "In this way, by reconfiguring sovereign, disciplinary and biopolitical power, the debt economy fulfils at once political, productive and distributive functions" (MIM, 104). Which brings us to the overlooked role of racialized indebtedness and the variegated dimensions of indebted subjectivities coloring segregated time.

But Wait, There's Less: The Temporal Arrears of Racial Debt

Gilles Deleuze writes that "man is no longer man enclosed, man is in debt," a phrase Lazzarato interprets as marking the shift from disciplinary governance to present-day neoliberalism; writing, "A man is no longer a man confined [as in disciplinary societies] but a man in debt [in a control society]" (MIM, 90). The statement is remarkable for a number of reasons, not least because it invites questions of what times and places its referents inhabit. More pointedly, to whom does the declaration refer? Surely not a great many of the temporal outcasts encountered in this study. Among the missing are proliferating multitudes subjected to carceral control and vast swaths of others swept into indefinite detention and refugee camps. Nor does it describe Aboriginal peoples living on Indigenous reservations resulting from their forced removal by settler states, or displaced peoples surviving under siege. All are well-documented phenomena that disproportionately impact populations racialized as nonwhite, albeit in different ways. In a present where everyone (gathered under the universal heading of "man") is in debt and guilty before capital, this presumably includes those whose bodies have historically not been considered human and have functioned *as* capital. Yet wealth accrues disproportionately over time as a result of power inequalities indexed by things like race, class, gender, and nationality. As Jodi Melamed puts it, "Capital can only be capital when it is accumulating, and it can only accumulate by producing and moving through relations of severe inequality among human groups ... procedures of racialization and capitalism are ultimately never separable from each other."[22]

Deleuze's quick move from past enclosure to present indebtedness segregates from memory the legacies of enduring racial injustice, thereby preempting a consideration of the present as segregated time.[23] This invites my inquiry into whiteness as a form of credit and racial stigma as branding others as always already in debt. In a political economy where white time is given time, racial debt is ultimately experienced as indispensable. With respect to my own debts, let me begin by acknowledging that I am hardly the first to foreground the issue of debt as it pertains to racial formation. In the American context, W.E.B. Du Bois's landmark *Black Reconstruction in America* was written against the backdrop of popular white sentiment that African Americans were the passive beneficiaries of white benevolence, and thus undeserving of credit for their own emancipation.[24] Du Bois excoriated popular notions that Black freedom evinced an enormous debt owed to whites who spilled so much blood and treasure on their behalf. In his famous account of the general strike, the Civil War hinged upon Black workers who withdrew their labor from the Confederate planters and transferred it to the Union at enormous cost. As a form of resistance cast in temporal terms, the strike represented a world-historical withdrawal and reapportioning of time. Du Bois's scholarship anticipated subsequent rejections of Black debt by figures like James Baldwin, who insisted, "I am not a ward of America, I am not the object of missionary charity, I am one of the people who built this country."[25]

Revealingly, the enslaved fashioned modes of resistance in temporal terms only to have their actions rebranded as Black moral failings. Work slowdowns, foot-dragging, and the stealing away of fugitives from slavery (the original "vagrants") were apprehended as stealing white property and white time. Since productive time was, by definition, time spent making white people money, time away was wasted time. Such histories of temporal reclamation—seen by whites as proof of Black sloth and racial untimeliness—would later be redeployed to denigrate emancipated workers as too lazy and too incorrigible to be fully free(d) labor. Indeed, during Reconstruction, the Freedman's Bureau was often tasked with adjudicating contract disputes where time was of the essence. For instance, time lost because of sickness was deducted from the worker's wage, or share, where time lost for idleness or unapproved absence was to be penalized at three times the normal rate. Such forms of accounting for time served as "a means of reenslavement insofar as it turned most Black farmers into debt peons."[26]

In *Scenes of Subjection* Saidiya Hartman writes of what she calls "the gift of freedom," referring to Reconstruction-era textbooks such as Isaac Brinckerhoff's *Advice to Freedman*, which made explicit the fact that "emancipation instituted indebtedness."[27] Brinckerhoff makes clear that the individual responsibility of the emancipated requires repaying those debts through proper conduct. Despite their past depredations, he advises freedmen to cultivate their latent capacities for "manhood" and make themselves "useful."[28] Usefulness was defined by being perpetually at the service of white power. From the prism of segregated time, Reconstruction's fashioning of the free(d) subject as indebted was moral suasion cotemporaneous with violent prohibitions against Black bodies as uniquely prone to wasting time—time over which whites refused to rescind dominion. In particular, Black freedom to move though space was severely restricted through vagrancy laws targeting those who squandered time.

Officially, an itinerant time-waster was marked as anyone without a labor contract (read: unemployed) and thus vulnerable to having their time seized in the form of forced servitude.[29] In some regions compulsory labor was a consequence for being unable to pay a fine. In places like Georgia, however, indolence, profligacy, and idleness were explicitly proscribed by the Black Codes, making freed people without contract or property subject to arrest.[30] Hence not only did the textbooks reiterate the Calvinist moralism of idleness as "the devil's playground" but "refigured enslavement through the fabulation of debt.... In short, the liberty and equality conferred by emancipation instituted the debt and established the terms of its amortization."[31] Hartman also references Nietzsche's account of bad conscience in her analysis of indebted servitude, but she quickly conjoins the psychic and the material dimensions to racialized indebted subjection. Narrated as a "gift" conveying individual responsibilities and duties, Black emancipation imposed the liabilities of freedom without its benefits. A "burdened individuality" utilized a fictional debt and racial amnesia to reconfigure Black servitude. At the same time, the debt imposed on the supposedly blameworthy individual reinstated the injuries of the past by attributing any vestiges of slavery's degradations to flaws of character and conduct. It amounted to a counsel of self-mastery in the form of indebted servility to white power.

This fabricated debt is incurred by virtue of the opportunity of the enslaved for self-improvement through bondage that can only come from serving one's betters. Borrowed time is paid *with, through, and throughout* one's life, making it a temporal imposition with material consequences. Booker T. Washington notoriously advocated respectability politics by referring to the "school of slavery" as a necessary historical step in Black advancement.[32] Then, as now, proper conduct was imagined as an appropriate currency of repayment—with the promised reward sometimes pitched as conversion into whiteness.[33] Despite promises that good behavior will allow debtors to catch up to whites, the racial debt imposed by white-time-as-given-time is ultimately indispensable. In the meantime, to be "one of the good ones," the subjugated must express gratitude for their own exploitation. On this point, Frantz Fanon observed that the colonizer claimed that the native was slow by nature when "what the colonist really wanted was for the slave to be full of enthusiasm."[34] Masters desire the enthusiasm of their enslaved not just because they want speedy work; they also want it done with grateful humility. The added emotional labor amounts to a compulsory expression of thanksgiving for the civilizational debt whites believe they are owed. Grateful subservience has the added benefit of not challenging the racial amnesia concealing white debt.[35] For those existing in a present caught between the unrequited injustices of the past and the unfulfilled promises of democratic futures, the demand for patience and gratitude modulates the rhythms of life on borrowed time.

The ideological and juridical fixation on idlers and shirkers during Reconstruction foreshadows those racially stigmatized as less creditworthy today. Recently, the journalist and author Ta-Nehisi Coates incited controversy with his book *Between the World and Me*. There were indictments that he distorted American history and that he was not sufficiently grateful.[36] Widely credited with mainstreaming the debate over reparations into center-left political discourse, Coates also registers how debt serves as an instrument of segregated time for African Americans. By creatively reworking popular tropes of the American Dream as connected with homeownership, Coates claims that the disposability of Black lives in America is "heritage," where Black death is a presumed "cost of doing business." Meanwhile, the willfully innocent whites Coates calls "Dreamers"

> accept our bodies as currency because it is their tradition. As slaves we were this country's first windfall, the down payment on its freedom. After the ruin and liberation of the Civil War came Redemption for the unrepentant South and Reunion, and our bodies became this country's second mortgage. In the New Deal we were their guestroom, their finished basement. And today, with a sprawling prison system, which has turned the warehousing of black bodies into a jobs program for Dreamers and a lucrative investment for Dreamers; today, when 8 percent of the world's prisoners are black men, our bodies have refinanced the Dream of being white. Black life is cheap, but in America black bodies are a natural resource of incomparable value.[37]

Coates's claim that slavery was a downpayment on the country's freedom, and the broken bodies of Reconstruction its second mortgage, is compelling rhetoric. On closer examination, his diction is also evocative of the French etymological roots of mortgage as *mort gage*, literally a "dead pledge."[38] The formulation also recalls Martin Luther King Jr.'s famous declaration on the centennial of emancipation that America's promise of black freedom and equality was a check that had been returned marked "insufficient funds."[39] Like Coates and Baldwin, King was marking white debt to Black benefactors—and not the other way around.

The metaphor of America as a house owned by white Dreamers, but bankrolled by Black bodies, evokes how the etymological root of the word "economy" comes from the Greek *oikos*, meaning "house."[40] The basement of the American house, fashioned from black bodies, is also its foundation. Its status as guestroom signifies the excess resources used to "finish" the space gleaned from the New Deal, a time *When Affirmative Action Was White*.[41] After having built the nation's house for nothing, white power threatens to evict Black labor to the jobs program of the prison big house to avoid paying the debt. Forced to wait in vain for what one is owed, the precarious meantime is spent as extorted basement tenants whose exorbitant rent pays the homeowner's mortgage. As Marx put it in 1844, "The cellar dwelling of a poor man is a hostile element . . . a dwelling which he cannot regard as his hearth where the renter cannot exclaim 'I am at home'—but instead finds himself in *someone else's house*, in the house of a *stranger* who always watches him and throws him out if he does not pay his rent."[42] Whatever the limits of the metaphor, it is revealing that when people of color demand what they are owed and refuse to wait for the goods, services, and standing accorded to whites they are so frequently told to "go home." In 2019, the sitting US president made headlines when he publicly said just that to a group of congresswomen.

Trump was obviously suggesting America is not the proper home for nonwhites in the first place, which brings us back to the homes impacted by the mortgage crisis. In the United States the default rate on non-fixed-rate mortgages quadrupled between 2006 and 2008, soaring from 10 percent to 40 percent. From 2007 to 2011 the country saw four million homes foreclosed upon, and 8.2 million foreclosures initiated.[43] Nevertheless, the impact of the subprime lending crisis was not evenly felt.[44] The Bank of America and Wells Fargo settled lawsuits for $355 million and $175 million, respectively, for targeting African Americans with predatory loans. The fallout revealed that the banks identified Black churches as sources of borrowers, and loan officers exploited their networks of trust, referring to black debtors as "mud people" to whom they sold "ghetto loans."[45] The city of Baltimore, where Coates is from (its population roughly 70 percent nonwhite), was eviscerated by the mortgage implosion. Settlements recouped from the banks came only *after* the evictions.[46] Baltimore's strife is emblematic of far broader devastation. In 2009, literally *every penny of wealth* accumulated by Black households during the post–civil rights era was lost in a single year.[47] Over a decade later, the percentage of Black homeownership was lower than when the Fair Housing Act was passed in 1968.[48]

Notice that the role of Black guilt in the debt crisis is conspicuously absent from Coates's prose. Like so many authors hailing from the Black radical tradition, he does not write from the position of one who feels guilty before capital. Nor does he think he should. He speaks in a voice that hails from a Black populace whose bodies, lives, and times have been used *as* capital to the point that they occupy the ontological status of a "natural resource of incomparable value." The subjugation of that "resource" has been sustained by white supremacy throughout the country's history, particularly through mass incarceration and brutal conditions under which people of color are overpoliced and underprotected. So Coates's description of the US penal system as a jobs program securitizing the white futurity colloquially known as the American Dream is not rhetorical polemic. I read him as gesturing to the history of how segregated time in the United States has been materially bankrolled by those racialized as subprime. Historian N.D.B. Connolly puts the point starkly by reminding readers that as early as the 1830s planter's banks sold slave-bundled mortgage-backed securities.[49] The emerging picture points to debt's asymmetrical distribution across races branded as indebted, conveying material inequities and the compulsory precarity of segregated time as life on borrowed time.

In an essay artfully entitled "The Subprime and the Beautiful," Fred Moten writes, "In the United States whoever says 'subprime debtor' says black as well."[50] When subjects are always already labeled subprime, they are effectively tethered to historically entrenched stigma of the past and preemptively denigrated in the present—even prior to being potential future borrowers. If we build on Moten, the temporal deficit of subprime time means being denied the chance to be afforded the credit for good behavior based on a past well-lived. This kind of credit is central to the promise of liberal individualism and equality before the law, not to mention any meaningful accounting of personal responsibility. Much of the same may be said of many of those who are denied credit altogether—subprime or otherwise. But the attenuated temporality of the subprime debtor differs from those who are excluded from the credit market. The borrowers predated upon by mortgage lenders were not cast out of time indiscriminately and immediately by being denied credit preemptively. They were subjected to subprime time. Nobody seems to have time for populations deemed immediately disposable in the short term, those who Deleuze refers to as "too poor for debt, too numerous for confinement."[51] Those subjects of subprime time, on the other hand, merit predatory interest in—and of—white time.

To better appreciate the dynamic of the predation, it is helpful to point out that although advocates of credit scoring pitch it as a colorblind means of providing an objective measure, it is more appropriately understood as a process of objectification by way of abstraction. When credit scores and actuarial data are deployed in ways that treat people as abstractions, it is not the case that everyone is necessarily turned into an anonymous vessel, a site of disinterest or disregard, or deracialized as an equal. For that matter, when we think back on the historical process of abstraction that turned time into equal units measured by the clock, it did not follow that everyone's time was valued equally. Ruth Gilmore contends that racism is a process of abstraction, a "death dealing displacement of differences into hierarchies that organize relations between planet's sovereign political territories."[52] As the phrase "death dealing" implies, racism also utilizes abstraction to organize temporal relations in morbidly differentiated ways. Racism's forces of abstraction are not impersonal, but target particular peoples for dispossession by debt as sites of what Miranda Joseph calls "disrespectful regard."[53] An antecedent politics of disrespectful regard was imposed on Indigenous peoples by early settlers in colonial America for purposes of seizing the land on which the nation's proverbial house was built.

Subprime Time

Up to this point the chapter has largely focused on experiences of temporal segregation that arise from the conjuncture of indebtedness and blackness in the United States. Yet the distinctions between the creditworthy and the incredible are not black and white. White colonials developed unique financial innovations specifically in order to dispossess American Indians of their land over time. The ease with which land is foreclosed upon today is a relatively recent development with origins in the predatory expropriation of

Indigenous lands. The context from which the American mortgage emerges as an apparatus of capture underscores the material, political stakes stemming from the abstractions of white time. By no means a granular history of finance, my intention is to glimpse the dynamic processes of racial abstraction over time that go missing in depersonalized accounts of debt. A brief sketch of debt foreclosure provides a sharper sense of the relays between past and present, segregated memory and segregated time.

In a rich essay entitled "Money, Mortgages and the Conquest of America," legal scholar K-Sue Park traces the contemporary practice of leveraging land for credit back to colonial America.[54] Park's analysis shows how land took on new liquidity when it became possible to use the land to securitize debts and obtain credit. For this to happen, land had to become real estate—meaning that the traditional line between real and personal property had to be undone in order for real estate to become a commodity that investors could speculate on, as so frequently happens today. In the centuries prior to colonialism, English property law had long made a clear distinction between land and chattel. This meant that land was not easily alienated for cash, and it was "virtually impossible" for it to be seized outright as a penalty for unpaid debts (MMCA, 4). In a genealogy of mortgages in America, Park explains the use of the gage (or pledge) as a financial instrument used by English lenders to secure the fruits of the land in question without running afoul of the prohibition against usury, or interest.

At least since the eleventh century, land was used to secure debts through mortgages in Europe, though not with the same foreclosure threats commonplace today.[55] Under the old model, mortgage lenders could take possession of the land for the life of the loan, but they had obligations for its upkeep and remained liable to the borrower for waste. A borrower could be thrown into debtors' prison for unpaid debts, and lenders could claim personal property from the land (such as crops) for debts in arrears, but it was extremely difficult for the land to be seized outright. If land was explicitly offered to securitize a loan that ultimately went unpaid, creditors could claim the land, but borrowers still held "an equity right to redemption" that allowed them to pay and redeem the land "within a reasonable amount of time, typically twenty years" (MMCA, 4). All the above underscores how difficult it was to separate landowners from their land, as English social and economic stability relied on the protection of estates across generations. This effectively meant "real property" (or real estate) was "practically inalienable," with chancery protecting land "even after the death of the debtor" (MMCA, 4). This brings us to the question: what augured the radical changes that have made real property seizure the commonplace occurrence it is today?

A proper grasp of the rationale behind the shift is impossible without appreciating how settlers' insatiable appetite for Indigenous lands necessitated jettisoning the old real estate laws that protected the propertied English gentry. In Park's analysis, the contemporary threat of mortgage foreclosure is an American innovation that begins as a tool of dispossessing Indians of their land through debt obligations. On the heels of the establishment of the Plymouth and Jamestown colonies in 1620 and 1607, respectively, the British Parliament abolished the remaining prohibitions against interest in 1623. The shift gave way to a range of new investment opportunities that arose from money's ability to grow with the mere passage of time (MMCA, 4–5). It also bequeathed powerful new currency that could circulate on the basis of credit, or promise to pay later, known as the negotiable instrument. Concurrently, the loosening of mortgage laws saw colonial lands increasingly subjected to foreclosure from failure to pay even unsecured loans. This amounted to a form of legalized theft, as the radical diversity of the participants in what Park terms "the contact economy" meant that the parties to the transactions did not share meaning across terms, nor was it generally the case that they negotiated as relative equals—to put it mildly.

Crucially, the emergent economy featured an economic repositioning of land as able to be enclosed and alienated like chattel—made so liquid that it could be used as a novel form of money. In fact, with the new liquidity it became common to refer to money as "coined land." By way of synthesis, Park writes:

> As the mortgage enacted a new equation between land and money, the money side represented debt. Indigenous debt created through colonial lending practices, often predatory in nature, enabled seizure of indigenous land. Land therefore became a money equivalent not through positive sale, but through debt and loss; foreclosure was a tool of indigenous dispossession. (MMCA, 3)

There was even a secondary market for third parties to buy and sell Indian debts, with speculators wagering on the likelihood of borrowers' defaulting and betting accordingly.[56]

Irrespective of *what* lending agreements are presumed and *when* they happen, the brokerage frequently occurs in the context of radical power inequalities—not least with regard to the creditor's and debtor's respective abilities to contest and enforce the terms of the contract. Liberal histories prefer to disavow the asymmetrical violence and inequities that are the contextual canvas upon which these loans were inked. Colonial lenders capitalized on Indigenous borrowers' misconceptions of the deal, such as deeded property as perpetually extinguishing rights of Native occupancy. The often deliberate misunderstandings and incommensurabilities (what she terms "miscomprehensions") foreshadow now-familiar strategies of predatory lending (MMCA, 3). Furthermore, Indigenous notions of belonging to the land—and not the other way around, as the settlers would have it—underscore the consequences of liberal property as enclosure. To reprise Deleuze, the inscriptions of private property make it possible to be simultaneously enclosed spatially and indebted temporally.

With respect to the alignment and disjuncture between tenses, notice what happens to the temporal vectors at play when the creditor–debtor relation is recast genealogically. Pondering foreclosure as a tool of Indigenous dispossession, the potential resources for historical revision are many. It allows us to hear, with new ears, James Madison's statement in the *Federalist Papers* that "the protection of different and unequal faculties of acquiring property . . . is the first object of government."[57] The gratuitous complexity woven into investment derivatives, together with our knowledge of who benefits from their opacity, make the resonance between past and present hard to miss. The past has been conceptually divorced from the present through willfully myopic scholarly practices that have focused on financial interactions between white colonial powers to the exclusion of the roles played by Indigenous peoples. Suffice it to say, the descent of American mortgages resituates present-day dispossession by debt by uncomfortably recontextualizing it within the racialized land grabs that built the country from the ground up. Beyond a laudable corrective to segregated memory, the legacy of contact economy speaks to the force of segregated time. It prompts us to consider the political stakes of deficiencies that might otherwise appear esoteric, antiquarian, or purely academic.

First, by overlooking the contact economy and starting instead with intramural exchanges among colonial whites as the primary, socially meaningful group worthy of study (a phenomenon Jean O'Brien calls "firsting"), one can easily miss core components of the time value of money, the monetization of time, and related innovations and continuities.[58] Not least is how, over time, one person's accumulated debt becomes another's accumulated capital. Second, notice how sharply this approach departs from ahistorical theoretical practices of focusing on transacting polities presumed to be composed of consent between so-called rational enlightened individuals—as defined by Anglo-European norms of self-interest maximization and so on—by instead centering its analysis on "specific rituals people use to authorize trade and binding diplomatic agreements."[59] The former is exemplified in economics textbooks that illustrate the time value of money with a story about how (infantile, stupid, backward) Indians sold the entire island of Manhattan to white settlers for a measly $24. The latter is only available by acknowledging that Indigenous peoples did not have notions of landownership and property commensurate with the Europeans.

Third, the presumed temporal flow through which the mortgage appears as a forward-looking vehicle progressing toward an ownership society now appears fraudulent, and indeed American Dream–like, from its inception. It looks especially fantastic if one is captive to the segregated memory of the United States as a nation whose founders aspired to create a transracial ownership society. Speaking to the political stakes of segregated memory and segregated time, Park writes that, as a "consequence of this omission, the story of the American mortgage appears as a narrative about generative credit, rather than one about dispossession" (MMCA, 2). Park's connection of mortgage and expropriation is trenchant and sustained. At the same time, I take the view that the racialized dispossession of the mortgage narrative *does* reveal a story of generative credit: the credit value of whiteness over time. The production of particular subjects as debtors implies creditors. Some brief remarks on *saving time* will help us approach the temporal economy whereby white time is credited as *given time*—in turn, branding racial others to subsist on borrowed time.

Saving Time

In Zygmunt Bauman's rendering of what he calls "liquid modernity," surplus populations are those relegated to the status of pariahs and treated as waste material. They include the unemployed, migrants, transient peoples, and so on.[60] Yet moving too quickly in the direction of liquidation risks a deficit in how we understand the dynamic channels and flows of human disposability in shaky times.[61] The civilizational debt imposed by white time is not always extracted through the outright extermination. After all, annihilated peoples can no longer be perversely exploited as "payback" for the injuries they have already suffered—injuries disavowed by segregated memory and compounded over segregated time. In the meantime of liberalism's "not yet," some subordinate subjects supposedly *saved* by the forces of Euro-modern progress and missionary colonialism coded as white can be *saved* in the sense of being held in reserve for future use. Rob Nixon observes that "the noun 'reserve' may refer to either a sanctuary or a place of involuntary confinement—a refuge or a cage."[62] Here reserves evoke Indian reservations with histories of being open-air prisons and veritable death traps that inspired Nazi concentration camps. Reserves also bespeak Indigenous territories and peoples regarded as set-asides, assets on loan to inhabitants, and hence subject to seizure and extraction over the long term. To the extent that the settler state treats even meager Indigenous survivance as an infinitely retractable pseudogift always open to repossession, the reservation "here and now" is on borrowed time.[63]

To name but a few colonial logics, reservations have alternately been regarded as bestowals of white beneficence, as a shorthand for reparations already paid, or territories sovereign in theory but not in practice. It should go without saying that crediting the Indian reservation system to white generosity is an erasure of Native agency and resistance—namely, the bloody wars that were instrumental for making the reservation system palatable to whites as viable solution to the so-called Indian problem in the first place.[64] All this evinces a mnemonic segregation long integral to the machinations of settler colonialism and segregated time.[65] Historically, European settlers frequently racialized aboriginal peoples as destined for extinction, and African peoples as rhythmically suited for labor.[66] However, it would oversimplify the flux and dynamism of segregated time to fix all Indigenous peoples as racially branded for dispossession of their space/land, and Afro-diasporic peoples as preyed upon for their time. The preceding scenes of Black property foreclosure suggest a more complicated dynamic. Relatedly, settler states often treat Native peoples and their lands as a kind of spatiotemporal *reserve*. I mean this in the sense that they can be marked as sites of extraction whose land, labor, and time are kept on hold for later acquisition to be appropriated accordingly—that is, when the time is white.

I refer to the imposition of white time as "given time" in the dual sense of a gift of time, and a temporal order taken for granted as universal. (The word "data" comes from the Latin word for "given.") At any rate, given time is premised on saving time. From the vantage point of would-be English settlers, Native Americans were in need of "saving" even before colonial savings accounts were engorged by Indian land, labor, and scalps. Before setting sail and signing the Mayflower Compact, in 1630 the English who would later make up the Plymouth Colony drew up an official seal depicting the figure of a near-naked Indian holding a small, benign-looking bow and arrow. In a revealing move that anticipated centuries of racially paternalistic imperialistic logic that continues to this day, underneath the image was the inscription "Come Over and Help Us."[67] Given that it was the Wampanoag Indians who later saved the inept Pilgrims from certain death, the statement emits a level of blind arrogance befitting the first act of a Greek tragedy. Even in a casual retelling of the history of the first Thanksgiving, settlers came to owe Native Americans an existential debt for saving *their* lives.[68] In one of the great scourges of history, whites repaid Indian generosity with genocide, stealing lives and land.

Segregated memory denies the long history of Indian reservations as sites willfully engineered by the settler state to induce death fast and slow through dependence on, and even addiction to, governmental powers augured by white supremacy.[69] Indeed, the colonization process in the United States was *deliberately* crafted to make Indigenous peoples beholden to white institutions of church and state spiritually, intellectually, cosmologically, and materially. Indian dependency would be officially inscribed when the issue of Native land rights intensified with the discovery of gold in Georgia in the late 1820s and the Indian Removal Act of 1830. In response to the Cherokee Nation's objection to the state of Georgia's theft of their land in 1831, the Supreme Court explicitly defined the "tribes" as "domestic dependent nations" who

> occupy a territory to which we assert a title independent of their will, which must take effect in point of possession, when their right of possession ceases. Meanwhile they are in a state of pupilage. Their relation to the United States resembles that of a ward to his guardian. They look to our government for protection; rely upon its kindness and its power; appeal to it for relief to their wants; and address the president as their great father.[70]

Notice the pseudo-benevolant, arrogant assignation of a title "independent of their will" with a "point of possession" happening in some later time. The "meanwhile" state of pupilage is contiguous with the present day. Not incidentally, the temporal roots of the ongoing deferral are evident in the Court's reference to the Euro-Christian doctrine of discovery, which has its origins in the papal edicts, or "bulls," dating back to the time of the Crusades.[71] Ultimately, the doctrine afforded priority title to European settlers, such that the transfer of land could only officially take place either *from* Indians *to* settlers, or between settlers.[72] In practice, this meant that the right of settlers to buy land always superseded the right of Indians not to sell.

Indian land that was parceled, collateralized, and borrowed against in desperate times could later be seized. Today, mining leases render Native inhabitants and their lands expendable destinations for uranium extraction and radioactive waste disposal. Ironically, the need for heavy metals was catalyzed by the country's quantum leap forward into the nuclear age. As Andrea Smith writes, "Military and nuclear testing takes place almost exclusively on Native lands."[73] It is a practice so prolific across time and space that it has given birth to what Gabriel Schwab calls "radioactive ghosts."[74] Radiation emitting from the ground beneath "hot houses" causes cancer, sterility, birth defects, and myriad long-term illnesses precipitated by nuclear seepage. And then there is the uprising over the Dakota Access Pipeline and the militant beatdown of water protectors who valiantly refused to be treated as a standing reserve of settler state resources. The need for cheap fuel to propel the US economy and empire led it to turn to Indigenous lands at Standing Rock in a time of perceived crisis. In that all-too-familiar dynamic of white time, settler acquisitiveness of time and territory is marshaled as a buffer against the bumpy temporalities that inconvenience the powerful with shortages, contingencies, and eventualities.

The injuries of environmental racism are at once concealed by the slowness of the violence and the spectral presence of their target: in this case, Indigenous peoples who have been fated for extinction since first contact and who are somehow always already in the process of disappearing. The flickering status of Indians as not quite present, but not quite absent from white time was articulated by Robert Durrenberger's writing in the 1972 *Annals of the Association of American Geographers*: "The Colorado Plateau was one of the last areas in the United States to be developed economically. Before the 1880s it was virtually empty except for Indians."[75] The phrase "virtually empty *except for Indians*" captures the spectrality of Native presence. It echoes

Locke's notion of America as vacant, yet somehow also populated by wasteful Indians.[76] Yet, as Mohawk anthropologist Audra Simpson has argued, the enduring presence of Indians here and now is embarrassing remainder—and reminder—of an incomplete genocide.[77] Acknowledging Indigenous presence threatens white racial amnesia that conveniently disavows Native land claims and debts to First Nations through segregated memory; acknowledgment that might chisel away at the willful ignorance sustaining segregated time. All of the above dramatizes contested issues of who has the authority to acknowledge and avow Indigenous presence in the first place.[78]

There is a discernable white psychoaffective attachment to racializing Native peoples as indebted. To the limited extent that whites acknowledge Indigenous presence at all, many regard tribal identity as already having provided access to special privileges in the form of entitlements like affirmative action and extravagant casino revenues. Deeper still, settler temporalities remain profoundly haunted by the racial stigma of Native debt to white society, preempting talk of aboriginal rights, reparations, or land return. Admittedly, I can only gesture to the vast range of conflagrations of civilizational debt and the political-theological colonization by salvation that represented a colonization of time with expansive material consequences. The Republic of Haiti, for one, has the dubious distinction of being the "first poor country to be placed in permanent debt peonage."[79] A soundbite of missionary conquest's planetary reverberations cannot hope to encompass its bandwidth of frequencies, themes, and variations. That said, when it comes to the resonance between the church as an instrument to colonize time and space, the mission bell is an especially appropriate symbol. From the "Great Father" in Washington to not-so-great "fathers" of the clergy, the pastoral power of the paternal white saviors was quite literal. It came with an unholy riot of abuses—sexual, epistemological, and cross-temporal incursions—that were the biopolitical precondition of being "saved." The missionaries' 'saving time' of redeeming souls for the next world also represented a saving of time that would otherwise be wasted unproductively in this one. It was time-saving in still another sense: they expropriated the times and territories of Others and then banked the proceeds.

Speaking to such dubious salvation, Lila Abu-Lughod writes: "When you save someone *from* something you're also saving her *to* something. What violences are entailed in this transformation, and what presumptions are being made about the superiority of that to which you are saving her?"[80] To this we might add, what debts are incurred in the meantime? Once again, the payback for the hard work whites expended on policies geared to "annihilate the Indian but save the man" was proper conduct befitting a "good Indian." The trouble is, then and now, that an Indian (bad, good, or otherwise) is still an Indian, just as the "good Negro" is still Black, the "model minority" is still Asian, the useful immigrant is still a foreigner, and on it goes. The fact that whites claim credit for singling out "the good ones" for salvation betrays notions of racial progress rendering people of color subprime in white time. In segregated white time, where redemption equals whiteness, the acceptable currency to pay back racial debt is the time of your life.

So, in response to Abu-Lughod's query, let us presume that the "you" doing the saving is directed toward white time itself. What, then, is the subject being saved *to* by the force of white time? The potential answers are many. However, by extension of the apprehensive logics of power at work—and to the extent she is being "saved" at all—at minimum we know what white time is saving her *for* . . .

It is saving her for later.

Given Time: On the Credit Value of Whiteness

Asking who, or what, is the supposed lender of borrowed time points back to how this chapter has complicated accounts of primordial debt as owed to a monotheistic God, or ancestral founding fathers who later become deified as gods (à la Nietzsche), or universal debt to the proverbial god of capital (Marx, Graeber, and Lazzarato). By considering white supremacy as another source of given time imposing debt, white time appears as an iterative apparatus of spatiotemporal capture that racially segregates conceptions of time and experiences of time, or temporality. The notion that given time is *not* free of charge is in keeping with Derrida's insight that what is typically called a "gift" is often really a time-sensitive exchange that makes demands on the recipient. "Where there is gift, there is time. What it gives, the gift, is time, but this gift is also a demand on time."[81] The gift of liberal freedom follows a missionary logic requiring a conversion of difference into sameness—an assimilation into life as a grateful liberal subject in synch with its prevailing tempos and notions of progress. As Mimi Thi Nguyen puts it, "The gift of freedom is not the end but another beginning, another bondage."[82] Those racially branded as recipients of the gift of "free time" who are "freed" into indebtedness to their saviors are patently *unfree* to deviate beyond the boundaries of liberal subjectivity, unfree to comport themselves as less than grateful for their own expropriation, and unfree to contest their precarity should they experience it as walking states of exception. Unmasked, the "gift" of white time is a euphemism for a nonconsensual conscription into racial indebtedness and life on borrowed time.

The prevailing notion of Euro-colonial temporal order as "given time"—in the dual sense of an order of time taken for granted as universal, as well as an offering bestowed—is a feature of *white time*. In this context, *white temporality* connotes affective experiences attaching to white time as a given providential *present*, in the sense of the present tense of now as well as the present as a white paternalist gift that indebts its recipients of color.[83] Recall that Du Bois speaks to white presence, and white *presents*, by theorizing white phenomenology as an expectation of perpetual ownership: "But what on earth is whiteness that one should so desire it? Then, as always, somehow, some way, silently but clearly, I am given to understand that whiteness is ownership of the earth forever and ever, Amen!"[84] Protected by power, whiteness as ownership of the world "forever and ever" conveys an expectation that the property value of whiteness is perpetual. With Cheryl I. Harris, let us examine how future expectations are relevant to whiteness as property as well as vehicles of white psychosocial credit.

Harris contends whiteness is constructed as a species of property "by recognizing the reputational interest in being regarded as white as a thing of significant value."[85] Credit is a store of value through time whose worth hinges on expectation. From the Latin *credere*, credit "is indistinguishable from one's personal reputation or status as worthy of being believed."[86] For its relation to time and property, Jeremy Bentham writes: "Property is nothing but *the basis of expectation* . . . consist[ing] in an established expectation, in the *persuasion* of being able to draw such and such advantage from the thing possessed."[87] The enclosure of property limbs off exclusionary *space* while also signifying a temporal enclosure that (p)reserves it for enjoyment at a future *time*. In Harris's analysis: "The relationship between expectations and property remains highly significant, as the law has recognized and protected even the expectation of rights as actual legal property."[88]

What is remarkable about the court protecting the *expectation* of rights as actual legal property is the promise of a judicial safeguard around how one experiences an anticipated future in any given present. One's affective orientation to time, or temporality, can be legally protected property.

Next, it is deeply intriguing that the property that gets hived off for future enjoyment by way of enclosure in this formulation is not just space, but time itself.[89] Bentham's so-called persuasion of being able to expect a future advantage is a protected right. Taken together, this arguably amounts to nothing less than a claim of sovereign ownership over time—an assertion of temporal sovereignty.[90] To synthesize the above, the reputational value of whiteness as elemental to its status as property deserving of protection over time makes legible the worth of whiteness as a form of credit.[91]

Of course, racialized creditworthiness hardly aligns with the *actual* past record of who makes good on promises, who keeps faith, or who upholds contracts.[92] The history of colonial settlement is a history of white theft, plunder, and countless broken treaties with Indigenous peoples. As Sioux Chief Red Cloud stated memorably, "The white man made me a lot of promises, and they only kept one. They promised to take my land and they took it."[93] White colonial power embodies the racist slur whites hurled at Native populations. It is the ultimate "Indian giver" that can reclaim its supposedly gifted reservation land at any time or finish its incomplete genocide.[94] So when Patrick Wolfe states that "property stops where Indianness starts," he is clearly referencing race and conquest, and not suggesting that whites' reputable behavior made them more qualified borrowers.[95] And the notion that bad credit always follows bad actors is patently absurd. Corporate bankruptcy protections unavailable to everyday people and taxpayer dollars spent on bank bailouts suggest otherwise. Credit and the related capacity to dispense with debt and start over are borne not by truth but by power. The signifying power of whiteness as a conduit of good faith and credit over time is underwritten by psychoaffective attachments to dangerous fictions of white beneficence and nonwhite deviance—myths altogether unhinged from history. The delusional belief in white trustworthiness is, as Baldwin might say, symptomatic of whites being the slightly mad victims of their own brainwashing.

Whiteness is a component of social creditworthiness that enables liquidity for some at the expense of others. Miranda Joseph defines liquidity in temporal terms as "the ability to move freely from one present to the next unburdened by a disabling past."[96] The liquidity of whiteness connotes the capacity to move fluidly across temporal spheres. It stands in stark juxtaposition to the racial fixity of those consigned to the undersides of segregated time and white supremacy, where redemption is racialized. To be racially branded as indebted often entails being disbarred from new beginnings and opportunities for self-refashioning according to one's own unique rhythms and sense of time.[97] This is not to erase or obviate, however, forms of resistance and creativity that are also figured in temporal terms. Asynchronous others use time they do not have to organize and contest the perception that the fault is theirs as subprime individuals, and insist on a collective accounting of systemic racism. In doing so, they actively contest their punishment as individuals accused of wasting their time unproductively by highlighting their membership in a group stigmatized for being irredeemable time-wasters.[98] Among Indigenous groups, it is hard to miss the temporal politics contesting racial stigma in the name Idle No More. Cut back to the mortgage crisis and, in its own way, taking on subprime debt for housing can be a temporary refuge delaying the impact of precarity imposed by white time. Moten calls that kind of deferral a "serial postponement of externally imposed contingency whose supposed intermittence is best understood as a whole other timeline's broken circle."[99] Contingencies that were *supposed* to be intermittent actually persist as elemental features of segregated time, undoing notions of (white) time's supposed universality.[100]

On the other side of subprime time is white time's liquidity. The liquidity of white temporality—with its expectation of owning a future unhinged from the past—is borne of present spaces and times apprehended as available for white ownership. Here is Fanon: "The white man wants the world for himself alone. He's predestined master of the world. He enslaves it. An acquisitive relation is established between the world and him" (BSWM, 128). With respect to the acquisitive relationship established between the world and white ownership, the symmetry between Fanon's prose and *Between the World and Me* is clear. Coates contemplates the possibility that white supremacy could end his son's life *at any given time*, asserting that "black bodies have refinanced the dream of being white," adding another inflection point to white apprehensiveness that underscores what I have termed the credit value of whiteness.[101]

One way that the American Dream has been refinanced by people of color is by the relative increase in the credit value of whiteness that occurs when the speed and spectacle of nonwhite disposability persists unabated. The frequently state-sanctioned theft of the lifetimes of racial others fortifies the exclusionary powers of whiteness. At the same time, stealing others' time further credits (or adds to) the staying power of whiteness to convey the expectation that white lifetimes will continually be inoculated against predation and attrition. This is embedded in the fiction of whiteness as inalienable and indivisible, its fortifications permanent.

Resisting the notion of market alienability as central to property, Harris writes that "the inalienability of whiteness should not preclude the consideration of whiteness as property. Paradoxically, its inalienability may be more indicative of its perceived enhanced value, rather than its disqualification as property."[102] Demagogues and political entrepreneurs capitalize on racial fantasies of white nationalism to blame widening inequalities on minorities, yet I remain unconvinced of the eternal stability of inalienable whiteness. Capitalism does not necessarily require *racial* dispossession. It does depend upon inequality, extraction, and human/nonhuman disposability—all of which make processes of racialization a going concern. A sense of expanding expendability among those whose whiteness is unstable fuels apprehension. Those who fear being sucked into the white underclass worry that they too might be living on borrowed time.

The student debt crisis took many middle-class whites by surprise in 2011, as it threatened their ownership of the future. Their surprise betrayed a consolidation of whiteness as expectation, as credit value, and as supposedly inalienable property. With innocent amnesia, some Wall Street Occupiers seemed genuinely perplexed by the monochromatic crowds and wondered why solidarity with nonwhite members of the 99 percent was not more readily forthcoming.[103] Remarkably, for all the florid and frequently public destruction of the lives of people of color, it does not seem to have prevented the increase in deaths of despair among whites and decreases in white life expectancy. In view of the heightened sense that the credit value of whiteness may be in decline, the next chapter takes up white precarity and disposability with respect to the segregated apocalypse now. This is not to imply that either the injuries or the entitlements have been evenly distributed over time. Far from it. It does, however, call attention to how white temporality is entrenched, defended, and sustained as a possessive tense.[104]

It also signals the dangerous fiction of faith in unlimited white credit: the presumption that the last shall always be first (to go). This sinister feature of segregated time is evident in the unfair burden borne by yet another form of contemporary liquidity, namely the aleatory weather catastrophes of the current climate crisis. Ecocatastrophe disproportionately affects Indigenous peoples and those residing in the Global South, particularly low-lying tropical regions especially susceptible to encroaching waters. The mainstream politics of the planet's biggest polluters have not yet seriously reckoned with sovereign climate debt. The existential urgency of doing just that makes the absence of race and climate debt from contemporary accounts all the more unsettling. While residents of low-lying, formerly colonized regions such as those of the Marshall Islands, the Maldives, and the Caribbean might not always be subject to outright extermination by way of guns and bombs, the recursive, surreptitious disasters pursuant to modern ecocide persist unabated. Viewed through the racist, biopolitical prism of settler states, these populations' vulnerability to mass death (fast and slow) might make it seem that they function as the proverbial canaries in the coal mine of contemporary climate change.[105]

By stating the disavowal of climate debt in biopolitical terms, we can illuminate contemporary borrowed time in still another way. The presence of populations as buffers who absorb the growing, increasingly brutal effects of the climate crisis allows the issue to be regarded as an endemic malady by the privileged. In view of the race of those disproportionately affected by climate change in the short term, it is little wonder that suffering is diminished and disappeared by the privileged as an endemic malady that can supposedly be managed over the long term as something they can live with—and off. In the meantime, the waters rise and storms intensify, with effects helpfully concealed by the segregated times and spaces of environmental racism. The powerful compulsively refuse to acknowledge that they, and the entire human estate, along with much of the nonhuman world, are now living on borrowed time.

Lastly, the temporal forces of racial capitalism chronicled here exceed the boundaries of the nation-state. The political implications of their concatenation make advocating for the downfall of any single government an anachronistic form of activism. As Santee Dakota activist, artist, and poet John Trudell writes, "I'm not looking to overthrow the American government, the corporate state already has."[106]

Interlude 2: Time Travel

In this short interlude I reflect on a dynamic whereby the racialization of many of the subjects in this study imbues them with the power to transcend temporal boundaries.[1] By taking up the interface of race and time travel as a cypher of segregated time, my purpose is to propose a hermeneutic identifying affective attachments that might otherwise remain encrypted. Toward that end, I locate an investment in race as a vehicle of transcending time as part of the spectrality of race. Simultaneously present and absent, the racial other as an instrument of time travel is an affectively imbued ascriptive identity that can become politically manifest when the time is right—or more pointedly—when the time is white. As such, I regard white apprehension of racial others as vehicles of time travel as a psychoaffective attachment in the Fanonian sense of an epidermalized past that (re)surfaces in nonlinear ways. From Frederick Jackson Turner's frontier thesis whereby settler encounters with Indigenous peoples allow them to go back in time in order to move forward and form a new American race; to immigrants who can alternately take the country back to its founding or act as agents of devolution; to African American female bodies as transcending time in the speculative fiction of Octavia Butler's *Kindred*: the capacity for racial others to serve as vehicles of time travel recurs as a potent (science) fiction of white temporalities.[2]

Frantz Fanon speaks to the strange fixation among whites to ascribe time travel to people of color as part of his own struggle to be rid of its contagion (BSWM, 35). Meditating on the immediacy of the epidermalized past, he recounts reading the poet Léopold Senghor and beginning to value his blackness for its ascribed proximity to rhythm, temporarily associating his difference with an alive, free, asymmetric energy that fuels great art. At first, his ecstatic description reads as the affirmation of a kind of necessary (Black) Dionysian counterpart to the (white) Apollonian. He remembers blushing with fleeting pride at the possibility that "from the opposite end of the white world, a magical Negro culture was hailing me. . . . Was this our salvation?" (BSWM, 123). In a painful turn, he confesses catching himself being seduced into accepting white standards of value, and recoiling: "I walk on white nails ... Black magic! Orgies, witches' sabbaths, heathen ceremonies, amulets ... from every direction" (BSWM, 126). Fanon emerges on the other side of the realization to see the fraudulence of ascribing rationality to whiteness and emotion to blackness. Rejecting the colonial dualism that renders the former human and the latter other, he turns again to acknowledge precisely what the supposedly all-seeing white rationality has overlooked with its rote Cartesian habits of thought. "*When the whites feel that they have become too mechanized, they turn to the men of color and ask them for a little human sustenance*" (BSWM, 129; my emphasis).

Fanon catches himself thinking, "At last I had been recognized, I was no longer a zero" (BSWM, 129). He steps back again in painful self-reproach, taking another beat to appreciate the toxicity of a condition in which the only way to see one's self as counting for something is by being a useful tool of white temporal flight. "I had soon changed my tune" (BSWM, 129). The quickness with which he evokes white modes of valorization tells him that disalienation requires grappling with the entwined psychic and material life of slavery and colonialism. This leads Fanon to recognize that the horror of the heathen ceremonies that breaths beneath "the Negro as a phobogenic object" also conveys the orgiastic eroticism and rhythmic musicality that reduces Blacks to objects of Negrophilia. Make no mistake, however: the specter of blackness as a mode of time travel haunts both the attraction and aversion. So long as whites apprehend racial others as available to help them transcend time, they imagine that, in the meantime, they can have it both ways.

For Fanon, such maddening racial fantasies must be overcome if a new humanism is to be born, a renaissance which would necessitate the birth of a new sense of time—and indeed a new world. White ascriptions of fixity to the nonwhite world have the familiar Césairean effect of returning to affix whites in a web of paralysis and dehumanization that they cannot articulate and cannot escape. So-called white civilizational maturity that projects a hypersexualized blackness ironically comes at the cost of white sterility.[3] In effect, many whites are fixed in the sense that one speaks of a neutered and sterilized pet as fixed—domesticated by civilizational forces they do not understand, largely unaware of what they are missing, and unable to birth a genuinely new humanism worthy of transracial affirmation. Such willful ignorance prompts Fanon to regard whites as "no less alienated (duping and duped)" (BSWM, 29).

To explore at least some of the expressions and complexities of racial time travel, I begin with the figure of the immigrant other as alternately threatening devolution to a prior time and also a regenerative resource for going forward by going backward. Thereafter I turn to the innovative Afrofuturism of Octavia E. Butler as addressing the dangerous subterranean investments in racial others as vectors of time travel. I interpret Butler's novel *Kindred* as critiquing the racial politics of transcending time by way of the Black female body. The African American protagonist Dana is repeatedly and involuntarily transported to a nineteenth-century plantation to save the life of her slaveholding ancestor, Rufus. To him she is a savior from the future, but for her white husband, Kevin, her touch can transport him back in time. Dana's status as a writer further positions the text at the intersection of literary and political imaginings of segregated time.

The Borders of Time Travel

In *Americans No More*, journalist Georgie Ann Geyer writes that "By the end of the 20th century, America itself had changed—it was in danger of drifting toward becoming a Third World nation, and crucially important parts of it, like once-glorious California, were actually moving backwards in time and backwards in development."[4] As she crudely suggests, the politics of migration is typically imagined in spatial terms but frequently amplified and contested with reference to time. Pondering the phrase as a site of intensification, the magical thinking radiating from this remarkable statement invites deeper inquiry. Just how, one might ask, is the "once glorious" California going to be hurled into history, and what does that have to do with its brown immigrants? Geyer was bemoaning a decline in American citizenship, adding another temporal vector by invoking the absence of adult decision-making among those clinging to a childish refusal to make tough judgments about immigration policy.[5] If one did not know the context, however, the remark would not seem at all out of place among white nationalists today. Neonativist calls for a border wall are conjoined to the time-sensitive injunction that such a fortification will augur a return to past greatness. Such voices cast insecure borders and pluralization as urgent threats to be scorned on the grounds that they portend a descent into incivility and cultural backsliding, even auguring a national jeremiad terminating in an apocalyptic hellscape. The political allegiances of these sources may differ, but they share a common presumption with respect to immigrant others as potential vehicles of time travel.

In the United States, the threat of a temporal reversal wrought by migrants is conjoined not just to their alleged hunger for undeserved resources, but the sense that they are mysteriously able to initiate nationwide time-travel by virtue of their presence. In *Democracy and the Foreigner*, Bonnie Honig offers an account of the powerful ambivalences at play with respect to the foreigner as alternately vilified and celebrated.

> In various versions of the myth of an immigrant America, it is . . . the immigrant's *foreignness* that positions him to reinvigorate the national democracy, and that foreignness is undecidable: our faith in a just economy, our sense of community or family, or our voluntarist vigor are so moribund that only a foreigner could invigorate them.[6]

On the other side of this ambivalence, Honig argues, is the sense that the otherwise admirable immigrant work ethic also spells a loss of jobs. What looks like vigorous community can also appear as ethnic enclaves, and the affirmation of traditional family values can look like a threat to gains in gender equality.[7] To make her case, Honig draws upon Ali Behdad's *A Forgetful Nation* to argue that Behdad acknowledges the politics of ambivalence at work in how Americans invoke the "nation of immigrants" mantra while also identifying themselves in opposition to the immigrants they simultaneously try to control. Honig affirms Behdad's analysis of this ambivalence and its array of contradictory stereotypes as productive of a muscular regime of immigrant discipline and regulation. Nevertheless, she thinks he misses the key oppositional stereotype of what she calls the "supercitizen immigrant."

> Neither needy nor threatening, as such, but always mirrored by and partnered with those others, the supercitizen immigrant is the object of neither American hostility nor charity but outright adoration . . . the supercitizen immigrant is an object of identification. He is the screen onto which we project our idealized selves. He works harder than we do, and he also fulfils our liberal fantasy of membership by way of consent.[8]

In the figure of the supercitizen, Honig perceptively captures a salient feature of the immigrant in the public imagination. The figure of the immigrant as subject of adoration is, as she acutely observes, "an agent of national reenchantment that might rescue the regime from corruption and return it to first principles."[9]

Notice that her formulation exists in a close, even asymptotic, relation to that of the immigrant as a vehicle of time travel. Honig's focus on the more general "foreignness" of the immigrant as fueling the engine that will take us back to the founding invites questions about the engine(s) driving the "undecidability" of the foreigner she theorizes. What attributes, specifically, give newcomers such regenerative prowess? Honig largely focuses on hard work, traditional family values, and religiosity as driving forces behind the superpowers of supercitizen time-travel. I would add that these aspects of identity are also invoked in the process of racializing immigrants, particularly when immigrant identities are tethered to the capacity to return those they encounter to a past time. As patriarchy and heteronormative bias are endemic to many religious traditions, calls for "traditional religion" on the right often sound like a shorthand for chauvinism to left progressives.[10] If employing religion as a political time machine to take us back to the founding sounds familiar, it is likely because it has had so many priests and practitioners—even among those who were less than devout—notably Niccolò Machiavelli.

Recall that, far from being concerned with "getting right with God," Machiavelli's *Discourses on Livy* famously held those who found a religion in highest esteem above all others, even the founders of a republic.[11] Why? In short, there is little glory in founding a polity that fails the test of time, and religion nurtures habits of obedience, sacrifice, and shared struggle necessary to craft continuity through the ages.[12] Machiavelli extolled religion's role in fortifying the republic by preserving order (his oft-repeated *ordini*), something that was in perilously short supply in sixteenth-century Italy.[13] Emphasizing religion in the contexts of habits of obedience, organizational practices, and institutions, he invoked religion as that which held the promise of returning a corrupt republic to its founding. To Machiavelli, religion is politically useful in the literal sense of the Latin *religare*, meaning "to tie back" to the past.[14] Fast-forward, and who better to take the polity back to the past than those racially coded as simultaneously anachronistic *and* religious?

Another point of access to race is available by dilating on immigration as abetting the "liberal fantasy of membership by way of consent" that Honig insightfully adumbrates. The move prompts an inevitable return to what the liberal fantasy replaces: the forgetting of the originary violence that Behdad theorizes. From there, we find ourselves at the intersection where racial extermination and subordination meet white supremacy and segregated memory. Amid such racialized amnesia, the fantasy of membership by way of consent keeps company with the abiding illusion that free market labor has always been consensual. Even for those avowing slavery, the postemancipation issue appears as free labor, not *freed* labor, in Robbie Shilliam's potent phrase.[15] Further, we ought not overlook that not just *any* traditional religious values are believed to get Americans (particularly whites) back to the "right" place. Were that the case, there would be no need for a travel ban targeting Muslims and no need to examine the representation of the Muslim as the demonized other of modernity.[16] I now want to shift from figures ostensibly from other places (and times) and turn to Black women whose presence portends time travel, despite their enduring presence far predating the country's founding.

Once You Go Black: Octavia Butler's *Kindred*

Octavia E. Butler's *Kindred* chronicles the story of Dana Franklin, an African American writer who is mysteriously ripped from her life and transported to a plantation in antebellum Maryland to save her white ancestor, Rufus Weylin, whenever his life is endangered.[17] Initially set in the bicentennial year of 1976, Dana is a temporary worker whose labor is farmed out to various blue-collar jobs through an employment agency the regulars call the "slave market" (K, 52). She has just moved to a new house in California with her husband, Kevin, a white writer whose recent success as a novelist helped leverage their mutual escape from the precarious life of itinerant work. Just when things are starting to look up for Dana, and her personal and professional life seems to be moving forward,[18] she is pulled back in time and into a crisis in 1815.[19] She immediately sees a drowning child, Rufus, whom she promptly rescues and returns to his parents, only to be staring down the barrel of a gun. Dana quickly realizes that when Rufus's life is threatened, she is yanked back in time and can only return to 1976 when she fears for her own life. Life-threatening occurrences are not infrequent given that her ancestors include both slave owners and the enslaved, and she is regarded as the latter. When she is summoned she is transported with whatever and whomever she is touching at the time. Irrespective of the duration of time that passes when Dana is pulled back, she always returns to roughly the same time and place in the mid-1970s. In Dana's attempt to intuit and navigate the strange logic that seems to govern her time travels, it quickly becomes apparent that any failure on her part to save the life of her cruel ancestor Rufus would result in her not being born.[20]

The preceding sketch is a rough premise of the logic of time travel that obtains throughout the novel. Published in 1979, *Kindred* appears before Afrofuturism became an academic destination.[21] The novel is typically read as a profound meditation on segregated memory more than segregated time. Speaking to segregated memory, Butler certainly offers a rich rendering of the complex humanity of Dana's enslaved ancestors, the variegated social and emotional ecology they inhabited, as well as the hideous labyrinth of domination, empathy, love, violence, and resistance of the plantation's residents. History in the abstract this is not. On my reading, *Kindred*'s challenge operates along a related, but different and more original, trajectory. With Dana as protagonist, Butler dramatizes the perversity, illogic, and fantastically fictional attachments of white time operative in American history and politics—with a special sensitivity to its gendered components. In what follows, I suggest that Butler offers a set of poignant reflections on the complex and contradictory aspects of racial subjectivities as they relate to matters of historicity and the possibilities of escaping one's temporal conditions. Critics regard *Kindred* as the first attempt by an author to "use the fictional conventions of time travel to transport an African American to an antebellum plantation."[22] Still, readers fluent in the time-travel genre popularized by H.G. Wells remark that there is no time machine in *Kindred* and miss the book's political intervention. Politically, the work advances a critique of segregated time as it pertains to the Black female body as an instrument of time travel.[23]

As a work of science fiction, the book is a notable commentary on race and segregated time on a number of levels.[24] Antebellum slavery was a condition of multiply segregated time. Alienation from one's homeland and ancestral ties was foundational to chattel slavery. Henceforth one could be ripped apart, uprooted, or torn asunder at any moment. The possibility of being arbitrarily subjected to innumerable forms of withering labors and horrors, sold away from one's family into a slave coffle, or summarily executed was ever present. Such displacements in space—but also time—return readers to an untimely question: what is the time of slavery? While the novel resists a single answer to the question of slavery's time, *Kindred* poses the question to the whites who have refused its burden time and again. A closer look at Dana's relationship to the two most prominent white men in the novel, Kevin and Rufus, brings to light what I take to be among *Kindred*'s less-heralded contributions.

Dana's husband, Kevin, is an educated, working-class white man whom she regards as a kindred spirit. Progressive and well intentioned, his imperfections in matters of race and gender are telling. The couple fights momentously when Dana, a writer in her own right, refuses to perform the secretarial function of typing his manuscripts. As a white man on the edge of poverty, Kevin's marriage to Dana wagers a slippage into the liminal status and precarity of the white underclass. More pointedly, because he literally travels back in time by touching Dana, Butler stages the very threat of time travel that racist discourse portends: whites who associate with racial others, especially as sexual intimates, can be seduced back into a prior stage of development. By "going Black" with Dana, Kevin goes back—in time.

When Kevin goes back in time with Dana to the Antebellum South, she is grateful for his presence but also has reason to be concerned that the time will shape him for the worse. She is suitably alarmed when, despite his disgust with the racial order of the day, he expresses a longing to go west and "watch the building of the country" (K, 97). Dana is outraged that he fails to register the obvious implications, exclaiming: "West . . . That's where they're doing it to the Indians instead of the blacks!" (K, 97). By romanticizing the past in the fashion of white innocents watching Westerns, Kevin enacts the adventurist desire for voyeuristic racial exoticism that Fanon scorched. The nomenclature of Edana (Dana) Franklin evokes both the Edenic garden of primeval nature echoed by Fanon, and the founding father and scientist Ben Franklin. Neither Dana nor the reader can reasonably write off Kevin's white nostalgia to his poor education, given that he is a man of letters. The fantasy of being the spectating umpire of history comes all too easily to him by way of white time. That it falls to Dana to bring to light what Kevin already knows is Butler's way of dramatizing a problematic reliance on women of color as salvific vehicles of time travel—particularly, if not exclusively, among white men.

As a comeuppance, Butler makes Kevin serve time in the past for five years and bear witness firsthand to the brutality whitewashed by American history. He sees vicious maiming and takes part in the Underground Railroad. The experience grows him morally, but ages him excessively, making him virtually unrecognizable to his contemporaries upon his return to a time and place that no longer feels like home. Performatively, *Kindred* asks the reader to contemplate what history might look like if whites' claim to temporal sovereignty were abruptly revoked. Involuntary time travel is clearly anathema to any pretense of owning or controlling time. Kevin is situated strategically in a powerful contrapuntal relation to Rufus in the novel; it is no accident that he adopts habits and characteristics that lead Dana to occasionally confuse the two. Just as Dana is a vehicle of time travel to the past for Kevin, to Rufus Dana is the embodiment of Afrofuturism in the literal sense of being a Black woman from the future.

As if she were not magical enough by virtue of her apparition, she also brings with her healing powers from the future in the form of knowledge and medicine unavailable in the nineteenth century. Yet despite her fantastical appearing and disappearing, her luminous erudition, lifesaving skills, and polished comportment, Rufus and his father cannot jettison their predisposition to see Dana as a subordinate whose inscrutable powers ought to be at their service in perpetuity. Even though she sometimes vanishes before their eyes, they are never fully convinced she will harm them by her presence. They fear only her absence.[25] This is particularly true for Rufus, whose life she repeatedly saves from catastrophes entirely of his own making. Without Dana, Rufus's time is up. Nevertheless, Dana's needs are only important to him as tools of manipulation. Ultimately, no generosity Dana expends can stop Rufus from violating her relatives and attempting to take possession of Dana herself. In the end, Rufus remains a man of his time and has to be taken out of time when Dana kills him in self-defense.

To further deepen the novel's reflections on racialized epistemologies, it is remarkable that Dana is a writer from the future who teaches Rufus how to read, yet her dignity and moral agency remains largely illegible to him. It is simply not in his interest to avow what his senses and experiences repeatedly prove demonstrably true. When it comes to matters of race, seeing is not always believing. Or, more precisely, even empirically conditioned perceptions do not necessarily overcome entrenched practices of racialized apprehension. Enlightenment rationality and even nonfiction history are no panacea in these pages. Dana mourns that, despite all her book learning, "Nothing in my education or knowledge of the future had helped me to escape" the Weylin plantation (K, 177). As Fanon put it, "Philosophy has never saved anyone" (BSWM, 29).

At the level of ontology, Butler lays bare how African presence is dehumanized by white evaluations of Black people as both less *and* more than human. A logic of anachronistic dehumanization prevails irrespective of whether racial others are behind the times as chattel or ahead of the times as "Magic Negroes."[26] As was typical of the biological racism of the day, Rufus regards the African Americans on his farm as less evolved and subhuman—this despite the fact that Dana teaches and shows him otherwise from a young age through her superhuman abilities. Her appearances give him pause, and even the occasional bout of generosity, but he never ceases to regard Dana's blackness, and that of her relatives, as making all available to his whims. Rufus largely regards the presence of Dana's enslaved eighteenth-century ancestors as instruments to help him exercise control over space, while Dana's twentieth-century presence largely serves as an instrument that promises to help him control time. By helping Rufus learn to read and get ahead of his peers, Dana affords him a chance to escape falling back into the sociohistorical dustbin of "white trash."[27] More poignantly, Dana becomes instrumental in preserving Rufus's lifetime and extending it in another way. His survival means he can father children with the enslaved.

Dana saves him just as he is outwitted and outmaneuvered by Isaac and about to lose a real-life "fight to the death" between master and slave.[28] Rufus is in love with Isaac's wife, Alice. He learns that while it is no shame to rape a Black woman, it is shameful to love one. He can no more make Alice love him than Dana can rewrite history so her very existence no longer hinges on Hagar, a progeny of rape. In the vernacular of James Baldwin, Rufus fails to avow that the relationship between Blacks and whites in America is a "blood relationship."[29] In the character of Rufus, Butler brilliantly gives her readers an image of a white man whose desires exceed his pretentions of sovereignty and self-control. He is torn apart by what, at some level, he knows but refuses to acknowledge: that his relationship to his Black counterparts is one of irreducible consanguinity. This brings us to a central question: where does Butler come down on the question of human agency in segregated time?

After Hagar is born and Dana kills Rufus, she returns home—but she doesn't return all the way. As she fends off Rufus's attempted rape, he grabs her arm, and she stabs him to death with her free hand. At that moment, she is transported home, but the arm he was gripping is lodged in the wall of her California house, contiguous with the plaster. In a self-liberating act of resistance, Dana has ensured the start of her family lineage, the freedom of at least some of her enslaved ancestors, and rid them of Rufus and his menace. Why then does she lose her arm? In Butler's own account, she offers, "I couldn't really let her come all the way back. I couldn't let her return to what she was, I couldn't let her come back whole and that, I think, really symbolizes her not coming back whole. Antebellum slavery didn't leave people quite whole."[30] Fair enough. But why her arm?

The answer, I think, lies in how the nightmarish horror of the novel's merciless logic reflects a continuity between antebellum and postslavery Black life. Dana's endurance of slavery's atrocities and her suffering is, unbelievably, an insufficient price to pay because the enduring injustice of white supremacy across time continually extracts an imagined, (fictive) debt from those stigmatized by slavery—but does so in "real time." Dana's heroism costs her an arm, if not (yet) a leg, because racial indebtedness is part of the lasting cost, or the not-quite-whole-ness, that Butler references as the afterlife of antebellum slavery. By portraying Dana's escape from slavery as costing her an arm and (not yet) a leg, Butler not only resists triumphal resolution but leaves the reader to ponder the fundamental injustices of slavery's many afterlives. The transition from institutional slavery to stigmatization by various ascriptions of racial indebtedness is imbricated in what Hortense Spillers terms a "hieroglyphics of the flesh whose severe disjunctures come to be hidden to the cultural seeing by skin color."[31] Importantly, Dana's missing arm also bespeaks the connection between temporal theft and her status as a writer and the story's narrator.

Dana is first called back to the nineteenth century as she is celebrating her twenty-sixth birthday, and her final return to the present happens on July 4, 1976, the year the United States is celebrating its bicentennial. By situating the time frame of the novel between personal and political commemorations, Butler provides an opening for the reader to contemplate the relation between identity and community transhistorically. It is no accident that *Kindred* begins at the end of the story, so it seems fitting that the reader should reflect back upon the narrative's starting point at the conclusion. That is, with Dana telling the police that what happened to her arm was "an accident" in order to convince them that Kevin did not belong in jail. "Who hurt you?" the police ask (K, 9), as if they were treating her missing arm like a scratch. "My fault, not Kevin's," she lies. But the question lingers as if it were put to American history and the nation itself by a hapless authority interrogating the grossly disfigured present tense as its subject—a white authority that is immature (Baldwin would say innocent) who can only speak in the idiom and tone that one addresses to a child with a scraped knee. As Lawrie Balfour writes, "Despite the fact that her injuries are fantastic, not easily explainable, Dana's words are intelligible to her would-be protectors only as long as she corroborates their interpretation, only as long as she fits the role of battered wife."[32]

The impossibly absurd conditions of radically nonlinear time, multiple temporalities, and racial time-travel admit no analytic explanation or causal inference. If there is any redemption in the novel, it comes not from triumphal resolution or dialectical synthesis but the imperfect authority of authorship of the text itself. The reader knows Dana is an outstanding writer because *Kindred* is written in *her* voice, the first-person singular. We learn that the novel emerges from Dana's pain and stands as her acknowledgment of ancestral debt, and presumably a gift to her descendants. We flash back again to Dana and Kevin as temporary workers at a place the regulars refer to as the slave market. Time travel takes something from Dana, but so does the modern wage slavery of contingent labor where her employers and white coworkers get to step back into history, effectively abridging past and present by treating her as a site of extraction. She is a passageway back to an earlier time available to be restaged in the present racial order.

Across the time of chattel and wage slavery, Dana's imperfect escape passage is a fugitive narrative that intersects with Butler's own biography and her belated recognition as a writer. Even though Butler wrote her first story at age twelve, she notes that she had every custodial and temp job that she gave Dana in *Kindred*. Just as Butler connects her own story with that of her protagonist, one can register the time stolen from both authors as represented symbolically by Dana's severed arm that leaves her to write the story after being maimed. Playing on a commonplace, Dana is forced to write with "one hand tied behind her back," with her missing arm tied back to an unbelievable past that continually extracts a voracious toll on her present and future. Her arm is gone, but the persistence of phantom pain are evocative of slavery's erasures and injuries across nonlinear time. Given Butler's impressive oeuvre, one can only imagine what was lost in the time she spent toiling doing menial jobs as a starving artist.

Debts to Octavia Butler's work are increasingly political, with organizers crediting Butler's speculative fiction as fueling their political imaginations of different futures.[33] Hers is also a creative intervention in how to inhabit the present moment other-wise. "Science fiction has long treated people who might or might not exist—extraterrestrials. Unfortunately, however, many of the same science-fiction writers who started us thinking about the possibility of extraterrestrial life did nothing to make us think about the here-at-home human variation."[34] That she wrote so much, using time she was certainly not given and that she did not "have," makes her accomplishments all the more laudable, even as her work—and indeed her life—challenge notions that time is able to be mastered and there is such a thing as temporal sovereignty. In a broader sense, Butler's (un)timely contributions point toward more generative conceptions of time travel. Her work spurs chronopolitical imaginings and creative practices that exceed the strictures, attachments, and linear vectors of heteropatriarchal, white timescapes.

5
End Times
The Segregated Apocalypse Now

Across deep ideological differences dividing contemporary segregated times, there seems to be agreement that the present tense is apocalyptic. Conservative evangelical Christians anticipate the coming end times as a Judgment Day when they, the chosen ones, will suddenly be sucked into heaven through the rapture.[1] Left environmentalists hold that unabated climate change will continue the planet's great acceleration toward a future that will resemble an infernal hellscape.[2] Security scholars and realists positioning themselves in the political center warn of nuclear fallout that could come fast or slow: whether by the mutually assured destruction of atomic warfare, or through radioactive seepage slowly penetrating our genetic material. Meanwhile, white religious nationalists support politicians who mendaciously claim that climate change is a Chinese hoax. Despite their political disagreements, all seemingly share an apocalyptic sense that the future is certain and the end is always near.

Etymologically, apocalypse means "revelation, of truth, *un-veiling*."[3] What might end times reveal about the politics of race and segregated time? Recall that white temporalities are affectively imbued with a sense of expectation and entitlement, the freedom to experience the present as opening onto a future horizon with a disposition that, in time, *all this can be yours*. Euro-colonials imposed an artificial end time by restarting the clock, making everything that comes next "discovered" and available for the taking.[4] American apocalypse might be understood as the dark underbelly of the shining mythology of the nation as a lit beacon, a geographical destination where the past tense is erased and new beginnings are everywhere—if not for everyone. In his 1992 book *The American Religion*, literary critic Harold Bloom called the United States "the most apocalyptic of nations."[5] In truth, an attachment to apocalyptic end times long predates the nation's beginnings and betrays a transcontinental, even ancient, pedigree. Christopher Columbus's *Book of Prophecies* affirms St. Augustine's notion of the world's clock end time, which informed his own calculations that the end times would come 150 years later.[6] Columbus understood the urgency of his quest as simultaneously political and cosmological—in the service of the end of Muslim domination, and in preparation for the coming of the Antichrist foretold in the book of Revelation—which is to say, the end of the world.[7] He also understood his mission in racial terms, as one predestined to "fulfil a number of prophecies" abetting "the salvation of the entire human race," a locution that recalls the limited scope of those included in the category of the human in those times.[8] Synchronizing racial and imperial agendas in the Americas would prepare Christian conquerors and their settler offspring for the apocalypse. Columbus's anemic humanism reflected the race-making projects underway in his era, and retained aspects of the long-standing ideology that placed Christians above heathen nonbelievers. During the so-called Age of Discovery, Euro-Christian categories of differentiation would be complicated by productions of "secular forms of human otherness," namely the race-ing of Indigenous peoples as irrational, savage, and marked for death.[9] Columbus's aspirations to unfetter himself from his pedigree in feudal Europe, which separated him as low-born from the blue-blooded nobility.[10] Wanting to slip the noose of his own social death in the European caste system, he created prolific temporal outcasts through imperial death-dealing. All of which is to say that the simultaneous coproduction of race, whiteness, and apocalypse has a long history of contributing to segregated time.

The preceding chapter addressed racialized political economies of segregated time where nonwhites were stigmatized as indebted and consigned to live on borrowed time. Extending the idiom of whiteness as property, this chapter explores the growing apprehension that the credit value of whiteness is under siege. Like any attachment to property, possessive investments in whiteness are frequently haunted by fears of repossession and credit devaluation that could render one's equity and standing obsolete. Hence I take up the fluid interlocution of race-making and waste-making that renders the threat of white disposability (the pejorative white trash) a politically meaningful form of time.

At the same time, insofar as white supremacy *produces* apocalypse, whiteness is inherently apocalyptic. If one takes apocalypse to also connote an end of a particular prevailing order of time, rather than just the end of some cosmic, theistic, or universal time, one might be prompted to ask: for whom, *exactly*, is apocalypse new?[11] In the reverberations of that question, the topic of race is unavoidable.[12]

The enslavement and diaspora of people indigenous to the African continent was effectively an apocalyptic project aimed at effectuating the end of many worlds by way of European conquest and plunder. The last great Crow chief, Plenty Coups, recounted the apocalypse of Indian removal in the Americas by saying, "After this nothing happened."[13] Given the intimacy between whiteness and apocalypse, perhaps it is little wonder that those who regard the potential end of white supremacy as world-ending overlap dangerously with those who fail to acknowledge or prioritize planetary existential threats like climate change.

The apocalypse, theologian Catherine Keller writes, "does not unfold *in* time—and certainly not outside of time—but rather constitutes a specific form *of* time."[14] We shall see that on the clock of white time, the ominous fear that white supremacy *might be coming to an end* can even take the form of a temporal race war. Murderous white terrorists motivated by a rancid rage over the fictional dystopia of "white genocide" and "replacement theory" are among the most visible defenders of temporal sovereignty.[15] Their violent extremism is indeed on the rise, with media spectacles weaponized to terrify and discipline. On another scale, even microabrasions against the white prerogative to control what happens next—and to enjoy a privileged meantime furnished with future expectation—are perceived as flagrant incursions on white temporal sovereignty. People of color who refuse to synch-up with the expected, preordained rhythms of servility risk provoking a metaphysical unraveling for whites, a shattering of the sense of stable reality that many whites might perceive as a violent affront. No matter how mundane the supposed offense, it can be apprehended by whites as a sign that the end of one world might give birth to another. As Frantz Fanon writes, a Black man who "says to you: 'I am in no sense your boy Monsieur'" radically ruptures the racial-temporal order, and there is "something new under the sun." In that new light, "The whole structure crumbles" (BSWM, 33).

The expectations of white time are embedded in that structure, and whites will "stand their ground" and kill Black children to stop it from crumbling. This knowledge compels James Baldwin to tell his young nephew that he was placed in a ghetto, where he was intended to perish.[16] The fact that the young man can spell his name and leave the squalor of his birthplace puts him at risk of being out of place, and therefore in danger of being cast out of time. He writes:

Try to imagine how you would feel if you woke up one morning to find the sun shining and all the stars aflame. You would be frightened because it is out of the order of nature. Any upheaval in the universe is terrifying because it so profoundly attacks one's sense of one's own reality. Well, the black man has functioned in the white man's world as a fixed star, as an immovable pillar: and as he moves out of his place, heaven and earth are shaken to their foundations.[17]

Why? Because "those [white] innocents who believed your imprisonment made them safe have lost their grasp on reality."[18] A sense of reality implies a sense of space as well as time, and Baldwin's point is that Black subordination is so central to prevailing white metaphysics that Black movement "*out of place*" *at any time* might be experienced as apocalyptic in white times. Radically ordinary actions can be shattering. *Where* one sits or looks, *when* one kneels and stands, and how fast or slow one walks can have world-ending consequences for people of color. This is in no small part because of their perceived threats to the fragile artifice of white cosmology that happen by simply being *present at the wrong—white—time*.[19]

This chapter begins with an account of white disposability (white trash) as segregated from political and theoretical memory of colonial America and Lockean liberalism, respectively. On the page and in political life, marginal whites were viewed as wasting time—and available to be wasted by those possessing the power and prerogative to define what time it is. This opens onto important tension between race as fixed and derived from space/land and constitution, as opposed to race as fluid and subject to variation by way of experience over time. I revisit Fredrick Jackson Turner's attempts to resolve this political/theoretical impasse by embracing a race-making project in his apocalyptic frontier thesis. By subjugating so-called primitive peoples and lands, settlers go backward in order to refashion themselves and move forward in segregated time as a new, distinctively white-American race. Still alive in contemporary imperial race-making projects today, we shall see that these biopolitical logics maintain that the vitality of whiteness necessitates the death of racial others.

I make those connections in part through a critical engagement with physician Jonathan M. Metzl's book *Dying of Whiteness*,[20] which illustrates how the impulse to preserve white supremacy can outpace the priorities of individual self-preservation assumed by Anglo-liberalism. To speak to the question of why individual whites would literally perish for whiteness in this day and age, I sketch an apocalyptic strain in white nationalist politics leading up to the present era. On the left and the right, the production of white backwardness—evocative of that which is projected onto people of color by white supremacists—perpetuates racial resentments and the segregated apocalypse now.

White Disposability in Segregated Memory

Prior to Winthrop's "City on the Hill" and Crevecoeur's *Letters from an American Farmer*, Old Europe regarded the New World of the Americas as a repository for deviants, ill-bred commoners, and the dregs of society. The colonies came to be so widely regarded as dumping grounds for criminals and lowlifes that Benjamin Franklin proposed returning the favor by sending back an equal number of rattlesnakes.[21] Eventually, the border with Mexico would be conceived as a spillover zone for North American waste, human and otherwise. But to Europeans the early Americas were wastelands, first in the sense of a trash repository, and then as a land of vast wealth being squandered. The territory was supposedly inhabited by idle Native peoples lazily wasting time by failing to cultivate the land and plunder its resources. Additional disposable people would be needed to extract its riches and become human sites of extraction. As I shall suggest in our brief encounter with historical discourses of white disposability below, these race-making logics frequently appear nonlinear, asynchronic, recursive, and even patently contradictory instabilities and ambiguities befitting the paranoid apprehensiveness of white temporalities. Since the overlap between disposability and whiteness could hardly be clearer than in the epithet "white trash," the historian Nancy Isenberg's eponymous study is an obvious starting point.[22]

Training her sights on how the New World inhabitants were "waste people" in the form of the "idle poor," criminals, orphans, and myriad deviants and outcasts, Isenberg takes as her ostensible focus *class* amnesia. Yet *White Trash* also acknowledges seemingly disparate sites of racial formation frequently segregated from memory, like the widespread belief that backward people came from substandard land, and that the poor of colonial America were a particular "breed" of person.[23] In vulgar vernacular, the book traces how yesterday's "waste people" (pejoratively called "clay-eaters," "lubbers," and "hillbillies") were the prototypes of today's trailer trash, troglodytes, and Trumptards. For an illuminating political and theoretical point of contact,

Isenberg turns to Locke as not just a problematic liberal, but an architect of colonial statecraft. Best known for the liberalism of his *Second Treatise* (1689), Locke also had a hand in authoring the deeply illiberal Fundamental Constitutions of Carolina (1669), which earned him the title of "Landgrave" and forty-eight thousand acres of Carolina land. The document granted "Freemen in Carolina" "ABSOLUTE POWER AND AUTHORITY over his Negro slaves of what opinion or Religion soever."[24] Locke's political and philosophical chauvinisms with respect to women and non-Europeans are increasingly well documented, to the point that they might serve as warnings about the potential (in)compatibility of liberal equality relative to human difference.[25] Yet he also spoke to inequalities among Europeans, to the point that his constitution amounted to a fundamental "declaration of war against poor settlers" that jealously guarded against "erecting a numerous democracy," ultimately fashioning North Carolina into the *"first white trash colony."*[26]

In Locke's formulation of what he termed "Leet-men," his constitution sanctioned a rigid hierarchy that protected the power of hereditary nobility, designating a peasant class above slaves but beneath nobles. Clearly influenced by feudalism, he imagined a servant caste who would be tied to the land and its lord, and for whom pedigree would determine destiny, as entire families of Leet-men could be inherited as part of an estate. In his *Second Treatise* Locke maintained that God had given the earth to the "rational" *and* "industrious." Such figures are not to be confused with the American Indians he denigrates for their failure to cultivate the land and maximize its productive capacity. As James Tully points out, Locke consolidates his theories of conquest and appropriation by arguing that any land that goes to waste can be rightfully seized by conquerors who can put it to its proper use.[27] Nor should industrious settlers be confused with the lazy poor who also waste time.

Locke's deep disdain for the impoverished is also moral. In addition to wasting their lives, poor people are shiftless and ethically degenerate. To the extent that he refers to the poor in terms of animal husbandry, accusing them of "loose ways of breeding," Locke's formulation is also racial insofar as he positions them beneath the human race.[28] In a revealing irony, it was the supposedly indolent Leet-men's labor that made them useful to him in the first place. Their productive capacity prompted Locke to carve out a liminal zone for those undeserving of the full liberal property rights typically ascribed to white European men. Not quite reducible to slaves, but servants nonetheless, they occupied a racial and temporal status that was ambiguous at best—hence their invocation in the context of the pejorative "white trash." The early colonial political analogues to Locke's Leet-men were indentured white servants, including European children who were sold, kidnapped (or "spirited") away to the New World to endure an often indefinite period of servitude.[29]

Historically, the possibility of perpetual white slavery officially ended in the colonies when skin color was codified as a racial marker separating the enslaved from free persons. Nevertheless, early colonial ideas of human procreation, figured in terms of animal husbandry and notions of the poor as backward, would have staying power. As historian Nell Irwin Painter contends, beliefs that the poor are ill-bred (or inbred) existed concurrently with the notion that inferior, undesirable land produced inferior, ungovernable people.[30] These racial mythologies had palpable implications for modernity, with precursors in ancient notions of autochthony that held that superior people grew out of superior land.[31] The coincidence of disposable whites and wasteland would recur repeatedly long after Locke's time, with various epithets associating rural populations with inbreeding and dysgenic qualities—such as those called "clay-eaters" for their yellowish skin.[32] Across the Americas, newcomers to the land experienced ghastly sicknesses that led them to think that a period of "seasoning" was required to fortify the settlers who would survive. Depending on where they were from, and where they were headed, a variety of guides for acclimation circulated among settlers. The guides' range of advice was expansive, reflecting how would-be Americans distinguished each other based on notions that people's constitution was derived from their respective geographical origin. Environmental and medical historian Conevery Bolton Valenčius quotes an 1843 medical text declaring, "Each man is primarily endued with a particular constitution, distinct from temperament. . . . The constitution may be modified by regimen, but not destroyed. In a word, the constitution is the foundation of the individual being."[33]

The question of whether whiteness was fixed or fungible across time and place was not soon resolved.[34] The breeding rationale of animal pedigree whereby that those of superior descent produced exemplary stock was deeply entrenched. It was so engrained that, in 1909 W.E.B. Du Bois declared the supposedly novel innovations of biological racism of the nineteenth century to be altogether unsurprising and unoriginal.[35] Given the prevailing racial order and its abiding fictions, Du Bois thought it followed logically that the spread of eugenics in the twentieth century would metastasize from evolutionary theory. After all, Darwin himself was a proponent of eugenics, an outrage that prompted Du Bois to publicly mock the bitter irony that *Origin of the Species* was released the same year John Brown was executed.[36] Since then, the "survival of the fittest" mantra has been naturalized and implicated in the extractivist logics of racial capitalism. Indigenous studies scholar Dion Million (Tanana Athabascan) maintains that contesting enduring Darwinism should be a central focus of contemporary environmental and racial justice movements. According to Million, "The notion of 'survival of the fittest' never existed except in Darwin's mistaken humancentric Eurocentric nineteenth-century theory of life's relations as a mirror of nineteenth-century capitalism—a mistake that could only be rendered by a capitalist mind."[37]

I am agnostic about whether *only* a capitalist mind could have made such a mistake. But in the midst of an economic system that institutionalizes disposability, the language where the fittest survive provides a convenient moral absolution in the face of all those lives laid to waste in the service of historical progress. A great deal of the utility of racial Darwinism stems from how it *does* provide a pathway toward resolving the tension between notions of human constitutions as relatively fixed, and beliefs that action and experience play a racially transformative role over time. The friction between racial stasis and flux resurfaces in white anxieties as a problem in the racial ordering of time. Fredrick Jackson Turner's frontier thesis incorporates racial and environmental encounters to make that tension generative. By granting that race is fluid, Turner tells a story of white racial progress and transformation. And by brutally turning Indigenous peoples into vehicles of white time-travel so as to be dispossessed, he fashions segregated white time as a productively apocalyptic form of biopower.

Apocalyptic Race-Making

For European immigrants, the gnawing possibility that race might be fluid intensified with their lived experiences of race-mixing and seeing their bodies changing with the climate, nutrition, and interactions with the land. An affective contagion of racial anxiety spread among whites who were particularly sensitive to bodily changes augured by the environment. "Such alteration especially threatened the 'people' and 'race' to which white newcomers understood themselves to belong."[38] By the end of the nineteenth century Frederick Jackson Turner had formulated his infamous frontier thesis contemplating the perceived racial changes wrought by Native lands and peoples. Widely credited with advancing the formative land-centered interpretation of the frontier as key to American distinctiveness, Turner made race-making key to his analysis. For him, it was settlers' dual interaction with the environment and its Native inhabitants that facilitated a physical and cultural transition that set the American race apart from its fusty European counterparts.

This transition was not just "seasoning" against climate and disease, or an adjustment to their white skin turning brown and copper in the sun. It ran far deeper, since the colonizer

> must accept the conditions which it furnishes or perish. . . . Before long he has gone to planting Indian corn and plowing with a sharp stick; he shouts the war cry and takes the scalp in orthodox Indian fashion . . . . Thus American development has exhibited not merely advance along a single line, but a return to primitive conditions on a continually advancing frontier line, and a new development for that area.[39]

In Turner's account, one finds the discourse of primitivism preserves the conflation of nature and Indian, not as inert or stagnating—or even unidirectionally regressive—but as a source of natality and generativity.

> American social development has been continually beginning over again on the frontier. This perennial rebirth, this fluidity of American life, this expansion westward with its new opportunities, its continuous touch with the simplicity of primitive society, furnish the forces dominating American character.[40]

Beneath the stench of racial Darwinism, notice how the encounter with Indigenous peoples and their land takes the settler back in time in order to go forward, recursively making the so-called primitives into vehicles of white time-travel. Progress is charted in terms of the westerly appropriation of Native lands, with Indigenous extermination made into fuel for cultivating American temporal advancement coded as white. In Indigenous bodies and territory, white settlers "discovered" a biopolitical mode of time travel among the extractable wealth available for the taking. Through their inescapable death, the so-called Indian naturals are portrayed as predisposed to be natural resources available to fertilize the cultivation of white settler race-making life. This profane form of biopolitical racial cultivation relied on a struggle between a white race capable of motion in time and Indigenous peoples ultimately produced—or "fixed" as Fanon would say—as inert material in space.

Haunting Turner's remarkable words is the spectral presence of First Nations whose scalps and land are reduced to fuel for the forces shaping the American character.[41] And what political end does this race-making-as-waste-making ultimately serve? Without a hint of irony, Turner tellingly marks the culmination of the frontier history in nothing less than the triumph of democracy itself. His racial amnesia has a history and continuity of its own that we do well to acknowledge, and that liberals prefer to forget: a narrative of (re)generation through violence and purification through bloodshed.[42] Relatedly, when Turner asserts that the American "land that has no history reveals luminously the course of universal history," he echoes the temporal cleansing of Hegel's colonial European historicism, as well as the strategy of colonial dispossession exercised through the prerogative to set the clock back to zero.[43] That conceptual violence is, of course, part of a well-worn colonial strategy of mapping wilderness onto land already inhabited and cultivated.[44] Such learned blindness via erasure corresponds to European philosophers who made a vacant wilderness of African and Native American histories though a timescape that also charted racialized human progress as moving from east to west. Turner's developmental account moves in a diachronic stagger, with the genocidal-biopolitical race-making struggle as the intermediate stage between *tempus nullius* (empty time) and *tempus plentitudinus* (time of abundance)—or as St. Paul would say, the "fullness of time."

In Turner's political philosophy European conquest brings a timeless land with no history into Time and History—but with key variations. His white time loops backward to go forward via a vortex hurling from east to west in a circular progression, expanding and spiraling outward while sucking up Indigenous peoples and Native spaces. Euro-invaders transform themselves into a new, distinctly American race by unabashedly (and necessarily) disposing of and dispossessing anachronistic Indians whose deaths propel the constant renewal of white temporal progress and vitality. With clear Hegelian overtones of a fight to the death, the necessity of *racial struggle* also inflects his philosophy of history with biopolitical content. The progress of the American race happens by way of a biopolitical logic whereby the more the Indian "they" dies, the more the proto-white American "we" lives.

I have dwelled on Turner's apocalyptic frontier thesis in part because its ghosts inhabit the present. A chronosophy propelled by the dialectic of race-making-as-waste-making resonates in enduring presumptions of racial capitalism. The frontiers of American empire have shifted since the time of Turner's writing, but the relevance of race as a neocolonial political force remains trenchant and sustained. In the twentieth-century school of "race realism," figures like George Kennan regarded the "bilious yellow and brown people" sitting on top of oil wealth as a "tax on American productive capacity."[45] By describing Indigenous nonwhites as asynchronous wastrels—sickly/jaundiced-yellow ("bilious") idlers, squandering time, space, and money—Kennan registers the haunting presence of manifold discourses in a single turn of phrase. Natives are sickly wastrels too lazy and unintelligent to exploit untapped fossil fuels, threatening civilizational progress and proving their own presumptive worthlessness by obstructing American (read: human) productivity—virtually justifying their own extermination. Fast-forward to 2001, and US president George W. Bush declared that Saddam Hussein had "something to hide from the civilized world." Vowing to waste no time invading oil-rich Iraq, Bush boasted, "We're steady, clear-eyed and patient, but pretty soon we'll have to start displaying scalps."[46]

Bush's thirst for a spectacular display of scalps and Kennan's vile racial imperialism suggest that features of Turner's ghostly political philosophy of racial history have been sublimated into a form of common sense pulsing through white temporality. Its aspects include the conflation of development with the proliferation of human disposability across time and space; the use of spectacle for disciplinary purposes serving race-making projects; the division of the civilized and barbaric into divergent time zones; temporal progress represented as seizing the lives and lands of racial others; the inauguration of new (white) times as parasitic on stealing time from (asynchronous) people of color; to name but a few. As temporal impulses, these discourses imbue what Keller calls an "apocalyptic unconscious" imbricated in contemporary politics and "living just below the surface of our self-image."[47]

This varient of white self-image betrays a dynamic whereby the forward progress of one party hinges upon the conquest, death, or temporal arrest of Others. The expectations of segregated time are such that white plentitude remains reliant on producing apocalyptic temporalities. As we shall see, the dynamics of race-making-as-waste-making can also result in the creeping sense among liminal whites that they might be next. Capitalism depends upon inequality, expendable people, and the theft of time. But it does not *necessarily* require the expropriated to be nonwhite. With that in mind, the temporal politics of proliferating white disposability is the subject to which we now turn.

The End of Whiteness and Whiteness as Death

Scholars estimate that the mortality rate among the white working class has risen a full 22 percent since 1999.[48] Studies suggest that a longing for the *expectations* of white time from a bygone era are key motivators in the politics of the white working class.[49] Still, the invocation of class raises thorny issues of how race and class articulate, and how and when they part company. To be clear, I do not take the view that class and race are mutually exclusive. Nor are possessive investments in white time explicable by economic status alone.[50] By shifting the temporal horizon to expectations, we are better positioned to acknowledge the presence of partisans of white nationalism who are *not* on the lower echelons of the economic food chain. On its own, widening wealth inequality and its concurrent impact on morbidity would seem to provide ample cause for dread. Yet a measurable sense of economic obsolescence, and the diminished political power that comes with it, are not the sole drivers of white radicalism or white resentment.[51] Whites disproportionately blame their perceived loss in political capacity and social centrality on immigrant and minority groups, leading to a potent sense of social depravation and marginalization.[52] All the more reason to consider white precarity in relation to ongoing racial states of exception and the proliferation of human disposability.

It is a macabre irony that the much-feared demographic changes trumpeted as threatening an apocalyptic end of whiteness compel individual whites to voluntarily hasten the end of their own lifetimes. In his book *Dying of Whiteness*, physician Jonathan Metzl connects whiteness's "promise of greatness" to a "biology of demise" through policies that, in effect, ask people to die on behalf of their whiteness (DW, 81). The study provides an intriguing evidentiary account of the deadly effects of white identity politics on the very communities that political entrepreneurs promise to empower through racial bigotry.

Unlike amnesiac media narratives that fail to contextualize white nationalism, Metzl surveys the historical precursors leading up to the present-day intensification of white death. Recalling that health insurance in the South was traditionally tethered to insuring enslaved Blacks as white property, he connects past and present opposition to government-sponsored expansion of health insurance under the Affordable Care Act, aka Obamacare (DW, 123). Long-standing racialized fears of government intervention have been mobilized to scare low- and middle-income whites. Remarkably, the opposition to free or lower-cost healthcare persists despite the reality that broader coverage would save a vast number of white lives. White aversion holds strong even where the program would have, say, merely provided government oversight of commercially made pharmaceuticals and private companies. In a deadly example of racial bribery, some whites choose against their biological self-interest out of fears that undeserving people of color might also benefit from receiving the very services that they themselves lack.[53]

Which brings us to Trevor, an uninsured, forty-one-year-old dying slowly of severe liver damage. He is in considerable pain, his skin is jaundiced yellow, and he needs a walker to get around. As a resident of Tennessee—a state that had refused the Medicaid expansion under Obamacare—Trevor is living out a veritable death sentence. But he does not bemoan the fact that had he lived a "simple thirty-nine-minute drive away in neighboring Kentucky, he might have topped the list for expensive medications called polymerse inhibitors, a lifesaving liver transplant, or other forms of treatment or support" (DW, 3). To the contrary, Trevor insists he would rather die than enroll in the program and support Obamacare. "We don't need any more government in our lives. And in any case, no way I want my tax dollars paying for Mexicans or welfare queens" (DW, 3).

Lots to unpack here. In turning to *Dying of Whiteness*, I want to amplify its biopolitical rendering of apocalyptic whiteness, which might sound counterintuitive. If biopolitical logic operates on the premise that "the more they die, the more we live," then how can this condition obtain amid all the white death like Trevor's chronicled in Metzl's study? The answer lies in the "we" and how it is figured racially. First, the unit of analysis is not the individual "I" of rights-based liberalism seeking self-preservation, but a collective mass. It follows that it can be the case that any one individual life might be worth losing, and indeed be lost, for the benefit of preserving the collective over time. Trevor certainly seems to think so. Moreover, this is the biopolitical point I take Metzl to underscore when he summarizes his argument as demonstrating that whiteness is something "worth living and dying for, and how . . . Americans bet their lives on particular sets of meanings associated with whiteness, even in the face of clear threats to mortality and common sense" (DW, 270). This stance is entirely consonant with a biopolitical ethos that says,

> The more inferior species die out, the more abnormal relationships are eliminated, the fewer degenerates there will be in the species as a whole, and the more I—*as a species rather than individual*—can live, the stronger I will be, the more vigorous I will be. I will be able to proliferate. (SMBD, 255; my emphasis)

Trevor's morbid calculus using "I as species" rather than "I as individual" reverberates loudly, a point to which I return. In addition to noting the meager time it would take to go to an insured state—and thus a state of being insured—Metzl accents the temporal dimension of biopolitics in *how* he dramatizes the mortal stakes of his argument. The consequence of Tennessee's refusal to expand Medicaid is that it cost "*every single* white resident of the state *14.1 days of life*" (DW, 13). Given that dropping out of high school supposedly reduces one's life expectancy by nine years, he correlates cuts to public education in Kansas with "*6,195.51 lost white life years*" (DW, 13). The fact that he is moved to make his case in these quantified racial/temporal terms underscores the depth and resonance of biopolitical rationalities. He figures the temporal horizon both quantitatively and racially, with lifetimes measured in terms of money, productivity, and longevity. Recall that biopolitics is a condition of racially segregated lifetimes, but also a mode of governmentality that seeks to manage populations quantitatively through the use of data and statistics so that "regulatory mechanisms must be established to establish an equilibrium, maintain an average, establish a sort of homeostasis, and compensate for variations within this general population and its aleatory field" (SMBD, 246). Although Metzl does not reference Foucault, the fact that he makes his argument in the idiom of biopower to maximize its impact testifies to the potency of biopolitical reasoning.

Unwittingly echoing Foucault's account of endemic threats to the population as sapping energy and shortening the workweek, *Dying of Whiteness* registers the cost of Missouri's lax gun laws between 2008 and 2015 in terms of $273 million in lost work, and the loss "of *over 10,506 years* of productive white male life" (DW, 12). A blunt reading of the takeaway lesson for people like Trevor might be the following:

The racial bribe of white supremacy promised to stabilize and extend your lifetime by making racial others contingent and disposable. In reality, the instability you are now experiencing is because you are being disposed of by the very system you spent your time defending—and for which you will ultimately pay with your expended life.

One might just as well say that the promises of white supremacy have failed to implement "security mechanisms [that] have to be installed around the random element[s] inherent in a population of living beings so as to optimize a state of life" (SMBD, 246). Or, more precisely, to the extent that security mechanisms *have* been implemented, evidence betrays forces safeguarding a population that excludes *certain* subgroups of would-be whites from those considered living beings. For liminal whites, morbidity is a "death tax" on the psychological wages of whiteness in the most literal sense of the phrase.

Dying of Whiteness dramatizes how the apocalyptic sense of contemporary white temporality is apprehended as the *end of whiteness*. I mean the *end of whiteness* in the plural sense. "End" references a purpose, telos, or a directional vector across time and space—as in what whiteness is for and against. Ends can also refer to inevitability or finality, such as when Fanon mocks liberal humanist notions of whiteness as destiny as tantamount to whiteness as death.[54] In Trevor's case, whiteness as death takes on multiple valences. The potential death of white supremacy is more politically meaningful than the end of any individual white life. Were he looking through a prism of liberal individualism that prioritizes self-preservation, Trevor would presumably be willing to travel the thirty-nine minutes to add years to his quantity of life— and vastly improve its quality. In Foucauldian parlance, however, he is not concerned with the *I as Trevor* but the *I as species*. Stated or implied, this is the logic of race war.[55]

It is also a rationale that operates under the presumption that wasting away slowly from liver disease is not the most insufferable future imaginable. Rather, what is unbearable is the possibility that nonwhites in the form of Mexicans and welfare queens might receive the same level of healthcare as whites.[56] Viewed from the prism of white nationalism, this is what dying for one's country looks like in the context of race war. The invocation of iconic tropes of racial parasites showcases how those fictions still function as disciplinary spectacles useful in aligning the policy preferences of the white underclass with wealthy white interests. Government and Medicare are depicted as subsidizing people of color and thereby sapping white livelihood. The dynamic also illustrates an eminently biopolitical logic whereby, without the social or forensic death of a racially subordinate population, "life" loses its meaning and vitality. Otherwise put, were it the case that healthcare or social standing were evenly distributed, and not viewed as a zero-sum game, a condition of biopolitics would no longer obtain. When biopolitics affirms the logic of "the more they die, the more we live," what is at stake is not only the relative longevity of white lifetimes, but also the affective *sense* of time across many who think of themselves as white. This is the perverse biopolitical context of white temporality where Trevor can only affectively "feel alive"—in the sense of regarding his decisions and morbid lifepath as vital—so long as his own imminent death forestalls the white apocalypse. In the throes of white temporality, one's lived whiteness means being entitled to experience present hardship and struggles as sufferable insofar as they will be redeemed by future white superiority.[57] And here Trevor's temporal logic reaches its tortured extreme. As we will see, contemporary morbidity also happens in the context of less dramatic psychoaffective attachments to whiteness and white subject formation that have been politically exploited, yet remain theoretically elemental to segregated time.

"The Smart Money Is on the Cavemen"

In 1996, the British publication *Searchlight* predicted "a fight to the finish for control of the conservative movement and the Republican Party: Pat Buchanan's neo-confederates versus William Bennett's and Bill Kristol's neoconservatives. *The smart money is on the cavemen.*"[58] The statement is remarkable for its frank acknowledgment of the politics of segregated time at work. Deploying the title of "cavemen" toward a subgroup of white conservatives as backward and primitive brings us full circle back to the idiom of degeneracy, unevolved brutes, and anachronism. Once again, the temporal orders of colonialism return to those who deploy them. In this case, the production of backwardness is weaponized against those for whom race was supposed to be a guarantor of being able to stay ahead of the times. From whence did these so-called cavemen come? Early productions of backwardness among disposable white trash tells part of the story. For a more updated account of how racial anachronism has been mobilized and the present political ends it might serve, here is Sam Francis, a neo-Confederate who served as an analyst at the Heritage Foundation and wrote for the *National Review*:

> Reagan conservatism, in its innermost meaning, had little to do with supply-side economics and the spread of democracy. It had to do with the awakening of a people who face political, cultural, and economic dispossession, who are slowly beginning to glimpse the fact of dispossession and what dispossession will mean for them and their descendants, and who also are trying to think about the processes and powers responsible for dispossession.[59]

Striking for their 1992 vintage, Francis's remarks seem prescient in retrospect. The idiom of colonial dispossession is strategically repurposed as Francis recasts whites as the *real* victims and *their* future white descendants as hanging in the balance. Capturing what I have called the declining credit value of whiteness, his language of dispossession and concern for future progeny anticipates today's apocalyptic racial paranoia. That anxiety ranges from "white genocide" to its only slightly more euphemistic intonations in white replacement theory. In Francis's view of Reagan conservatism, resistance to white disposability and the preservation of white supremacy are of the essence. His statement also offers critical purchase on how the politics of resentment is so usefully weaponized by political entrepreneurs to capitalize on the sentiment that whites are *the only endangered species worthy of concern*.

Importantly, Sam Francis was also an ally of Patrick Buchanan, a figure whose ideological influence on the right has long been underestimated. I have made the point elsewhere before, but Buchanan's imprint takes on a weightier valance with Trumpism.[60] For Buchanan "mass invasion" of immigrants is a key engine of American decline and "the end of white America," to which he devotes an entire chapter in his book *Suicide of a Superpower*.[61] Needless to say, it is also a catalyst for the politics of racial resentment. For those seeking to contextualize *Dying of Whiteness*, Buchanan's *The Death of the West: How Dying Populations and Immigrant Invasions Imperil Our Country and Civilization* is an unsettling precursor.[62] The titles leave little doubt that Buchanan's nationalism is *white* nationalism. And his apocalyptic outlook is not subtle.[63] The fact that his connection to the Trump regime has largely gone unnoticed is symptomatic of a broader failure of public memory regarding the legacy of white nationalism. When Buchanan says he thinks Trump's presidency is the "last chance for these ideas" today, he means *his* ideas—a poignant indicator of all that preceded Trump's regime and what will most certainly outlast his presidency.[64]

As arguably the closest ideological precursor to Trumpism, the rhetorical symmetry between the two is unmistakable. Buchanan has long championed "forgotten Americans" as shafted by trade deals, he criticized foreign nations as economic predators taking advantage of the United States, and he repeatedly invoked the need to "take back" the country from racial others and even invoked "America first" first. Buchanan and Trump were opposing candidates for the Reform Party in 2000. Before Trump was soundly defeated, he criticized Buchanan for his "intolerance," anti-Semitism, and "bigotry and prejudice." Especially rich in hindsight is Trump's accusation that Buchanan "has systematically bashed Blacks, Mexicans and Gays."[65] After trying on the neoconservative mantle of paying lip service to racial inclusion, Trump reverted to his public racism that had been on display for decades—since 1973, in fact, when the Trump Management Corporation was sued by the Nixon administration for refusing to rent apartments to African Americans. He later called for the death of the "Central Park Five" (one Latino and four Black teenagers) who were wrongly convicted of raping and murdering a female jogger.[66] The accused men were exonerated after serving decades-long prison sentences, but Trump never apologized for taking out a full-page ad in the *New York Times* demanding their execution. Having criticized President Barack Obama for being on a perpetual international apology tour, it is instructive that one of the only apologies of which there is a public record of Trump ever having given is to none other than Pat Buchanan.[67]

To whites cast as backward by liberals and conservatives alike, Trump's embrace of the "forgotten man" as shat upon by coastal elites played well rhetorically. He lifted a page from Buchanan's repertoire, but it was a role Trump was well suited to play as one long disdained by New York society as too boorish, too vulgar, and too crude for admission. The subtext of Trump's rallies often approximated what Roxanne Dunbar expresses bluntly:

> We [white trash] ARE PROOF OF THE LIE OF THE AMERICAN DREAM. However, self-blame, a sprinkling of white-skin privilege with license to violence against minorities, scapegoating, and serving as cops and in the

military (give them a gun and point to the enemy) conspire to neutralize and redirect our anger.[68]

The redirection of anger toward racial Others, and away from wealthy whites and capitalist modes of economic dispossession more broadly, is a useful strategy for legitimating the existing system that took the form of chants of "We want our country back."[69]

The stigma of white trash makes poor whites "bad" others who have failed to perform adequately in a system that ostensibly favors them. The shame magnetized by the white trash stigma is ascribed to those who waste time or otherwise fail to keep up within a system that is geared to their advantage. This, in turn, reinforces the myth of liberal capitalist meritocracy. Shamed, liminal whites are on the receiving end of a politics that stages a version of the dehumanization and othering that white supremacists visit upon people of color.[70] As with the distinction between neoconservatives and neo-Confederate "cavemen," casting white supremacy as an intraracial issue makes it a problem of certain whites who are behind the times. They are not to be conflated with their more enlightened, civilized white counterparts. On this score, we ought not forget that Bill Kristol's neoconservatives were the architects of the neocolonial invasion of Iraq that became a venue for displaying the aforementioned scalps.[71]

As Nancy S. Love observes, "The label 'white trash' challenges norms of whiteness, including whiteness itself as an unmarked race. By associating poor whites with the already racialized categories of primitive and savage it effectively turns white supremacy into an 'intra-racial affair.'"[72] By rhetorically outsourcing the brutality of white supremacy on "white trash," wealthier whites can assume a veneer of cultivated innocence that distances them from the ugliness of racial violence—all while simultaneously preserving their status as beneficiaries of the very racial hierarchy that such "uncivilized" violence affirms.[73] And, as I argued earlier, the property value of whiteness increases with heightened racial terror. It bears repeating that *all* white people benefit from white privilege. Making white supremacy an in-group issue distracts from nonwhite poverty and suffering. It also allows the various ways that not all whites benefit equally from white supremacy to go underacknowledged, thus leaving the racial bribe firmly in place.

With this in mind, I find Metzl's claim that "the systems of inequality we build and sustain aren't benefiting anyone" far too strong.[74] In addition to overlooking wealthy whites benefiting from those systems of inequality—a key distinction with respect to how whiteness articulates with class—the broad generalization misses the variegated levels of whiteness in flux in an age of proliferating disposability. The failure to consider temporal politics inadvertently risks concealing the dynamics of racial bribery.[75] Specifically, neglecting the political economy of time misses how gilded whites benefit massively in the (relatively) short term through a politics of forcing their "cavemen" racial underlings past their expiration date.[76] It risks obscuring how elites use racial disposability to securitize their futures, leaving others on borrowed time. In sum, the production of white backwardness acts as an accelerant of the race of segregated time. Though far from its sole cause, the manufacture of asynchronous white trash sketched above dramatizes the dynamism of ongoing race-making projects as apocalyptic—the *racing* of race, if you will.

Postscript: White Apocalypse Now and Again

In view of the ongoing racial "plague dream" of immigrant infestations, job losses, climate change, and wealth inequalities, Keller's invocation of an "apocalyptic unconscious" seems more of a conscious centerpiece of public awareness by the day. "The desire for and deferral of apocalypse," she writes, "may be an organizing force behind the tenses of what we know as time."[77]
White racist dystopias have distinctive ends, even as they demonstrate affective and spiritual affinities with a more general sense of end times permeating the apocalyptic zeitgeist of contemporary political life. Here again is Baldwin: "It can be objected that I am speaking of political freedom in spiritual terms, but the political institutions of any nation are always menaced and ultimately controlled by the spiritual state of that nation."[78]

Against the backdrop of the expansive writings of Christian millennialism, there are ample reasons to be wary of the whiteness of apocalyptic thinking in popular culture—a genre unto itself. In the film *Melancholia*, the end of the world comes by way of an asteroid strike. By placing the white protagonists in a makeshift teepee right before the final impact, director Lars von Trier (almost) says the quiet part out loud, if not quite loud enough, when the film evokes the prior end times of colonialism that enabled the protected lifestyle they stand to lose. Viewers are tacitly invited to reflect on how whiteness has recursively produced apocalypse through various strategies of world-ending to shore up white temporal uncertainty. Series like *The Walking Dead* can be read critically, and ironically, as featuring predominantly white people forced into conditions typical of many people of color in the world, in the form of food shortages, fear of being invaded and dispossessed, terrorized at the prospect of being killed or assaulted, left without healthcare, and wasting away.

Apocalyptic portrayals are not revelatory because they disclose the *actual* end of time, but because they illuminate the present state of the world that those invested in the contemporary social hierarchy would seek to preserve. Such racial imaginaries risk distracting from the actual, material, waste-making factors of capitalism and empire producing the human disposability that white time promises to inoculate against.[79] The perils of apocalyptic genres are intensified when, to many, the world of fiction becomes virtually indistinguishable from political reality. The political rhetoric of immigrant invasions and infestations exposes the present tense of (im)migrants, refugees, and noncitizens to lived horrors of segregated time—not science fiction. In the context of these dangerous fictions (re)presented as real in white time, cinematic invasions of contagious zombies, animal uprisings, and robot insurrections are more than apolitical fantasies. Akin to Nietzsche's notion that anyone who has ever imagined heaven has done so from their own hell, these dystopian hellscapes can be read as apocalyptic visions produced by white time.

As political imaginaries, robot insurrections and animal uprisings arguably stand in for slave revolts against their masters. Zombie infestations evoke nightmarish terrors of a *reconquista* and ghastly returns of the supposedly vanquished. All might be viewed as possible incarnations of long-standing white American horrors voiced from Jefferson to Lincoln that—in the face of the country's tortured racial history—the judgment of the almighty might be "just indeed." Jefferson's fears that there might be a price to pay for slavery and colonial genocide, and Lincoln's worry that every lash thrust upon the enslaved would be matched with the blood spilled by Civil War soldiers, represents a trembling in the face of apocalyptic justice entirely consonant with long-standing apprehensions. Herman Melville's white whale (based on Owen Chase's real-life story of the voyage of the *Essex*) and the *Planet of the Apes* keep company with a seemingly ever-expanding genre of dominated species slipping the leashes of their assigned roles to torment and overtake their once masters. The epic takedown of race-making Promethean hubris is especially alive in the first science fiction book and archetype of its genre, Mary Shelley's *Frankenstein: Or the Modern Prometheus*.[80] Alive beneath the ongoing coproduction of race-making and monster-making in each of these tomes are horrific fantasies of so-called reverse colonialism.[81]

In abbreviated form, reverse colonialism might be shorthanded as white fears that the insights of Césaire and Fanon were right all along; colonial white supremacy—including the domination of nature and those figured as less evolved and closer to it—always comes home. The evidence of the power of colonialism to haunt is manifest in the very ghosts, monsters, and apparitions bedeviling white temporalities and threatening to lay to waste its culpable beneficiaries. These monsters are of white supremacy's own making. With the capacity to disclose that which is latent or concealed, apocalypse keeps company with the monstrous insofar as the linguistic roots of monster (*monstrum*) mean "to show." With that in mind, what counts as monstrous can diverge significantly across peoples and times, along with the terror in the face of what various apocalyptic visions reveal. In keeping with the function of monsters to show what their makers are made of, the monsters of reverse colonialism demonstrate the hellish end times opposite the desired "heaven" of white times.

It is hardly any wonder that the failed Hollywood screenwriter and former presidential chief strategist Steve Bannon regularly invokes the racist fiction of Catholic explorer and author Jean Raspail's *Camp of the Saints*.[82] A sensationalized version of what might happen if the spatiotemporal borders of white supremacy are not protected, the book culls its title from an apocalyptic passage in the book of Revelation (20:7–10) where Satan mounts a final battle against the "camp of the saints" before being defeated. In Raspail's novel, however, the "saints" are white residents of continental Europe and "Satan" is a swarm of fornicating, irredeemably dirty, lazy, ravenous subhuman Indian immigrants led by a figure known as "the turd eater." Shortly after arriving in France, the savage invaders quickly go viral, reproducing and outnumbering whites while devouring all in their path.

It is harrowing, if not surprising, that *Camp of the Saints* has become a favorite of the radical Right. More interesting, albeit deeply disturbing, is how the call-and-response of that fiction radiates across levels of power from the White House to the white poor house—and points in between. At stake politically is what that wide breadth of reception foreshadows for the possibility of transracial democratic futures, particularly since so many white Christians support racist, xenophobic, misogynist forms of governmentality. And what of the other political implications? Per Fanon, "The problem is to create, with the help of psychoanalytical, geological, political lessons, a new family environment capable of reducing, if not eliminating, the proportion of waste in the asocial sense of the word" (BSWM, 49). The work of mobilizing the insights of critical race theory (broadly conceived) to track the movement of ongoing race-making-as-waste-making projects in real time remains on the horizon for political theory. By venturing into these unruly crosscurrents, I have made no pretense of having divined a monolithic causal inference, nor have I sought anything approaching a comprehensive history. By staging a brief encounter with these rich themes, my hope is to raise their tensions and correspondences to the level of a question in an effort to convene a broader, transdisciplinary inquiry as the clock-tick of ecological crises and environmental racism grows louder.

Among the many potential points of future intervention this chapter anticipates is the temporal politics of environmental racism. Typically conceived in terms of the spatial proximity of racial others to waste, the preceding discussion suggests that environmental racism entails its own politics of temporal hygiene. In other words, there are salient relays between dirt as "matter out of place," as Mary Douglas famously put it, and populations who are racially coded as matter out of time, those who do not matter, or who only matter as sites of extraction. Even more directly related to this discussion are its implications for the economy of the pleasure that whites take in racial waste-making processes.

Specifically, the segregated apocalypse now is rife with toxic racial attachments that accelerate the coming of the fire *this* time in the form of planetary climate catastrophe. The economy of pleasure at work in the presence of nonwhite suffering in these pages enables a politics of refusal of collective goods such as healthcare. Assuming this chronobiopolitical logic of refusal continually extends to the massive investments needed for green infrastructure, the prognosis for a planetary future in common is dire indeed. The toxic sociocentric racist thinking of "I as species" that haunts aspirational whiteness imperils nonhuman species and ecologies as well. The deadly presumption that human and nonhuman disposability can always securitize white time betrays a will to temporal sovereignty—the subject before us now.

Epilogue

Other Times

In his last Sunday morning sermon, Martin Luther King Jr. openly lamented that he had become "absolutely convinced that the forces of ill will in our nation, the extreme rightists of our nation—the people on the wrong side—have used time much more effectively than the forces of good will."[1] Like his observation that the most segregated hour of the week is eleven o'clock on Sunday morning, King's reflections still hold true. *Segregated Time* invites the question of whether contesting its dynamics politically and theoretically means striving for what might be called an *integrated time*. I do not think so. As James Baldwin asked, "Do I really want to be integrated into a burning house?"[2] Today Baldwin's "The Fire Next Time" takes on an intensely prophetic significance, as the *burning house* is the planet, the *fire* is atmospheric, and the *time* is now. As presaged in the preceding discussion of end times, the desire for a segregated time endemic to white temporality is fomenting an integrated time of mass extinction across species. Notably, it was also Martin Luther King Jr. who declared that we shall either learn to live together as brothers (*sic*) or die together as fools. With that in mind, what does it mean to avow the "fierce urgency of now" given the multiple temporalities and denials of copresence discussed in these pages? Rather than a singular "now," I shall take the impulse to build a symbiotic, agonistic coexistence as calling us toward an improvisational politics of temporal relationality.

My hesitation toward calls for copresence may seem surprising, especially given Johannes Fabian's influential critique of the denial of others' right to be coeval. Yet a key pretense of white time as I have theorized it is the presumed prerogative to set the terms of what counts as presence and absence politically and phenomenologically. Without an attunement to the power relations that define what counts as cotemporaneous in the first place, even well-intentioned calls for integrated time in the form of a universal right to be coeval risk reinstating the problematic impositions of white racial time chronicled here.[3] One political pathology recurring throughout this study

Segregated Time. P.J. Brendese, Oxford University Press. © Oxford University Press 2023.
DOI: 10.1093/oso/9780197535745.003.0009

is the accelerating sense of temporal uncertainty that is increasingly combustible in the wake of legacies of racial hierarchy—what I have phrased "the race of segregated time." This entails the chronobiopolitical leveraging of racial others in order to securitize white temporalities. Another way of putting that securitization is that the time of nonwhites is leveraged to solidify white time as property—or white temporal sovereignty. Consonant with Du Bois's and Fanon's association of whiteness with a desire for perpetual ownership of the world, this book has argued that the time of whiteness is a possessive tense. White apprehension, the acquisitiveness that contributes to that which racializes temporalities as white, is imbued with a will to temporal sovereignty. Bids for temporal sovereignty might be understood as a desire to own—and belief in the capacity to define, partition, quantify, and command—that which is called time.

Among the investments in temporal sovereignty surfaced in the preceding chapters are notions that permanent-temporary laborers will insulate the racially dominant population from economic shocks, the use of race as a predictive technology to reinforce carceral temporalities, the belief that racial others will bear the brunt of the rising tides of climate change, whiteness as a store of credit negotiable over time, racial others as vehicles of time travel, as perpetually indebted, and the presumption that the free time of whites is parasitic upon the multiply arrested times of people of color. Against that grim backdrop, my hope throughout has been that a critical engagement with the drives toward temporal sovereignty will serve as an aspirational bridge onto desegregated and relational—if not integrated—chronopolitics. This is no substitute for a extended exposition of relational temporalities or a catalog of the various modalities of inhabiting time differently, which would require at least another manuscript. Still other works could productively focus on strategies of temporal resistance through time, with an extended index of political actors using time they do not have.

Asking after what time one does, or does not, have returns us to the issue of temporal sovereignty. Can one really "own" time? Does a presumption that time can be owned represent a kind of epistemic entitlement, perhaps a companion of capitalist acquisitiveness? Last, what are we to make of temporal sovereignty with respect to the white possessive sense of entitlement, itself historically conditioned, which presumes the capacity to own material things along with the prerogative to own—and to define—time? A few hesitations regarding temporal sovereignty seem appropriate. In view of sovereignty's spatial orientations, its intellectual descent, its supposed utility in policing boundaries, along with its corresponding crises and "walled" insecurities, one might ask: are we well-served by mapping sovereignty onto time?[4] It would seem that temporal sovereignty is a political-theoretical instantiation of the problem Bergson identified by noting that when we say time, it is space that answers the call. Further, what are the attendant political and theoretical benefits and liabilities of a collective investment in time as that which can be possessed?

I do not raise these as merely rhetorical questions, nor do I pretend to resolve them in these last few pages. Hardly. Rather, I do so because temporal sovereignty is one of the potential resolutions recently posed for temporal theft and erasures of presence. I certainly seek solidarity with efforts to resist temporal redistribution and insidious modes of colonizing time—both of which parade under the banner of temporal sovereignty, as I discuss in what follows. And in the context of the world-ending powers of colonial dispossession that claim nonwhite lands, bodies, and futures—along with looming ecocide that threatens life forms on a planetary scale—the possibility of sovereignty over time and temporality is understandably seductive. Nevertheless, I hold that temporal sovereignty is a flawed vessel for a politics capable of conceiving temporal plurality differently and inhabiting time otherwise. Conceptions of time as something to be possessed are colonial in the sense that, pace Césaire, colonization is thingification. But there is more to it than a performative contradiction. A politics of temporal sovereignty where everyone is on their own time strikes me as antithetical to a relational sense of time and political possibility. It seems an inadequate counter to the race of segregated time, in the triple sense of race as identity, race as acceleration, and race as a zero-sum competition. Temporal sovereignty promises to desegregate time, only to be integrated into the burning house of relating to time in terms of property.

Why make an issue out of adding sovereignty to time? Isn't this just another conceptual cream-puff war among academics? There are political stakes of owning time, which I sketch. For the sake of concision, I engage Mark Rifkin's *Beyond Settler Time*. I do so in part because Rifkin has explicitly argued on behalf of temporal sovereignty in the service of a kind of aspirational decolonial politics with which I am generally sympathetic. To illustrate the dangers of possessing time, I move between accelerationist modes of relying on technology to own the future and cognate presumptions that innovations like geoengineering will shore up uncertainties around climate change. In this epilogue my hope is to initiate a broader dialogue around creatively contesting temporal impositions, and to do so in the service of asynchronous and untimely innovations that interrupt and exceed the recursive strictures of white time.

Beyond the Pale of Temporal Sovereignty

The *Merriam Webster Dictionary* defines *pale* (in the noun form) as

1 an area or the limits within which one is privileged or protected (as from censure) //conduct that was beyond the pale
2 a: space or field having bounds: ENCLOSURE
//the cattle were led into the pale
b: a territory or district within certain bounds or under a particular jurisdiction
//British culture survived even within the Roman *pale*.
3 a: one of the stakes of a palisade
b: PICKET [a pointed or sharpened stake]
4 : a perpendicular stripe on a heraldic shield
5 *archaic*: PALISADE, PALING

In the vernacular adjective form, of course, pale refers to a deficiency of color or light; that which is pallid, faint, or feeble even. At risk of being pedantic, this means that the phrase "white picket fence" is triply redundant. Ludwig Wittgenstein's analogy for language was a city. Appropriately, the multiple meanings and uses of *pale* across time and space draw us to reflect back on urban spaces as delineating the historical boundaries between white settler properties and Indigenous territories—those literally *beyond the pale* of white spacetimes. I use the word "spacetime" deliberately, because many are still surprised to learn that the majority of Native Americans live in cities, not on reservations or in rural areas. Long before "urban" became a codeword for "black" and "brown," cities were conceived as segregated spaces as well as segregated times.[5] To encounter the frontier and nature was to transgress into the "primitive." It meant encountering Indigenous peoples associated with nature as "the Naturals" whose extinction was inevitable—itself a temporal orientation of whiteness as destiny that facilitated a genocidal weaponization of white time. Native bodies and spaces existed in contrast to concentrated settler spaces, coded as modern and white—not because they lacked significant numbers of nonwhites (particularly Blacks) but because they were controlled by white power.

Unlike Native Americans, the projected destiny of Blacks was generally servility, labor, and slow death and attenuated attrition, not removal to a reserve or outright extinction. Preserving the time value of Black labor required different modes of racialized "keeping watch," since the movement of Black bodies had to be carefully managed in the interest of economic productivity and white security. This is another way of saying that differential impositions of temporal sovereignty functioned as part of ongoing projects of racialization. Practices such as slave patrols, passes, curfews, and sundown towns have all regulated racial rhythms and corporeal flows as expressions of white desire to command African American time. Underwriting that temporal regulation, of course, is the necropolitical right to violently cast racial others out of time entirely—a prerogative scholars have increasingly recognized as historically coextensive with white popular sovereignty.[6] The upshot is that the securitization of white time is contingent on the institutionalized precaritization of nonwhite temporalities. As an elemental vector of white time, the desire for temporal sovereignty seeks dominion over the timescapes of others who are "beyond the pale," reinforcing and elevating the property value of whiteness. The politics of subject formation that figures racial others as multiply "out of time," or living on borrowed time, is directly related to the credit value of whiteness.

In *Beyond Settler Time*, Mark Rifkin rejoins what he calls Johannes Fabian's "well-worn" critique that the discipline of anthropology is implicated in the broader politics of denying its "Others" the right to be coeval that it would profess to critique.[7] Much of the force of Rifkin's argument (the entirety of which I do not reconstruct here) stems from his rightful concern that the definitional power required to constitute what it means to be "coeval" risks effectively reproducing the temporal structure and corresponding impositions he refers to as "settler time." Likewise, he is critical of the temporal politics of recognition whereby the figure of the Indian appears as an anachronism who must be refigured as equally "modern" and "part of a shared present" in order to be an intelligible subject (BST, x). Such maneuvers run the risk of presenting a patina of ecumenical pluralism while actually effectuating yet another compulsory assimilation into a dominant temporal structure. In place of such calls for a shared, cotemporaneous present he proposes to "gesture toward temporal sovereignty—the need to address the role of time (as narrative, experience, as imminent materiality of continuity and change) in struggles over Indigenous landedness, governance and everyday socialities" (BST, x).

Rifkin takes pains to traverse disciplinary boundaries in an effort to enrich his readers' sense of Indigenous peoples' lived experiences of time beyond their presumed "settler" formations. A textural, dimensional mode of addressing the heterogeneity of Indigenous temporalities forms a key part of Rifkin's analysis of Indigenous texts, as well as the body as a kind of text that is conditioned by time.[8] This sensibility also allows him to theorize the overlap between the heteropatriarchal order of the settler state, which prioritizes a "repro-sexual marital union" that "was conjoined with the acceptance of private property and construction of non-kinship-related governance as (racialized) markers of progress toward the achievement of civilization" (BST, 121).[9] He contends that a key benefit of the study's attention to Indigenous temporal sovereignty is its capacity to reveal the prevailing, heterotemporal, linear, progressive assumptions of how time supposedly operates universally and how it ought to be inhabited (BST, 26). This opens onto his analysis of the chrononormativity of the nuclear family that naturalized a particular order of time as it relates to, and is advanced by, a chronobiopolitics of race (BST, 120). What, then, does Rifkin mean by temporal sovereignty?[10]

Promising to offer "less an explanation than a hermeneutic," he proposes at the outset to engage a range of "Native texts and Native scholars and that hopefully can contribute to the pursuit of Indigenous self-determination by proposing additional conceptual tools for marking the force, effects, and endurance of settlement. In this vein my insistence on the potential distinction between Native and non-Native experiences of time may be aiming to facilitate possibilities for temporal sovereignty" (BST, 4–5). In the context of Indigenous peoples, considering temporal sovereignty entails attending to "how sensations and articulations of time take place in Indigenous peoples' operation as polities and their pursuit of self-determination" (BST, 3). At each step, Rifkin carefully honors the alterity of Indigenous experiences and orientations to time as nonderivative of settler time and not reducible to a "unitary flow" of "a singular given time" (BST 3). He notes that wants to explore latent possibilities for considering "Indigenous temporal sovereignty" "in terms of both the relative autonomy of Native experiences and articulations of time" as well as "Native experiences of time . . . assaulted, denied and reordered" through the violence of imposed settler time (BST, 16).

Neither seeking an overarching conception of "Indigenous temporality," nor attempting to measure the distance between "traditional" authentic Indigenous lifeways and their deviations in order to delimit the boundary for being truly Native, Indigenous temporalities are plural. As such they are "discrepant" but not "hermetically sealed" from "white forms of experience," but rather "can be understood as affecting each other, as all open to change, and yet as not equivalent or mergeable into a neutral, common frame—call it time, modernity, history, or the present (BST, 3).[11] Rifkin contends that Indigenous temporal sovereignty is expressed in the retelling of stories through dynamic processes that do not necessarily presume stability across content, storytellers, or those to whom the stories are told. Relationships to the land and its care, upkeep, and history all interact through "storied landscapes" that convey a sense of collective belonging and "connections to the land" lived as "forms of bodily sensation, intimately a part of temporal experience" (BST, 36).[12]

Remarkably, Rifkin follows his opening affirmation of temporal sovereignty as a seemingly unqualified good with a discussion of how prevailing forms of temporal recognition have served to cast Indigenous peoples as either extinct or embodied anachronisms on the verge of inevitable extermination. This is notable since, on the one hand, he carefully cautions against the dangers of interpolating Indigenous subjects into the time signatures of the dominant discursive order. On the other hand, Rifkin reads Indigenous lifeways as expressions of not just self-determination, but *temporal sovereignty*. Moreover, the heavily freighted conceptual, and deeply political, sociohistorical legacies of sovereignty include its spatial/geographic renderings, its material and bodily connotations traversing the king's body and the body politic, and its colonial connection to liberal individual sovereign self-possession—to name but a few familiar touchstones.[13] At a minimum, this baggage invites misunderstanding. At worst, it threatens to undercut the very sensibility Rifkin counsels and admirably demonstrates in the text's many laudable movements.

Rifkin's ethnographic account of temporal multiplicity, itself buttressed by a phenomenologically conditioned sense of duration informed by Merleau-Ponty and Bergson, respectively, adds theoretical ballast for a compelling case of divergent experiences of time—as does Einstein's landmark theory of special relativity by way of its departure from Newtonian time. Yet, on my reading of these thinkers, it does not *necessarily* follow that time is—or could be—the stuff of sovereign possession.[14] Furthermore, the desire to command ownership over time in general, and the time of racial others in particular, is a core component of the colonial subjectivity to which Rifkin objects. If time is read alongside Indigenous claims of peoples "belonging to the land" (and not the other way around, as liberal sovereignty would have it), it seems quite a stretch to imagine time in terms of property, be it Indigenous or otherwise.

Rifkin claims that temporal sovereignty seeks to open spaces to articulate Native lifeways in accordance with Glen Coulthard's notion of grounded normativity as "the modalities of Indigenous land-connected practices and longstanding experiential knowledge that inform and structure our ethical engagements with the world and our relationships with human and non-human others over time."[15] Accordingly, the examples in *Beyond Settler Time* do not reflect Indigenous peoples seeking mastery over time the way their colonial counterparts seek mastery over nature, or proposing an imperious sense of temporal dominion. Rather, the chapters illustrate differential modes of understanding and inhabiting time to disclose the violence of settler colonial desires for temporal command—and the consequences of settlers arrogating to themselves the power to "standardize" time in the first place.

Yet I worry that Rifkin's stance toward temporal sovereignty risks implication in a different concern that Coulthard and many other Native scholars caution against: that of responding to the problems of colonialism by reinstating its categories.[16] In the shadow of the Peace of Westphalia, there is an enduring tendency to theorize politics from within chrononormative timescapes already predisposed to regard sovereignty as a form of common sense. Yet, as Césaire puts it, "The tenses of colonialism are never conjugated with the verbs of an idyll."[17] However inadvertently, Rifkin's invocation of temporal sovereignty invites a "temporal interpellation" into settler categories and timescapes that his argument would seem to oppose, as those frames convey time signatures unto themselves. The political and theoretical stakes of thinking sovereignty in terms of time surpass what he regards as a more modest "gesture" toward temporal sovereignty (BST, 186).

Last, it remains unclear why redeploying sovereignty in temporal terms represents the best means of "envisioning Native being and becoming as non-identical to these imposed frames of reference, even as Indigenous temporalities are affected and shifted by such colonial imperatives" (BST, 179). Temporal sovereignty has understandable attractions for those, like Rifkin, seeking generous receptivity—and not just those seeking to cast peoples regarded as autochthonous out of time altogether. With the forces of instability and uncertainty increasingly feeding off one another, the seductions toward making the future a knowable entity (which I take to be a liability of a temporal sovereignty) intensify and multiply with our anxieties.

No Time to Lose

Perhaps the presumption of temporal sovereignty explains why it comes as such a shock to learn that paleontologists, geologists, and evolutionary biologists with a long view of planetary life testify that humankind is currently living through earth's sixth mass extinction. Extinctions are not identical to apocalypses, but sociocentric theorists should take note that they overlap in the present moment. According to Elizabeth Kolbert, the ongoing extinction in progress includes human life itself.[18] The collective disavowal of the five prior mass extinctions amounts to yet another incarnation of segregated time that holds the temporality of the human estate apart from that of the earth in peculiar ways. Conventional notions of planetary history have long maintained that the geological formation of the earth exists apart from the age of humans. Discrete divisions between planetary and human time can echo creation mythologies and theistic stories of progress wherein the culmination of the natural world's development is human life, with the arrival of humanity effectively resetting the clock to zero.[19]

Such profoundly linear senses of time assume a course between the evolution of the natural world that more or less culminates in planetary stability. Geological equilibrium, in turn, conveniently provides a staging ground for human flourishing and human consciousness of itself as a higher-order life form above and apart from that blue sphere underfoot. Planetary gradualism entails a belief that evolution happens over a prolonged duration, which, in turn, is enticingly suggestive of a future of equally incremental changes—shifts so minute that they're likely to escape notice.[20] The preceding chapters suggest that there is a similar habit of thought in the white investment in racial fixity across time. The recent spate of unprecedented climate disasters alone should make any wager on planetary gradualism seem like a losing bet.[21] From the opposite vantage, those who acknowledge the threat of climate change are tempted toward their own version of temporal sovereignty by projective calculus. Dipesh Chakrabarty takes issue with the probabilistic thinking of economists and environmental policy wonks who inject a veiled mode of temporal certainty into their projections. Through what he calls a "physics of global warming" they assume "a kind of stability or predictability—however probabilistic it may be—on the part of a warming atmosphere that paleoclimatologists, focused more on the greater danger of tipping points, often do not assume."[22]

Chakrabarty notes that it is not that such analysts are ignorant "of the nonlinear nature of the relationship between the greenhouse gasses and the rise in the planet's average surface temperature," nor is it the case that they simply do not care. Rather, their methodology converts "uncertainties to risks that have been acknowledged and evaluated," "while working out options that humans can create for themselves."[23] The upshot is the world climate system has "no significant capacity to be a wild card insofar as they can make policy prescriptions; it is there in a relatively predictable form to be managed by human ingenuity and political mobilization."[24] The erasure of contingency that converts uncertainties into risk takes the form of a financial hedge, with public policy leveraging the planet as too big to fail. Chakrabarty dryly observes that "climate change is a problem defined and constructed by climate scientists whose research methods, analytical strategies and skill sets are different from those possessed by students of political economy."[25] Presumably, the capacity to grapple with multiple temporal forces in the context of a condition where the earth and humans are coactors is also not among the skills of most political economists. In the place of any wild card, faith in temporal sovereignty functions as the imaginary ace up the sleeve of the human estate.[26]

Any certainty about end times presumes to know too much about the relation between human and nonhuman forces to give a precise date for the coming apocalypse. Just consider the repeated revisions by climate scientists about the velocity of polar ice melt and glaciers that no longer move at a glacial pace. Previous extinctions were augured by forces human and nonhuman, and planetary times are among the multiple temporalities with which humans interact. Asteroids, methane vents leaking toxicity, and volcanic eruptions are among the forces that prompt Connolly to theorize what it means to "face the planetary" in terms of "bumpy temporalities."[27] These range from the literal bumps of tectonic shifts and terraforming, to the emergent pluripotentialities that issue forth from synergistic interactions between the biological and geological, to their respective bearing on human evolution and creativity. To varying degrees, Chakrabarty and Connolly take positions that contrast to thinkers such as Žižek, Foster, Clark, and York, who ascribe a much stronger role to humans when it comes to climate change vis-à-vis capitalism and colonialism.[28] Yet neither lets human forces like imperial capitalism off the hook. Varying in emphasis and expertise, they converge in their dissent from positions that reduce ecological crises to a problem entirely in the wheelhouse of human ability to resolve.[29]

For Connolly, such a posture risks a politics of existential ressentiment as well as the onset of nihilism, be it active or passive.[30] Chakrabarty notes climate scientists' use of vitalist metaphors to stress the inability to predict and control the planet and chronographically map its unknowable tipping points.[31] All of which is to say that we are not entitled to the presumptions of sovereignty over time or in time. Humans play a role in the ongoing crisis and must actively work to address it, but there are no guarantees. If you have accelerationist tendencies, however, you likely disagree.

There are avowed accelerationists and those so labeled for purposes of insult, with subsets of each on the left and right.[32] Generally speaking, left accelerationists advocate a political economy of speeding up in order to push the contradictions of capitalism to their limits to realize a postcapitalist future.[33] By my lights, several assumptions about time are typically at play: (a) capitalism is in its late stages; (b) effectuating its collapse quickly will produce *something* desirable—with the specifics of precisely what that something is remaining vague or undefined; and (c) the providential nature of technology will provide what humans lack, presumably filling in the aforementioned lack of specificity. Perhaps the most widely cited example of left accelerationism is Alex Williams and Nick Srnicek's *The Accelerationist Manifesto*, which has come under fire for, among other things; its flawed application of Marx as well as its "Eurocentric eschatology of Progress, that is nostalgic for its rationalist, imperialist, triumphalist past," it is said to erase otherness through a "forgetfulness which is perfectly humanist" and arguably racist.[34] Left accelerationism deploys a strong messianic relationship to time through a range of suppositions that the future belongs to innovators who depart from the backward "folk politics of localism."[35] It suggests a politics of segregated time that is oracular in its conceits of temporal sovereignty.[36]

The disappearance of duration in the digital age of instantaneous exchange compounds concerns over economic class and access to neoliberal capital flows that intersect with technology, race, and place. There are abundant sociological studies on the transformation affected by clock time, while research on time in the internet age has emerged only recently. In what media studies scholar Robert Hassan has termed "network time," the "times of the networks are infinitely fragmented" and the speeds of one's connections and interactions may vary; they are all governed by a "network logic" or "techno logic driven by commercial competition" that "orients almost all network users to an *accelerated existence* within network time."[37] Hassan's concerns about the correspondence between technological saturation and temporal inundation are compelling, but his answer to resisting the impositions of an accelerating present is also temporal sovereignty.[38]

The rhythms, habits of thought, and temporal grammar at play in accelerationism offer occasions for reflection not limited to the staying power of late capitalism since the (also late) Karl Marx. The technology that so many presume will save us has a voracious appetite for fossil fuels and mineral resources. Widely billed as a timesaver despite its often planned obsolescence, technology beckons us to consider the colonization of temporalities (asymmetric, aggregative, syncopated, and modulated) relative to the internet specifically and technological advancement more generally. With respect to geoengineering our way out of climate change, the legacy of white colonial bids for temporal sovereignty is a good place to start "for understanding why putting giant mirrors into space or intentionally manufacturing large-scale algal blooms are beginning to be considered less utopian means to address climate change than reducing greenhouse gas (GHG) emissions."[39] Mark W. Driscoll takes bold steps in this direction by theorizing the role of whiteness in the current climate crisis, with the Opium Wars as a key point "when white racial capitalists assumed global control over nonliving minerals like fossil fuels, nonwhite humans, and extrahuman nature."[40] Rather than pretend that everyone was always considered human and all are equally responsible for climate change, he views time and space differently, to explore when "white men transcended their role in the Holocene as one biological actor among others and became the dominating geological force" of what he provocatively calls "climate Caucasianism."[41]

As we look forward, some of the most urgent work to be done is arguably in the relays between environmental racism, whiteness, and temporality—particularly in an age where many think the real existential threat is the end of white supremacy, not the climate crisis. There are no easy ways out of these entanglements, but some closing reflections anticipate the way toward relational modalities. Untimely temporal castaways call theorists to complement the reflective, the spatial, and the visual with the affective and improvisational in order to mine the present for emergent modes of solidarity and agonistic ways of becoming otherwise. King himself knew well how to use rhythm to convene a public by building a temporary community of shared pleasure around his words. The work of demonstrating how others are placed "out of time" by exclusionary modes of empowered temporality needs to be conjoined with constructive companion projects. Such generative efforts would be aimed at compelling wider audiences to sense the countertempos that confine those upon whom white time depends. But this kind of untimely theory would also have to be critically reflective in order to acknowledge how what seems to be a counterrhythm might actually exceed the conventional dialectic and be emergent and instructive. It might be a practice of freedom, "an art of being free" from which we have something to learn.[42]

In the wake of the affective turn recently timely among theorists, thinking affectively in untimely ways is a good place to start feeling those who are out of time. The impulse to undertake such a project would be as much intuitive as reflective. It is at least as affective as it is cognitive. Likewise, political theory has tended toward an idiom centered on the ocular, with an emphasis on sight and vision. Vision can certainly connote imagination as well as a teleological projection, but fully embodied modes of theorizing do well to take into account the sonic registers of being and becoming. Vision is well suited to the spatial, while temporal politics requires a different sensory field. The music that opens each chapter of Du Bois's *Souls of Black Folk* is not incidental, the poetry in Fanon's and Césaire's texts is not ancillary, and music is not mere escapist entertainment.[43] All are creative modes of resounding prevailing orders of time and making more habitable, humane, and embodied temporalities that dimensional publics might relate to. Jettisoning the attachments to owning time and temporal sovereignty, relational modes of cohabiting time otherwise favor improvisational approaches with a sense of polyphony, tonic, play, rhythm, and productive resonances and dissonances. I do not draw stark boundaries between politics and aesthetics, and this is not a suggestion to abandon the former for the latter. It is, however, an invitation to expand our conceptual sensorium toward a broader range of frequencies, an improved sense of the time we do not have, and possibilities for inhabiting time otherwise.

We have no time to lose.

Notes

Prelude and Acknowledgments

1. Baldwin, quoted from *James Baldwin: The Price of the Ticket*, PBS/American Masters, (documentary), originally aired August 14, 1989.
2. James Baldwin, "The Fire Next Time," in *The Price of the Ticket: Collected Nonfiction 1948–1985* (New York: St. Martin's Press, 1985), 350.
3. For intellectual historians working under the heading of political theory who might think there is not room for all of us at the table, here is John Pocock: "The understanding of time, and of human life as experienced in time, disseminated in a society, is an important part of that society's understanding of itself—of its structure and what legitimates it, of the modes of action that are possible to it and in it. There is a point at which historical and political theory meet, and it can be said without distortion that *every society possesses a philosophy of history—a set of ideas about what happens, what can be known and what done, in time considered as a dimension of society—which is intimately part of its consciousness and its functioning*" (my emphasis). J. G. A. Pocock, "Time, Institutions and Action: An Essay on Traditions and Their Understanding," in *Politics and Experience: Essays Presented to Professor Michael Oakeshott on the Occasion of His Retirement*, ed. Preston King and B. C. Parekh (Cambridge: Cambridge University Press, 1968), 233.
4. For that matter, I am also aware that any discussion of the human race is always in relation to its constitutive outsides, interspecies boundaries, and virtual interfaces, as well as a range of nonhuman actants—which are themselves subject to temporal dynamism.
5. Malcolm X, quoted in George Lipsitz, *The Possessive Investment in Whiteness: How Whites Benefit from Identity Politics* (Philadelphia: Temple University Press, 1998), 183.

Introduction

1. I am grateful to Lawrie Balfour for this illuminating formulation.
2. Michael Hanchard, "Afro-Modernity: Temporality, Politics and the African Diaspora," *Public Culture* 11, no. 1 (1999): 245–268. Hanchard's pathbreaking work represents one of the few attempts to work at the intersection of race and time with a sustained attention to power. Notable exceptions are cited accordingly.

3. See Martin Luther King Jr., *Why We Can't Wait* (New York: Harper and Row, 1963); Martin Luther King Jr., "Negroes Are Not Moving Too Fast," in *A Testament of Hope*, ed. James M. Washington (San Francisco: Harper Collins, [1986] 1991), 176–182.
4. Martin Luther King Jr., "Letter from Birmingham City Jail," in *A Testament of Hope*, 295.
5. King, "Letter from Birmingham City Jail," 292.
6. King, "Letter from Birmingham City Jail," 292.
7. Martin Luther King Jr., "Remaining Awake through a Great Revolution," in *A Testament of Hope*, 270.
8. Roxanne Dunbar-Ortiz, *An Indigenous People's History of the United States* (Boston: Beacon Press, 2014), 49.
9. For instance, US president George W. Bush argued on behalf of invading Iraq by insisting that Saddam Hussein had something to hide from the civilized world.
10. Thomas McCarthy, *Race, Empire and the Idea of Human Development* (New York: Cambridge University Press, 2009), 171–189. J.S. Mill endorsed an enforced paternalism that he acknowledged was despotic but would nevertheless serve the ends of progress. See John Locke, *Second Treatise of Government*, ed. C.B. McPherson (Indianapolis: Hackett, 1980), 19–22. Note Locke's references to America as a "vacant land" whose "savages" had not heeded God's command to make it productive and fruitful, as would befit those who were "rational," "industrious," and, not coincidentally, English.
11. McCarthy, *Race, Empire*, 180. What that liberal past's future looks like is visible in the scenes of contemporary segregated time and temporality taken up in this volume. Also see Uday Sinha Mehta, *Liberalism and Empire* (Chicago: University of Chicago Press, 1999); Jeanne Morefield, "Empire, Tragedy and the Liberal State in the Writings of Niall Ferguson and Michael Ignatief," *Theory & Event* 11, no. 3 (2008).
12. Johannes Fabian, *Time and the Other: How Anthropology Makes Its Object* (New York: Columbia University Press, 2003), xxxvii.
13. Dipesh Chakrabarty, *Provincializing Europe* (Princeton, NJ: Princeton University Press, 2000), 8.
14. Frantz Fanon, *Black Skin, White Masks*, trans. Charles Lam Markmann (New York: Grove Press, 1967), 130. Hereafter citations appear in text as BSWM.
15. I discuss this at length in P.J. Brendese, "A Race of Devils: Race-Making, *Frankenstein* and the Modern Prometheus," *Political Theory* 50, no. 1 (February 2022): 86–113.
16. On the fraught political descent of Christian generosity, see Romand Coles, *Rethinking Generosity* (Ithaca, NY: Cornell University Press, 1997).
17. The phrase is often attributed to Richard Henry Pratt, army officer and architect of the Carlisle Indian Industrial School (1879), which was regarded as the first off-reservation Indian boarding school. See Ward Churchill, *Kill the Indian, Save the Man* (San Francisco: City Lights Bookstore, 2004).
18. Recent studies that reflect on the politics of imposed durational time include Javier Auyero, *Patients of the State: The Politics of Waiting in Argentina* (Durham, NC, & London: Duke University Press, 2012); and Elizabeth Cohen, *The Political Value of Time* (Cambridge: Cambridge University Press, 2018).

NOTES 189

19. Valerie Rohy, *Anachronism and Its Others: Sexuality, Race, Temporality* (Albany: SUNY Press, 2009).
20. Ruth Wilson Gilmore, *Golden Gulag: Prisons, Surplus, Crisis and Opposition in California* (Berkeley: University of California Press, 2007), 247.
21. Zygmunt Bauman, *Liquid Modernity* (Malden, MA: Polity Press, 2000), 94.
22. See Thomas Friedman, *Thank You for Being Late: An Optimist's Guide for Thriving in the Age of Accelerations* (New York: Farrar, Straus & Giroux, 2016). The title is a gesture to the additional time for reflection the author got when someone else was tardy for a meeting. From the vantage of segregated time, however, the "thank you" can be read quite differently when one considers that the prevailing temporal flows of white time are leveraged on the exploitation and demise of anachronistic temporal outsiders: carriers of criminalized residual difference who embody a past time, violate the chronology of present time, and represent a threat to future time. "Thank you for being late" can be heard as an expression of what the dominant time says to the temporal outcasts rendered disposable—with "late" as the appellation naming those left behind and the recently deceased.
23. Paul Virilio, *The Great Accelerator* (Malden, MA: Polity Press, 2012); Simon Glezos, *The Politics of Speed: Capitalism and the State of War in an Accelerating World* (New York: Routledge, 2012). The emphasis on the accelerating speed of contemporary time can create the impression that everyone is being pushed ahead, or forced to keep up, at the same pace and even in the same way.
24. The statement that "the future is already here—it's just is not evenly distributed yet" is often attributed to the science fiction writer William Gibson, but I (and others) have not been able to source it to him. See Pagan Kennedy, "William Gibson's Future Is Now," *New York Times*, January 13, 2012. Online at https://www.nytimes.com/2012/01/15/books/review/distrust-that-particular-flavor-by-william-gibson-book-review.html.
25. Rob Nixon, *Slow Violence and the Environmentalism of the Poor* (Cambridge, MA: Harvard University Press, 2013), 18, 152, 162.
26. Giordano Nanni, *The Colonisation of Time: Ritual and Resistance in the British Empire* (Manchester: Manchester University Press, 2012), 8–10.
27. Elizabeth DeLoughrey and George B. Handley, eds., *Postcolonial Ecologies: Literatures of the Environment* (New York: Oxford University Press, 2011), 12.
28. The phrase is Deborah Bird Rose's.
29. Mark M. Smith, *Mastered by the Clock: Time Slavery and Freedom in the American South* (Chapel Hill: University of North Carolina Press, 1997).
30. W.E.B. Du Bois, *Black Reconstruction in America* (New York: Free Press, 1998), chap. 4.
31. Patrick Wolfe, *Traces of History* (London: Verso, 2016), 2. Wolfe makes such a distinction as a historically entrenched form of racial coding. Note that Indigenous peoples have also been enslaved and the capture of their lands has also resulted in an extraction of time. See Andrés Reséndez, *The Other Slavery: The Uncovered Story of Indian Enslavement in America* (Boston: Mariner Books, 2017).

32. Ghasson Hage, *Is Racism an Environmental Threat?* (Malden, MA: Polity Press, 2017), esp. 9–12.
33. Maddeningly repetitive instances of absurdity and illogic is what I take Frantz Fanon to indicate by his contention that philosophy has never saved anyone. See BSWM, 29
34. See BSWM, 118. As Fanon puts it, "For a man whose only weapon is reason there is nothing more neurotic than contact with unreason." Fanon's theory of sociogeny identified historical disavowal in psychology that naturalizes afflictions among colonized peoples when, in reality, no human being is born neurotic.
35. James Baldwin, "The Fire Next Time," in *The Price of the Ticket: Collected Nonfiction, 1948–1985* (Boston: Beacon Press, 1985), 336.
36. I discuss the manufacture of time at length in Chapter 1.
37. See David Scott, *Conscripts of Modernity* (Durham, NC: Duke University Press, 2004); David Scott, *Omens of Adversity* (Durham, NC: Duke University Press, 2014); McCarthy, *Race, Empire*; Nanni, *Colonization of Time*; Zygmunt Bauman, *Wasted Lives: Modernity and Its Outcasts* (Malden, MA: Polity Press, 2004).
38. On multiple modernities, see Chakrabarty, *Provincializing Europe*. The reference to Afro-modernity is indebted to Michael Hanchard. On the denial of coevalness, see Fabian, *Time and the Other*, 25–35.
39. See Michel Foucault, *"Society Must Be Defended": Lectures at the Collège de France, 1975–1976*, trans. David Macey (New York: Picador Books, 2003), 247 (hereafter citations appear in the text as "SMBD"); Lauren Berlant, "Slow Death: Sovereignty, Obesity and Lateral Agency," *Critical Inquiry* 33 (Summer 2007): 754–780; Achille Mbembe, "Necropolitics," *Public Culture* 15, no. 1 (2003): 11–40.
40. Katherine McKittrick, ed., *Sylvia Wynter: Being Human as Praxis* (Durham, NC: Duke University Press, 2015), 31. Wynter contests the taken-for-granted, somatic facticity that is the outcome of a long history of bourgeois Western Man, who "overrepresents" himself as *the human* and projects himself as the referent that encompasses all humanity.
41. Take, for instance, attempts to depoliticize racial difference by speaking of it in terms of animal speciation.
42. Didier Fassin, "The Biopolitics of Otherness: Undocumented Foreigners and Racial Discrimination in French Public Debate," *Anthropology Today* 17, no. 1 (2001): 3–7. Fassin is careful to acknowledge that racial distinctions are products of power relations, not nature or biology.
43. Hence when Donald Trump calls Hispanic people "animals" and Black people "dogs," his rhetoric is contiguous with a long and tortured history of strategies seeking racial purity by denigrating the lesser-evolved, the degenerate, or the savage.
44. Édouard Glissant, *Poetics of Relation*, trans. Betsy Wing (Ann Arbor: University of Michigan Press, 2010), 72.
45. Elizabeth Freeman, "Introduction," *GLQ: A Journal of Lesbian and Gay Studies* 13, nos. 2–3 (2007): 160. Freeman is reflecting on the asynchronies of "queer time."
46. Such dissonance is audible in courtrooms where prosecutorial discretion is deployed to decide whether, and whom, to charge criminally. It is palpable in the

politics of entitlement where inherited white privilege is disavowed by those who act as if "they were born in a log cabin they built themselves." A sense of entitlement speaks to expectations, which are relationships to future time. In other words, to be "out of time" is a means of being relegated to the margins of political space.

47. P.J. Brendese *The Power of Memory in Democratic Politics* (Rochester, NY: University of Rochester Press, 2014).
48. For instance, think of when the European Enlightenment is taught as the era when Reason vanquished the authority of religious revelation once and for all. As if. It also can appear in the impression that the cleavage between ancient and modern politics is supposedly marked by the historical abolition of the notion that "might makes right."
49. With respect to the politics of truth commissions and public apologies, there is a pernicious tendency to speak of injustice as existing in the past tense and sealed off from the present.
50. Stuart Hall, "When Was 'the post-colonial'? Thinking at the limit," in *The Postcolonial Question: Common Skies, Divided Horizons*, ed. Iain Chambers and Lidia Curti (New York: Routledge, 1996), 242–260.
51. James Q. Whitman, *Hitler's American Model: The United States and the Making of Nazi Race Law* (Princeton, NJ: Princeton University Press, 2017).
52. The Texas school board is once again omitting from elementary school curricula core aspects of America's history of race, gender, and imperialism, thereby connecting segregated memory and temporality. The board argued that it was redacting the material in order to *save grade-schoolers time*. Despite those concerns, Texas *did* agree that third graders still had enough time to learn that "Arab rejection of the state of Israel has led to ongoing conflict." See Dana Milbank, "Texas Creates the Perfect Curriculum for the Trump Age," *Washington Post*, September 18, 2018, online at https://www.washingtonpost.com/opinions/texas-creates-the-perfect-curriculum-for-the-trump-age/2018/09/18/32358f4c-bb7b-11e8-a8aa-860695e7f3fc_story.html?utm_term=.1d3305320505. The Texas school board decided that Hillary Clinton, Helen Keller, and Betty Friedan were "not necessary" historical figures for children to learn about and that omitting lessons on how government services are paid for was prudent because it would save a full *forty minutes* of third graders' time. The board estimates it will save fourth graders another thirty minutes by omitting a lesson on "holding officials to their word" because it was ostensibly not "grade appropriate."
53. This is known as the "principles/ideals" theory of American history à la Gunnar Myrdal. For a lucid discussion of the various renderings of the national creation myth and its descent, See Joel Olson, *The Abolition of White Democracy* (Minneapolis: University of Minnesota Press, 2004), xii–xvii.
54. Brendese, *Power of Memory*, 8–9.
55. Note those populations accused of making poor choices are conspicuously consonant with those previously denigrated by biological racism: those long criminalized and made deviant under other signs.

56. Martin Heidegger, *Being & Time*, trans. John Macquarrie and Edward Robinson (New York: Harper & Row, 2008). See esp. sections 72–77.
57. For Heidegger, the history of Western philosophy since Plato is a history of the forgetting of *Being*—that which all beings share.
58. A range of critics, spanning Charles Mills, Susan Moller Okin, and Sheldon Wolin, have argued that the existing inequalities attaching to particular differences put pressure on the "veil of ignorance" as a metric of justice since it effectively asks individuals to momentarily forget they are, say, women or persons of color when what matters is how their particular difference will be treated. See Charles Mills, *The Racial Contract* (Ithaca, NY: Cornell University Press, 1999); Susan Moller Okin, *Justice Gender and the Family* (New York: Basic Books, 1989), and "Political Liberalism, Justice and Gender," *Ethics* 105 (1994): 23–43; Sheldon S. Wolin, *The Presence of the Past: Essays on the State and the Constitution* (Baltimore: Johns Hopkins University Press, 1990), 38.
59. This is by no means a study of Heidegger. But note that Barbara Adam, for one, contends that "in social theory much lip-service is paid to the importance of [Heidegger's] work, but we search in vain in theories and studies of social time for the implications of his conceptualization." See Barbara Adam, *Time* (Malden, MA: Polity Press, 2004), 59.
60. Tommie Shelby, "Justice, Deviance and the Dark Ghetto," *Philosophy & Public Affairs* 35, no. 2 (2007): 126–160.
61. W. James Booth, *Communities of Memory: On Witness, Identity and Justice* (Ithaca, NY: Cornell University Press, 2006), 151. "Seen from that standpoint the weight of the weight of the past is not germane. . . . Not only does it not figure, but Locke can be read as supplanting it with an egalitarian, rights-based, and non-particularistic counter-memory."
62. Brendese, *Power of Memory*, 10–12. Despite his penchant for presentism in theory, Locke remained committed to preserving the right to inherit wealth across generations in practice.
63. John Paul Lederach, *The Moral Imagination* (New York: Oxford University Press, 2005), 131–147. Lederach, a reconciliation scholar and professional peacemaker, identifies a recurring overlap between space and time as a crucial part of the knowledge he has absorbed from a range of Indigenous peoples. Since Lederach's work involves negotiating hotly contested disputes among opposing parties, the political consequences of segregated time and temporality are seldom far from view.
64. If it seems difficult to imagine such a transgenerational sensibility in Washington, DC, it is because of segregated time.
65. Audra Simpson, *Mohawk Interruptus: Political Life across the Borders of Settler States* (Durham, NC: Duke University Press, 2014), 100. In her discussion of the Oka crisis, Simpson registers how what counts as an event in the eyes of the white settler state is apprehended as structural to the Mohawk.
66. This is how, for instance, America can alternately see itself as both "a nation of immigrants" *and* express fiercely anti-immigrant sentiment—and also move between each competing narrative without critical reflection on Native American presence

and absence. I discuss spectrality in relation to Derrida, Benjamin, and the critique of the metaphysics of presence in *The Power of Memory*, 104–125.
67. Walter Benjamin, "Theses on the Philosophy of History," in *Illuminations: Essays and Reflections*, ed. Hannah Arendt, trans. Harry Zohn (New York: Schocken, 1968), 254. To the extent that we expect something to happen next, but do not presume to know the content of the future in advance, we participate in what Walter Benjamin called "weak Messianic" time—or messianism without the Messiah.
68. Benjamin, *Illuminations*, 261.
69. Against the segregated memory of prevailing historicism, I shall contest the temporal logics implicated in theories of history by attending to their implication in lived experiences of race.
70. Nell Irvin Painter, *The History of White People* (New York: Norton, 2010), 388. American society at large also views whites as individuals in ways that people of color are not. Hence the people who massacre schoolchildren are overwhelmingly white and male, yet no matter how frequent the shootings are, there is not a call for a national conversation about derelict white culture and pathology. There is no equivalent to the *Moynihan Report* on the crisis of whiteness and the transgenerational delinquency among whites that produces such sociopathic behavior. In the main, those acts of terror are regarded as the acts of individual "lone wolves" without much question of how many wolves it takes to make a pack.
71. Among the consequences of segregated time and the carceral temporality of white time is that racialized grievances are registered as unintelligible in the hegemonic discourse, received as what Saidiya Hartmann and Steven Best call "Black noise" in conditions of fugitive justice. Stephen Best and Saidiya Hartman, "Fugitive Justice," *Representations* no. 92 (Fall 2005): 9.
72. The supposedly progressive proimmigrant statement that immigrants "do the jobs Americans can't do, or *won't* do" resonates as a form of biopolitics insofar as such jobs are undesirable precisely because they are often physically debilitating over time; entail dangerous, undercompensated, life-risking labor; and leave workers disproportionately exposed to human rights violations, isolation, and other maladies.
73. Latinx family separations dramatized today as unprecedented have historically been a terrifying reality for migrants as well as Indigenous peoples whose children were killed, kidnapped, enslaved, and sent away to abusive boarding schools. Chattel slavery devastated Indigenous and African American families for hundreds of years, violently severing bonds of kinship. Also, less dramatized, but arguably no less objectionable, is the deportation of undocumented parents of children who are US citizens, which the government has undertaken with the presumption that the children will accompany their parents back to their countries of origin. Some critics have even argued this amounts to a contemporary form of ethnic cleansing. See Adam Serwer, "Cruelty Is the Point," *The Atlantic*, October 3, 2018, online at https://www.theatlantic.com/ideas/archive/2018/10/the-cruelty-is-the-point/572104/.
74. Annie McClanahan, *Dead Pledges: Debt, Crisis, and Twenty-First-Century Culture* (Stanford, CA, Stanford University Press, 2017), 100.

Chapter 1

1. Simone Weil, *Lectures on Philosophy* (Cambridge: Cambridge University Press, 1978), 197.
2. Judith Butler, *Precarious Life* (London: Verso, 2006); Judith Butler, *Frames of War: When Is Life Grievable* (London: Verso, 2009).
3. Henri Bergson, *The Creative Mind: An Introduction to Metaphysics* (Mineola, NY: Dover Publications, 2007), 4.
4. Jennifer Mendelsohn, "Voices: We Won't Be OK While There Are Still Two Baltimores," *USA Today*, April 28, 2015, online at https://www.usatoday.com/story/news/nation/2015/04/28/we-are-not-ok-in-baltimore/26529001/.
5. While my treatment of time draws from a range of references, I have deliberately avoided anchoring the discussion to any single discourse of physics, phenomenology, historicism, etc., in favor of elucidating time and temporality as dynamic functions of contingent social formations.
6. Dan Thu Nguyen, "The Spatialization of Metric Time: The Conquest of Land and Labor in Europe and the United States," *Time & Society* 1, no. 1 (1992): 30.
7. W.E.B. Du Bois, "The Souls of White Folk," in *Darkwater: Voices from within the Veil* (New York: Harcourt Brace, 1920, Kindle ed.), 17.
8. Carlo Rovelli, *The Order of Time* (New York: Riverhead Books, 2018).
9. Yet, somewhat paradoxically, Einstein publicly argued against Bergson that "the time of the philosophers does not exist." There are many interpretations of the statement, but my bet is that Einstein misunderstood Bergson as advancing an understanding of time and duration incompatible with the principles of relativity as applicable across the board. See Jimena Canales, *The Physicist and the Philosopher: Einstein, Bergson and the Debate That Changed Our Understanding of Time* (Princeton, NJ: Princeton University Press, 2015), 19, 48.
10. Or a human divination with cosmic implications.
11. Adam, *Time*, 114–115.
12. Dean Buonomano, *Your Brain Is a Time Machine: The Neuroscience and Physics of Time* (New York: Norton, 2017), 35. In the seventh century, Pope Sabinianus decreed that monks should be summoned to prayer seven times a day. The coincidence between pastoral power of the clergy and that of the clock was a connection that would not be lost on later thinkers like Weber and Foucault.
13. Nanni, *Colonisation of Time*, 16; also see Eviatar Zerubavel, *The Seven Day Circle* (New York: Collier Macmillan, 1985).
14. All are the subjects of some of the most eminent theorists of modernity, not least Marx and Weber. For a seminal account, see E.P. Thompson, "Time, Work-Discipline and Industrial Capitalism," *Past & Present* 38 (December 1967): 56–97. For a contemporary study that builds on the interlocution of Marx and Weber in the context of present-day labor, see Benjamin H. Snyder, *The Disrupted Workplace: Time and the Moral Order of Flexible Capitalism* (New York: Oxford University Press, 2016).
15. Nanni, *Colonisation of Time*, 29.

16. Cedric Robinson, "Slavery and the Platonic Origins of Anti-Democracy," *National Political Science Review* 5 (1995): 31.
17. Rovelli, *The Order of Time*, 67–68.
18. Joe Sachs, *Aristotle's Physics: A Guided Study* (New Brunswick, NJ: Rutgers University Press), 121.
19. Descartes was intrigued that both the mind and the external world at large are in motion. Unsurprisingly, he deeply disliked history for its lack of precision.
20. As Aristotle puts it, "For we perceive time together with motion, and even if it were dark and we experienced nothing through the body, but a certain motion were present in the soul, immediately, a certain time would seem to happen along with it" (*Physics*, XI.219a). Quoted in Sachs, *Aristotle's Physics*, 121. For a thoughtful discussion of Aristotle's "vulgar" notion of time, see Nathan Widder, *Reflections on Time and Politics* (University Park: Pennsylvania State University Press, 2008), 13–21.
21. Rovelli, *The Order of Time*, 65. True time is accessible only through calculations such that even "natural days" are used for a measure of time and typically considered equal, though really they are not. For this reason, Newton contended, astronomers have to correct this inequality for a more accurate measure of celestial motions.
22. John G. Gunnell, *Political Philosophy and Time: Plato and the Origins of Political Vision* (Chicago: University of Chicago Press, 1987), 21. "In this way Kant avoided the relativism of the empiricists and made time meaningful for science while preserving its internal base. But the internalization of time inevitably put its 'reality' in jeopardy and made it a problem for psychology."
23. Of course, the move opens onto a number of questions about time's metaphysical standing, its status as a concept, linguistic representation, and experience.
24. Metaphysically, Kant argues in favor of an immortal soul even though he admits we cannot be certain of our immortality. Still, believing so allows us to pursue an approximation of moral perfection without presuming to do what would otherwise be impossible for fallible people in a lifetime. See David Couzens Hoy, *The Time of Our Lives: A Critical History of Temporality* (Cambridge, MA: MIT Press, 2009), Ch. 1.
25. Immanuel Kant, "The Idea for a Universal History with a Cosmopolitan Intent," in *Perpetual Peace and Other Essays on Politics, History, and Morals*, trans. Ted Humphrey (Indianapolis & Cambridge: Hackett Publishing Co., 1983) Charting a course of improvement from the ancient Greeks onward, Kant ultimately holds that nature's supreme objective is a universal cosmopolitan state.
26. Édouard Glissant, *Caribbean Discourse: Selected Essays*, trans. J. Michael Dash (Charlottesville: University Press of Virginia, 1999), 73. "For the Western mind, it is a matter of learning the natural Genesis, the primordial slime, the Eternal Garden, and embarking—even at the risk of condemnation . . . on a journey to an ordering-knowledge. History and Literature agree (with the rare episodes of a blending of the two that quickly came to an end, as with the pre-Socratic philosophers) to separate man from the world, to subject nature to culture. The linear nature of narrative and the linear form of chronology take shape in this context."

27. Kimberly Huchings, *Time and World Politics* (Manchester: Manchester University Press, 2008), 6. "Newton's theory of time did not presume an 'arrow of time,' but eighteenth- and nineteenth-century developments in physics (thermodynamics) and biology (evolution) suggested that time was not only infinite and linear but also unidirectional and irreversible."
28. Huchings, *Time and World Politics*, 6.
29. Just as important, albeit less remarked upon, *kairos* also includes all those random, seemingly trivial things that can snowball into an avalanche if the planets align just right. But to acknowledge as much suggests that the division starts to self-destruct as soon as it emerges.
30. Huchings, *Time and World Politics*, 7. As Huchings puts it, "Theories of history complicate the idea of *chronotic* time. The whole point of these theories is that the principle according to which the past, present and future is divided does not reflect the idea of time as a neutral measure of undifferentiated flow. Rather than world history being divided up into lumps of equal length, it is divided according to principles of comparative value, in which some times become seen as more significant, better, or worse, than others."
31. Thomas Friedman, "Foreign Affairs: The Real War," *New York Times*, November 27, 2001, online at https://www.nytimes.com/2001/11/27/opinion/foreign-affairs-the-real-war.html. Note that Friedman's claim is different from the argument that the resources of modernity are not evenly distributed. See Muqtedar Khan, "This Is What Happens When Modernity Fails All of Us," *New York Times*, December 6, 2015, online at https://www.nytimes.com/roomfordebate/2015/12/06/how-can-america-counter-the-appeal-of-isis/this-is-what-happens-when-modernity-fails-all-of-us.
32. See William E. Connolly, *A World of Becoming* (Durham, NC: Duke University Press, 2014); William E. Connolly, *The Fragility of Things* (Durham, NC: Duke University Press, 2014); William E. Connolly, *Facing the Planetary: Entangled Humanism and the Politics of Swarming* (Durham, NC: Duke University Press, 2016); William E. Connolly, *Pluralism* (Durham, NC: Duke University Press, 2014); William E. Connolly, *The Ethos of Pluralization* (Minneapolis: University of Minnesota Press, 1995).
33. David Christian, *Maps of Time: An Introduction to Big History* (Berkeley: University of California Press, 2004), 467.
34. See Jacqueline Stevens, "Political Scientists Are Lousy Forecasters," *New York Times*, June 23, 2012, online at https://www.nytimes.com/2012/06/24/opinion/sunday/political-scientists-are-lousy-forecasters.html.
35. Jairus Grove, "Of an Apocalyptic Tone Recently Adopted in Everything: The Anthropocene or Peak Humanity?," *Theory & Event* 8, no. 3 (2015).
36. See Jairus Grove, "The New Nature," *Boston Review*, January 11, 2016, online at http://bostonreview.net/forum/new-nature/jairus-grove-jairus-grove-response-jedediah-purdy. Françoise Vergès, "Racial Capitolocene," *Verso Books Blogs*, August 30, 2017, online at https://www.versobooks.com/blogs/3376-racial-capitalocene.

37. Katheryn Yusoff, *A Billion Black Anthropocenes or None* (Minneapolis: University of Minnesota Press, 2018).
38. Catherine A. MacKinnon, "Difference and Dominance: On Sex Discrimination," in *Theorizing Feminisms*, ed. Elizabeth Hackett and Sally Haslinger (New York: Oxford University Press, 2006), 244–253; Rohy, *Anachronism and Its Others*, xvi. Also see Lee Edelman, *No Future: Queer Theory and the Death Drive* (Durham, NC: Duke University Press, 2004); Jose Esteban Muñoz, *Cruising Utopia: The Then and There of Queer Futurity* (New York: New York University Press, 2009); Judith Halberstam, *The Queer Art of Failure* (Durham, NC: Duke University Press, 2011).
39. Aimé Césaire, *Discourse on Colonialism* (New York: Monthly Review Press, 2000), 46.
40. Achille Mbembe, *On the Postcolony* (Berkeley: University of California Press, 2001), 17.
41. Timothy Mitchell, *Carbon Democracy: Political Power in the Age of Oil* (London: Verso, 2012), 239; Connolly, *Facing the Planetary*.
42. Robbie Shilliam generatively resists this impulse in order to illuminate spaciotemporal relationships that disclose the cosmological conceits of colonial categories. See Robbie Shilliam, *The Black Pacific: Anticolonial Struggles and Oceanic Connections* (London: Bloomsbury, 2015), esp. 21–30; 135–137. See also Sanjay Seth, "'Once Was Blind but Now Can See': Modernity and the Social Sciences," *International Political Sociology* 7, no. 2 (2013): 136–151.
43. Musab Younis, "Race, War and Time: Haiti, Liberia and Ethiopia (1914–1945)," *Millennium* 46, no. 3 (2018): 352–370. Less recent, but no less relevant, is Siba N. Grovougi, "Come to Africa: A Hermeneutics of Race in International Theory," *Alternatives* 26, no. 4 (2001): 427–435.
44. For this reason, I avoid the language of a white "epistemic community" in favor of white time as a social artifact and white temporality as a normalizing political force. While I reference scientific studies of time perception, duration, phenomenology, etc., I do so modestly, as my focus will be on the politics and social formations that condition experiences and understandings of time—rather than seeking a universal metaphysic of time. Likewise, power can go missing in accounts that center on experiences of time as subjective. On this see Samuel A. Chambers, "Untimely Politics *Avant la Lettre*: The Temporality of Social Formations," *Time & Society* 20, no. 2 (2011): 197–223.
45. Hoy, *Time of Our Lives*, 235.
46. See Glen Sean Coulthard, *Red Skin / White Masks: Rejecting the Colonial Politics of Recognition* (Minneapolis: University of Minnesota Press, 2014); David Harvey, "The 'New' Imperialism: Accumulation by Dispossession." *Socialist Register* 40 (2004): 63–87; Cedric J. Robinson, *Black Marxism: The Making of the Black Radical Tradition* (Chapel Hill: University of North Carolina Press, 1983); Lisa Lowe, *The Intimacies of Four Continents* Durham: Duke University Press, 2015).
47. I am grateful to Samuel Chambers for bringing this to my attention.
48. After the Revolution, Indigenous land originally claimed by European powers became part of the United States.
49. Wolfe, *Traces of History*, 142.

50. On the discovery doctrine and its reverberations, see Wolfe, *Traces of History*, esp. 142–150. Formulated in response to the conquest of the Americas, the "doctrine" actually encompassed a range of defenses of European sovereignty that would become the law of nations, then simply international law. While the singularity implied by the term is misleading, it represents what Wolfe takes to be constant across an "apologetic repertoire." Also see Robert A. Williams Jr., *The American Indian in Western Legal Thought: The Discourses of Conquest* (New York: Oxford University Press, 1990). On the Salamanca School and the Spanish priests, see George E. Tinker, *Missionary Conquest: The Gospel and Native American Cultural Genocide* (Minneapolis: Fortress Press, 1993), esp. 7.
51. Wolfe, *Traces of History*, 142. Also see Evitar Zerubavel, *Time Maps: Collective Memory and the Social Shape of the Past* (Chicago: University of Chicago Press, 2003), 63–82. With respect to descent, Francisco de Vitoria intervened in the religious crisis precipitated by Columbus's discovery of peoples whose relationship to Adam was unclear. The tortured legal logic offers us a rendering of the privileged form of land title afforded to whites, and financial tools like the American mortgage that serve as vehicles of Indigenous dispossession, as I discuss in Chapter 4 on race and debt. Here, my interest is in the conditions of possibility that make such legal theft possible and actionable—and that raise questions about settler subjectivity and the entitled sense of time colonials would impose in order to get the title to the land.
52. Wolfe, *Traces of History*, 145.
53. Wolfe, *Traces of History*, 145.
54. As Wolfe notes, this cleaving of sovereignty would seem to present legal difficulties when it came to treaty negotiation; the reason being only sovereign nations could enter into negotiations and become signatories of international agreements. I do not reconstruct the tortured logic here, but the upshot was a convenient ascription of sovereign nation when it suited dispossession and removal and, as was the case in *McIntosh*, a relegation wto the status of "domestic dependent nations" as per the discovery doctrine.
55. Wolfe, *Traces of History*, 145–146. In this juridical sleight of hand, time really is of the essence. Blink and you'll miss the slick moves. First, the Court redeploys the instantaneity of the discovery doctrine's subordinate status of Indigenous people as having only rights of "occupancy" after the moment of European sovereign dominion. The problem this would seem to present is that only sovereign nations can enter into treaties and consensual agreements to alienate land.
56. See Kevin Bruyneel, *The Third Space of Sovereignty: The Postcolonial Politics of US-Indigenous Relations* (Minneapolis: University of Minnesota Press, 2007). On the hyperpaternalist discourse, see Michael Paul Rogin, *Fathers and Children: Andrew Jackson and the Subjugation of the American Indian* (New York: Routledge, 2017).
57. Wolfe, *Traces of History*, 155.
58. Mark Lamont Hill, *Nobody* (New York: Atria Books, 2016).
59. Jodi A. Byrd, *The Transit of Empire: Indigenous Critiques of Colonialism* (Minneapolis: University of Minnesota Press, 2011), 64; Aileen Moreton-Robinson, *The White*

Possessive: Property, Power and Indigenous Sovereignty (Minneapolis: University of Minnesota Press, 2015), 29–30.
60. Simpson, *Mohawk Interruptus*, 100.
61. On resetting the chronometer to zero as a strategy of power, see Eviatar Zerubavel, *Time Maps: Collective Memory and the Social Shape of the Past* (Chicago and London, University of Chicago Press, 2012), esp. pp. 2, 91–92.
62. Jean O'Brien, *Firsting and Lasting: Writing Indians out of Existence in New England* (Minneapolis: University of Minnesota Press, 2010).
63. Roxanne Dunbar-Ortiz and Dina Gilio-Whitaker, *"All the Real Indians Died Off": And 20 Other Myths about Native Americans* (Boston: Beacon Press, 2016).
64. Cheryl I. Harris, "Whiteness as Property," *Harvard Law Review* 106, no. 8 (1993): 1721. For an influential historical accounts refuting the myth of Europeans encountering wilderness in the Americas, see William Cronon, *Changes in the Land: Indians, Colonists, and the Ecology of New England* (New York: Hill & Wang, 2003); Charles C. Mann, *1491: New Revelations of the Americas before Columbus* (New York: Alfred A. Knopf, 2005).
65. I discuss this in the introduction.
66. For an account of the development of whiteness as property in the US context, see David R. Roediger, *How Race Survived US History: From Settlement to the Obama Phenomenon* (London: Verso Press, 2008).
67. Charles Mills, "White Time: The Chronic Injustice of Ideal Theory," *Du Bois Review* 11, no. 1 (2014): 27–42.
68. With respect to resonances, Mills and I share intellectual debts to Michael Hanchard, Lawrie Balfour, and Evitar Zerubel. Regarding my development of the concept independently, see P.J. Brendese, "Black Noise in White Time: Segregated Temporality and Mass Incarceration," in *Radical Future Pasts: Untimely Political Theory*, ed. Romand Coles, Mark Reinhardt, and George Shulman (Lexington: University Press of Kentucky, 2014), 81–111.
69. On this point, I follow Michel Foucault, *The Birth of Biopolitics: Lectures at the Collège de France, 1978-79*, trans. Graham Burchell (New York: Palgrave Macmillan, 2008), 63, 65. For Foucault, freedom is both consumed and produced by liberalism: the "art of government consumes freedom, which means it must produce it." "So freedom in the regime of liberalism is not a given, it is not a ready made region which has to be respected, or if it is, it is so only partially; regionally, in this case or that case, et cetera. Freedom is something which is constantly produced."
70. James Baldwin, "The Fire Next Time," in *The Price of the Ticket*, 378.
71. Du Bois, "Souls of White Folk," 19.
72. Du Bois, "Souls of White Folk," 26. "Where sections could not be owned by a dominant nation there came a policy of "open door," but the "door" was open to "white people only."
73. Du Bois, "Souls of White Folk," 17.
74. Harris, "Whiteness as Property," 1721. Harris is referencing the United States, but as Moreton-Robinson elucidates, this observation exceeds the United States.

75. When Rousseau famously observed that mankind is born free but is everywhere in chains, he conceded that his goal was not to unchain (hu)mankind, but to make those chains legitimate and even "force" subjects "to be free." The position I advance here is that it is long past time to ask what subjective experiences of temporality such risky propositions have bequeathed to a racialized world.
76. Du Bois, "Souls of White Folk," 27.
77. Ella Myers, "Beyond the Psychological Wage: Du Bois on White Dominion," *Political Theory* 47, no. 1 (2019): 12.
78. Harris, "Whiteness as Property," 1730.
79. Fanon troubles Marxist/Hegelian, materialist/idealist dialectical divides to locate the fixity in terms of temporality—a past that never seems to be completely digested by the dialectic under the prevailing order of time. For a thoughtful account that reads Fanon's work against the grain, while retaining Fanon's investment in dialectics without the teleological determinism with which dialectics are conventionally understood, see George Ciccariello-Maher, *Decolonizing Dialectics* (Durham, NC: Duke University Press, 2017).
80. Moreton-Robinson, *White Possessive*, 33–46; Du Bois, *Souls of Black Folk*; George Lipsitz, *How Racism Takes Place* (Philadelphia: Temple University Press, 2011).
81. Moreton-Robinson, *White Possessive*, xii.
82. Moreton-Robinson, *White Possessive*, xvii.
83. Jeremy Bentham, "Security and Equality in Property," in *Property: Mainstream and Critical Positions*, ed. C.B. Macpherson (1978), 51–52. Quoted in Harris, "Whiteness as Property," 1729.
84. Harris, "Whiteness as Property," 1729–1730.
85. Georg Lukács, *History and Class Consciousness*, quoted in Harris, "Whiteness as Property," 1730.
86. Radin, quoted in Harris, "Whiteness as Property," 1730.
87. Moreton-Robinson, *White Possessive*, xix.
88. I develop this point in the coming chapters.
89. Butler, *Frames of War*, 5.
90. This is what I take to be undergirding the dynamic Paul Butler elucidates as *Chokehold*. See Paul Butler, *Chokehold: Policing Black Men* (New York: New Press, 2017).
91. Barrington Moore, quoted in James C. Scott, *Domination and the Arts of Resistance* (New Haven: Yale University Press, 1990), 220.
92. See Richard Iton, *In Search of the Black Fantastic: Politics and Popular Culture in the Post-Civil Rights Era* (New York: Oxford University Press, 2008).
93. On subjectivity as temporality, see Mbembe, *On the Postcolony*, 15. "There is a close relationship between subjectivity and temporality—that, in some way, one can envisage subjectivity itself as temporality." For a sharp dilation on the implications of heterogeneous temporalities for decolonial political thought, see Gary Wilder, *Freedom Time: Negritude, Decolonization and the Future of the World* (Durham, NC: Duke University Press, 2015).
94. Locke, *Second Treatise of Government*, 19–22.

95. Glissant, *Caribbean Discourse*, 73; Kim Tall Bear, *Native American DNA: Tribal Belonging and the False Promise of Genetic Science* (Minneapolis: University of Minnesota Press, 2013).
96. Shannon Sullivan, *Revealing Whiteness: The Unconscious Habits of Racial Privilege* (Bloomington: Indiana University Press, 2006) Notably, Sullivan's critique of white entitlement extends beyond the usual suspects of the Far Right to address white liberals who transit into Black spaces to expand their (ontological) horizons. See also *Good White People: The Problem with Middle Class Anti-Racism* (Albany: State University of New York Press, 2014).

Chapter 2

1. Adam Gopnik, "The Caging of America," *New Yorker*, January 30, 2012, online at http://www.newyorker.com/arts/critics/atlarge/2012/01/30/120130crat_atlarge_gopnik.
2. Glen Loury, *Race, Incarceration and American Values* (Cambridge, MA: MIT Press, 2007), 5–6.
3. Gopnik, "The Caging of America." See also Vesla M. Weaver and Amy Lerman, "Political Consequences of the Carceral State," *American Political Science Review* 104, no. 4 (November 2010): 817. Weaver and Lerman write that "on any given day, about 1 in every 31 adults is currently in custody, on parole, or on probation."
4. Loïc Wacquant, "Deadly Symbiosis: When Ghetto and Prison Meet and Mesh," in *Mass Imprisonment: Social Causes and Consequences*, ed. D. Garland (Thousand Oaks, CA: Sage, 2001), 105.
5. W.E.B. Du Bois, *The Souls of Black Folk* (NY: Cosimo Classics, 2007), 1.
6. Angela Davis, *Are Prisons Obsolete?* (New York: Seven Stories Press, 2003), 44.
7. Amy E. Lerman and Vesla M. Weaver, *Arresting Citizenship: The Democratic Consequences of American Crime Control* (Chicago: University of Chicago Press, 2014). Lerman and Weaver call the phenomenon "custodial citizenship."
8. Fabian, *Time and the Other*, 25–35.
9. Freeman, "Introduction," 160.
10. Pierre Bourdieu, *Outline of a Theory of Practice* (New York: Cambridge University Press, 1977), 167.
11. Despite historically being racialized as closer to nature and as wasting time, the majority of Indigenous peoples in the United States live in cities, not on reservations.
12. See Mike Mills, "Who Are Police Killing?," Center on Juvenile and Criminal Justice, August 26, 2014, online at http://www.cjcj.org/news/8113.
13. Segregated time is apparent when, for instance, acts of racial terror are conceptualized as flashbacks, episodic and isolated, or part of a present divorced from a society historically constituted on such violence.
14. See P.J. Brendese, "Worlds Neither New Nor Brave: Racial Terror in America," *Theory & Event* 20, no. 1 (January 2017): 24–43.

15. The expression of surprise is itself revelatory of segregated temporality. As an affective reaction to an interruption of temporal continuity, shock can betray one's subject position and orientation to time. The whiteness of surprise was apparent when, for instance, the attacks of 9/11 were billed as the first instance of terrorism in the United States. Asking for whom, exactly, terrorism is new discloses the intersection between segregated memory and segregated time.
16. Ruha Benjamin, *Race after Technology: Abolitionist Tools for the New Jim Code* (Cambridge: Polity Press, 2019), 13–17.
17. While it is certainly true that the discourse of rehabilitation is no longer operative, the prison abolition movement is indebted to a long and established literature by inmates that is a genre unto itself.
18. Places like Baltimore, which the American president declared not desirable for human habitation—with "human" conspicuously tantamount to "white." Wilborn P. Nobles III, "Trump Calls Baltimore 'Disgusting . . . Rodent Infested Mess,' Rips Rep. Elijah Cummings over Border Criticism," *Baltimore Sun*, July 27, 2019, online at https://www.baltimoresun.com/politics/bs-md-pol-cummings-trump-20190727-chty2yovtvfzfcjkeaui7wm5zi-story.html. In the case of post-Katrina New Orleans, I remember hearing one NPR commentator going back further, describing it as a Hobbesian state of nature.
19. James Baldwin, "A Report from Occupied Territory," in *Price of the Ticket*, 415–424.
20. Frantz Fanon, *The Wretched of the Earth*, trans. Richard Philcox (New York: Grove Press, 2004), 6, 15, 43. Studies and debates over the legacy of colonialism as inhabiting present-day spaces of internal colonization are increasingly resurgent with the militarization of police. See, for example, Chris Hayes, *A Colony in a Nation* (New York: Norton, 2018). I say "resurgent" to acknowledge the vibrant tradition of Black scholars and activists who have long theorized the imprint of colonialism, spanning Aimé Césaire and the Black Panthers to Harold Cruse's 1962 essay "Revolutionary Nationalism and the Afro-American," to the work of Marcus Garvey and his acrimonious disagreements with W.E.B. Du Bois, Paul Robeson, and Eric Williams's *Capitalism and Slavery* (Philadelphia: Great Library Collection, 2005), to name but a few. Also see Nikhil Pal Singh, *Black Is a Country: Race and the Unfinished Struggle for American Democracy* (Cambridge, MA: Harvard University Press, 2014), esp. 174–212.
21. Lawrence Brown, "Two Baltimores: The White L vs. the Black Butterfly," *City Paper*, June 28, 2016, online at https://www.citypaper.com/bcpnews-two-baltimores-the-white-l-vs-the-black-butterfly-20160628-htmlstory.html.
22. Michelle Alexander, *The New Jim Crow: Mass Incarceration in the Age of Colorblindness* (New York: New Press, 2010), 6; emphasis mine. Alexander also notes that, in less than thirty years, the US penal population grew from around three hundred thousand to over two million.
23. Michael Tonry, *Punishing Race* (New York: Oxford University Press, 2010), 1; Weaver and Lerman, "Political Consequences," 817. "Carceral contact is not randomly distributed, but is both spatially and racially concentrated. On any given day, 11% of

black men aged 25 to 29 years are incarcerated ... and one third of black men aged 20 to 29 years are under some type of correctional supervision."

24. Michelle Alexander, "The Age of Obama as Racial Nightmare," March 8, 2010, blog post at Tom Dispatch.com, online at http://www.tomdispatch.com/archive/175215/.
25. To be sure, African Americans are not the only racial others whose spatiotemporal presence posed a challenge. And racial advances were not the only kinds of progress that were viewed as accelerating threats.
26. See also Thomas Edsall and Mary Edsall, *Chain Reaction: The Impact of Race, Rights and Taxes on American Politics* (New York: Norton, 1992).
27. The urgent need to bring these arguments to the fore is further underscored by the erasures of segregated memory that work to conceal the state-sponsored fortification of segregated time. See Brendese, *Power of Memory*.
28. Hannah Arendt, *Between Past and Future: Eight Exercises in Political Thought* (New York: Penguin Books, 1968), 10.
29. Joseph Lowndes, *The Southern Origins of Modern Conservatism* (New Haven: Yale University Press, 2008).
30. Edsall and Edsall, *Chain Reaction*, 224.
31. Vesla Weaver, "Frontlash: Race and the Development of Punitive Crime Policy," *Studies in American Political Development* 21 (Fall 2007): 230.
32. Weaver, "Frontlash," 234, 247–250.
33. Weaver, "Frontlash," 238. The political capital gained by conservatives through advocacy of harshly punitive policies was especially available from lower- and lower-middle-class whites. Working-class whites felt that they bore a disproportionate share of the costs of racial equality and integration, and might be left behind in an increasingly uncertain future. Affluent whites who could afford private schools were less likely to be affected by measures of enforced integration such as busing. Lower- income whites were also more likely to feel their tenuous grip on the American Dream was threatened by affirmative action and competition with Blacks for blue-collar jobs. Hence affirmative action was an instrumental wedge-issue that proved especially useful in dividing the electorate, accruing to a Republican advantage. See Edsall and Edsall, *Chain Reaction*, 186.
34. Weaver, "Frontlash," 238.
35. Edsall and Edsall, *Chain Reaction*, 148.
36. See David R. Roediger, *How Race Survived U.S. History* (London: Verso, 2008), 207. Roediger notes that Reagan's proficiency and ease with "code words such as 'states' rights,' 'welfare moms,' 'quotas,' and 'reverse racism' were key to his success at winning over 'Reagan Democrats' via racial appeals." In effect, he used a tried and tested racial bribe to build upon the reaction to the 1964 Civil Rights Act that Earle and Merle Black term the "Great White Shift in Presidential Voting." Earle Black and Merle Black, *The Rise of Southern Republicans* (Cambridge, MA: Harvard University Press, 2002), 205–240.
37. Stuart Schrader, *Badges without Borders: How Global Counterinsurgency Transformed American Policing* (Berkeley: University of California Press, 2019), 40–42.
38. Gilmore, *Golden Gulag*, 247.

39. Michel Foucault, *Security, Territory, Population: Lectures at the Collège de France 1977–1978*, ed. Michel Senellart, trans. Graham Burchell (New York: Picador, 2007), 118.
40. Roger-Pol Droit, "Michel Foucault, on the Role of Prisons," trans. Leonard Mayhew, *New York Times*, August 5, 1975, unpaginated interview, online at http://movies2.nytimes.com/books/00/12/17/specials/foucault-prisons.html. Foucault writes: "Lawbreaking is not an accident, a more or less unavoidable imperfection. Rather, it is a positive element of the functioning of society. Its role is part of a general strategy. Every legislative arrangement sets up privileged and profitable areas where the law can be violated, others where it can be ignored and others where infractions are sanctioned."
41. Schrader, *Badges without Borders*, 41.
42. Kahlil Gibran Muhammad, *The Condemnation of Blackness: Race, Crime and the Making of Modern Urban America* (Cambridge, MA: Harvard University Press, 2010). Especially compelling is Muhammad's analysis of the nineteenth-century labor movement's invocation of a "white slavery" narrative and sympathetic, and politically effective, portrayals of European immigrants by advocates such as Jane Addams. This is in relative contrast to powerful and compelling works addressing the enduring imprint of *actual* slavery by authors like Ida B. Wells and W.E.B. Du Bois, which did not gain the same political traction. On the role of the federal government in subsidizing European immigrant progress, see Ira Katznelson, *When Affirmative Action Was White: An Untold History of Racial Inequality in Twentieth-Century America* (New York: Norton, 2005).
43. Kevin R. Johnson, "How Racial Profiling in America Became the Law of the Land," *Georgetown Law Review* 98, no. 4 (2010): 1005–1077.
44. Note that, even in cities like Baltimore where homicides have increased over the past decade, there is little compelling evidence that more police would lead to less murders. Not only does Baltimore have an outsized police force relative to its population, almost 70 percent of homicides committed in 2019 remained unsolved. See Jessica Anderson, "Baltimore Ending the Year with 32% Homicide Clearance Rate, One of the Lowest in Decades," *Baltimore Sun*, December 30, 2019, online at https://www.baltimoresun.com/maryland/baltimore-city/bs-md-ci-crime-policy-20191230-zk2v2auuhbgq3f7zsh3t7rt6cm-story.html.
45. Janet Lauritsen and Robert J. Sampson, "Minorities, Crime and Criminal Justice," in *The Handbook of Crime and Punishment*, ed. Michael Tonry (New York: Oxford University Press, 1998), 58–84. Quoted in Lawrence D. Bobo and Victor Thompson, "Racialized Mass Incarceration: Poverty, Prejudice and Punishment," in *Doing Race: 21 Essays for the 21st Century*, ed. Hazel Rose Markus and Paula M.L. Moya (New York: Norton, 2010), 335–336. The notorious federal "100-to-1" law instituted in 1986 punished the sale of crack cocaine one hundred times as severely as that of powder cocaine—even though the substances have virtually identical pharmaceutical properties. As criminologists Janet Lauritsen and Robert Sampson write, while "crack cocaine has generated an intense law enforcement campaign in our nation's

Black ghettos, 'powder' cocaine use among whites is quietly neglected (perhaps even portrayed as fashionable). These differences cannot be attributed to objective levels of criminal danger, but rather to the way in which minority behaviors are symbolically constructed and subjected to official social control." See Marvin D. Free Jr., ed., *Race and Criminal Justice in the United States* (New York: Praeger Publishers, 2003), 6. Also see Bruce Western, *Punishment and Inequality in America* (New York: Russell Sage Foundation, 2006), 64.

46. Alexander, *New Jim Crow*, 6–7.
47. Tonry, *Punishing Race*, 1, 22. By 1992 African Americans and Hispanics accounted for almost 90 percent of all drug sentences to state prisons. See Marc Mauer, "Young Black Americans and the Criminal Justice System," in *States of Confinement: Policing, Detention and Prisons*, ed. Joy James (New York: St. Martin's Press, 2000), 80.
48. See the interview in *Bill Moyers Journal*, Brian Stevenson & Michelle Alexander, PBS. April 2, 2010. Online at https:// www.pbs.org/ moy ers/ jour nal/ 04022 010/ tran scri pt1.html.
49. Gilmore, *Golden Gulag*, 108.
50. Legal definitions of status offenses vary, but the term most frequently refers to juvenile crimes that cannot be committed by adults. More broadly, status offenses apply to a certain class, sex, religion, or race of people—such as laws prohibiting men from using a women's restroom or antimiscegenation laws. Gang membership, for example, is a status offense.
51. In a precursor of things to come, the law mandated a creation of a rolling database of alleged gang members liable for elevated persecution if they had future encounters with law enforcement. See Gilmore, *Golden Gulag*, 107. Gilmore notes that Maxine Waters (D-Los Angeles) sponsored sentence-enhancing legislation, and "almost everybody sponsored some law, collectively creating a plethora of new crimes for the state's fifty-eight district attorneys to prosecute." See also Naomi Nakamura, *The First Civil Right: How Liberals Built Prison America* (New York: Oxford University Press, 2014).
52. Allen Feldman, *Formations of Violence*, cited in Gilmore, *Golden Gulag*, 235; Douglass quoted in Philip S. Foner, *The Life and Writings of Frederick Douglass*, vol. 4, *Reconstruction and After* (New York: International Publishers, 1955), 379. In the context of slavery (a condition of legal/social death if ever there was one) the extent to which an enslaved individual's humanity was acknowledged bore a direct relationship to one's criminal culpability.
53. Desmond S. King and Rogers M. Smith, *Still a House Divided: Race and Politics in Obama's America* (Princeton, NJ: Princeton University Press, 2011), 7.
54. Bobo and Thompson, "Racialized Mass Incarceration," 339.
55. Counting prisoners in the census tracts where they are incarcerated reduces the political power of their home region, while enlarging the representational power of district where the facility is sited. See Gary Hunter and Peter Wagner, "Prisons, Politics and the Census," in *Prison Profiteers: Who Makes Money from Mass Incarceration*, ed. Tara

Herivel and Paul Wright (New York: New Press, 2007), 80–90. To be clear, none of this implies that the grim evolution of late twentieth-century racialized mass incarceration is without historical precedent. Nor is imprisonment itself an especially recent means of perpetuating racial domination. See Douglas A. Blackmon, *Slavery by Another Name: The Re-Enslavement of Black Americans from the Civil War to World War II* (New York: Anchor Books, 2009); and Scott Reynolds Nelson, *Steel Drivin' Man: John Henry, The Untold Story of an American Legend* (New York: Oxford University Press, 2006). Richard Nixon's 1968 "law and order" campaign deliberately conflated criminal activity with the Vietnam War protests, race riots, and the civil rights movement to gin up support for heightened government control with an emphasis on African Americans. See Marc Mauer, *Race to Incarcerate* (New York: The New Press, 2006), 52.

56. Marie Gottschalk, *Caught: The Prison State and the Lockdown of American Politics* (Princeton: Princeton University Press, 2015), 254–256.
57. Note that many of the titles cited here connote a disruption of linear, progressive time: *The New Jim Crow*, *Slavery by Another Name*, *The Unsteady March*, *Still a House Divided*, and so on.
58. See the interview in *Bill Moyers Journal*, Brian Stevenson & Michelle Alexander, PBS. April 2, 2010. Online at https://www.pbs.org/moyers/journal/04022010/transcript1.html.
59. Lauren Berlant, *Cruel Optimism* (Durham, NC: Duke University Press, 2011).
60. Jeff Manza and Christopher Uggen, "Punishment and Democracy: Disenfranchisement of Nonincarcerated Felons in the United States," *Perspectives on Politics* 2, no. 3 (September 2004): 494–495.
61. Western, *Punishment and Inequality*, 193.
62. Nikhil Pal Singh, *Race and America's Long War* (Berkeley: University of California Press, 2017), 45, 140–150; Michael Gorup, "The Strange Fruit of the Tree of Liberty: Lynch Law and Popular Sovereignty in the United States," *Perspectives on Politics* 3, no. 18 (September 2020): 819–834.
63. The phrase is Michelle Alexander's. See *New Jim Crow*, 34.
64. See Alex S. Vitale, *The End of Policing* (New York: Verso Press, 2018).
65. Phillip A. Goff, Matthew C. Jackson, Brooke Allison Lewis Di Leone, Carmen M. Culotta, and Natalie A. DiTomasso, "The Essence of Innocence: Consequences of Dehumanizing Black Children," *Journal of Personality and Social Psychology* 106, no. 4 (2014): 526–545.
66. Examples are numerous, with many not widely reported. To date there is no federal requirement for the ongoing maintenance of a database of police killings.
67. From "Ella's Song," written by Bernice Johnson Reagon of Sweet Honey in the Rock. With so many cast violently out of time surreptitiously, and so many survivors with publicly ungrievable losses, activists from Rev. William Barber II to Alice Green, director of the Center for Law and Justice in Albany, New York (where I interned as a college student), have called for truth commissions to address relatively invisible police violence.
68. Esp. see Dorothy Roberts, *Killing the Black Body: Race, Reproduction and the Meaning of Liberty* (New York: Vintage Books, 2017); Davis, *Are Prisons Obsolete?*, 60–83.

69. Gottschalk, *Caught*, 257.
70. Race-making projects innovate and uncannily even seem to incorporate elements of science fiction futures. The film *Minority Report* is set in a dystopian time when authorities use technology to arrest subjects before they commit a crime. The fictional story of precrime prevention foretold much of what is happening in real life today as power infuses racial fictions with cybernetic innovations.
71. Jackie Wang, *Carceral Capitalism* (South Pasadena, CA: Semiotext(e), 2018), 48–50. Also see Safiya Umoja Noble, *Algorithms of Oppression: How Search Engines Reinforce Racism* (New York: New York University Press, 2018); Ruha Benjamin, ed., *Captivating Technology: Race, Carceral Technoscience, and Liberatory Imagination in Everyday Life* (Durham, NC: Duke University Press, 2019); Bernard Harcourt, *Against Prediction: Profiling, Policing and Punishment in an Actuarial Age* (Chicago: University of Chicago Press, 2007).
72. Fabricated notions of Time pretending to be neutral and universal leave little or no room for thinking and living time otherwise—and thus are not accommodating to those whose very presence evokes a different sense of time. The possibility of encountering different times and different peoples is the pluripotentiality of *kairotic* becoming.
73. Wang, *Carceral Capitalism*, 48.
74. O'Neil, *Weapons of Math Destruction* (New York: Broadway Books, 2017).
75. Harcourt, *Against Prediction*, 24.
76. Jackie Wang, *Carceral Capitalism*, 43. Reflecting on the *technes* of predictive policing in relation to race, she notes that her brother is serving a four-year prison term while she completes a doctorate at Harvard.
77. Errol Morris, "Who Is Dangerous, and Who Dies?," *New York Times*, June 7, 2017, online at https://www.nytimes.com/2017/06/07/opinion/errol-morris-interview-death-penalty.html?_r=0.
78. Bill Chappell, "California Prison Sterilizations Reportedly Echo Eugenics Era," *NPR News*, July 9, 2013, online at https://www.npr.org/sections/thetwo-way/2013/07/09/200444613/californias-prison-sterilizations-reportedly-echoes-eugenics-era.
79. Friedrich Nietzsche, *On the Genealogy of Morals* and *Ecce Homo*, trans. Walter Kaufmann and R.J. Hollingdale (New York: Vintage Books, 1989), 81.
80. Peter Osborne, *The Politics of Time: Modernity and the Avant-Garde* (London: Verso Books, 1995), xxii.
81. See Meagan Parker Brooks, *A Voice That Could Stir an Army: Fannie Lou Hamer and the Rhetoric of the Black Freedom Movement* (Jackson: University Press of Mississippi, 2014). A bold and fearless advocate, Hamer was known for being as silent about her personal problems as she was vocal about racial justice.
82. As I discuss in the next chapter, racial others are also categorized as expendable tools for shoring up the contingencies of white time.
83. Rohy, *Anachronism and Its Others*, 34. Also see Hanchard, "Afro-Modernity," 267. From the vantage of subordinate temporalities, Hanchard makes a related point in his exposition of what he calls "racial time": "Afro-Modernity is at once a part of and apart from the parameters of Western modernities."
84. Berlant, "Slow Death," 754.

85. Berlant, "Slow Death," 760.
86. Davis, *Are Prisons Obsolete?*, 17–18.
87. Dent, quoted in Davis, *Are Prisons Obsolete?*, 18.
88. Interestingly, Davis recalls interviewing women in Cuban prisons whose awareness of prisons prior to incarceration came from Hollywood films. Davis, *Are Prisons Obsolete?*, 18.
89. Berlant, *Cruel Optimism*, 101.
90. J. Peter Euben, *Platonic Noise* (Princeton: Princeton University Press, 2003), 12–13. White noise has multiple meanings for Euben. It represents the distortion and vertigo produced by a present-centered culture intoxicated by streams of endless information vacant of historical context.
91. Euben, *Platonic Noise*, 12–13.
92. Euben, *Platonic Noise*, 168.
93. Stephen Best and Saidiya Hartman, "Fugitive Justice," *Representations* no. 92 (Fall 2005): 9.
94. Chuck D, quoted in David Thorpe, *Bomb* no. 68 (Summer 1999), online at http://bombsite.com/issues/68/articles/2251. For an illuminating account of the limits and possibilities of hip-hop for Black politics, see Lester K. Spence, *Stare in the Darkness: The Limits of Hip-Hop and Black Politics* (Minneapolis: University of Minnesota Press, 2011). Regarding racialized strategies employed to disrupt sonic contributions such as jazz, see Michael Paul Rogin, *Blackface / White Noise* (Berkeley: University of California Press, 1996).
95. Euben, *Platonic Noise*, 12–13. "It is supermarket labels that erase the origins of white man's food and the lives of people in twenty countries that produce it."
96. Euben, *Platonic Noise*, 168.
97. N.W.A., *Straight Outta Compton* (LA: Ruthless Records, 1988), Track 2; Public Enemy, *It Takes a Nation of Millions to Hold Us Back* (New York: Def Jam / Columbia, 1988), Track 2.
98. For an account of its more subversive elements, see Bruce Banhart, *Jazz in the Time of the Novel: The Temporal Politics of American Race and Culture* (Tuscaloosa: The University of Alabama Press, 2013).
99. Frederick Douglass, *My Bondage and My Freedom* (New York: Miller, Orton & Co. 1857), 100.
100. Saidiya V. Hartman, *Scenes of Subjection: Terror, Slavery and Self-Making in Nineteenth Century America* (New York: Oxford University Press, 1997), 25.
101. Baldwin, *Price of the Ticket*, 65.
102. Baldwin, *Price of the Ticket*, 65.
103. Michel Foucault, *"Society Must Be Defended" Lectures at the College de France 1975––1976*, trans. David Macey, ed. Mauro Bertani and Alessandro Fontana (New York: Picador, 2003), 247. Hereafter abbreviated in text as SMDB. This is not to say there are not white modes of perception that register racial grievances with a sense of history, and even righteous indignation.
104. Hartman, *Scenes of Subjection*, 35.

105. Hartman, *Scenes of Subjection*, 47.
106. Hurston, quoted in Tracey Morison, "Trans: Transgender Life Stories from South Africa," *Culture, Health and Sexuality* 15 (2013): 111. Speaking politically, my thinking is informed by a range of scholars in the Black radical tradition from Solomon Northrup and Frederick Douglass through Ralph Ellison, James Baldwin, Saidiya Hartman, Claudia Rankine, Christina Sharpe, and the many others who have variously registered the long history of racialized suffering as occasions of profane white leisure and enjoyment.
107. Euben, *Platonic Noise*, 168.
108. Kimberly "Sweet Brown" Wilkins speaks to this aspect of white time in her tragicomic catchphrase "Ain't nobody got time for that." I am grateful to Chris LeBron for this connection.
109. At risk of overextending the metaphor, people purchase white noise machines because they provide comfort—even the chance to sleep and dream.
110. Nietzsche, *On the Genealogy of Morals and Ecce Homo*, 69.
111. With respect to First Nations, critics of how Native Americans are portrayed, such as Philip J. Deloria, Michael Paul Rogin, Ward Churchill, and Cree filmmaker Neil Diamond (to name but a few), have sought to interrupt the ease with which Native peoples are dissimulated through symbols, artifacts, and caricatures while actual Indigenous existence and voices are denied. See Philip J. Deloria, *Playing Indian* (New Haven: Yale University Press, 1998), Rogin, *Fathers and Children*; Ward Churchill, *Indians Are Us: Culture and Genocide in Native North America* (Common Courage Press, 1993); Neil Diamond, *Reel Injun: On the Trail of the Hollywood Indian*, PBS Documentary, November 2, 2010. Online at https://www.pbs.org/independentlens/documentaries/reel-injun/.
112. For example, in Frank B. Wilderson's study of race and cinema, *Red, White and Black*, he distinguishes white supremacy from antiblackness, with the latter connoting a structure of feeling that is nonidentical to ideology or political institutions as they are conventionally conceived. In so doing, he parses ascribed racial distinctions that make a difference aesthetically and politically. See Frank B. Wilderson III, *Red, White & Black: Cinema and the Structure of U.S. Antagonisms* (Durham, NC: Duke University Press, 2010).
113. Hanchard, "Afro-Modernity," 265.
114. Instances like police executions that remain largely unchecked and recursive demonstrate the breadth and continuity of a possessive investment in whiteness. In Chapter 4 I contend that they serve to increase the credit value of whiteness as property over time.
115. Bauman, *Liquid Modernity*, 94.
116. I am grateful to William E. Connolly for generative conversations around the issue.
117. Droit, "Foucault on the Role of Prisons."
118. Droit, "Foucault and the Role of Prisons." One could easily go down the list of criminalized drugs in the United States and identify the specific racial populations to be managed by the criminalization of each substance through history; marijuana (Hispanics), opium (Chinese), cocaine (African Americans).

119. Michel Foucault, *Discipline and Punish: The Birth of the Prison*, trans. Alan Sheridan (New York: Vintage Books, [1977] 1995), 173. Hereafter citations appear in the text as "DP." Recall that the dream of the panoptical society was the simultaneity of the gaze, the capacity to ultimately make everyone visible *at the same time.*

120. Note that Foucault's ultimate intellectual destination was neither the spatial architectonics of Bentham's panopticon nor its particular articulations in places like Philadelphia's Eastern State Penitentiary. See Droit, "Foucault and the Role of Prisons." Foucault was writing at a time when the discourse of prison as rehabilitative was still in the air, a rationale that made him fear that criminal psychiatry and psychology "risk becoming the ultimate alibi behind which the prevailing system will hide in order to remain unchanged."

121. I say this because the discussion of Indian schools as cultural re-education camps tends to obscure the fact that these were sites of physical violence, torture, and murder.

122. Andrea Smith, *Conquest: Sexual Violence and American Indian Genocide* (Durham, NC: Duke University Press, 2005), 35–36.

123. Smith, *Conquest*, 35–54. Smith notes that "primary role of this education for Indian girls was to inculcate patriarchal norms into Native communities so that women would lose their place of leadership in Native communities" (37).

124. Smith, *Conquest*, 36.

125. Coulthard, *Red Skin / White Masks*, 127.

126. Best and Hartman, "Fugitive Justice," 3.

127. This is not just due to my own lack of time and space, but because treating the subject with fidelity, I think, means convening a community—as opposed to being the work of a single author.

128. The phrase is often attributed to Indigenous scholar-activist Winona LaDuke.

129. Hanchard, "Afro-Modernity," 252–253, 267; Homi K. Bhabha, ed., *Nation and Narration* (London: Routledge, 1990), 306; Elizabeth Grosz, *The Nick of Time: Politics, Evolution and the Untimely* (Durham, NC: Duke University Press, 2004), 258–261; Richard Iton, *In Search of the Black Fantastic* (New York: Oxford University Press, 2008), 290; Neil Roberts, *Freedom as Marronage* (Chicago: University of Chicago Press, 2015); Chakrabarty, *Provincializing Europe*.

130. George Cicarello-Maher's *Decolonizing Dialectics* invokes a vision of the dialectic that avoids this circularity.

131. Robert Nichols, "The Colonialism of Incarceration," *Radical Philosophy Review* 2, no. 17 (2014): 436. In Canada, aboriginal peoples comprise only 3–4 percent of the population but make up 27 percent of the provincial incarcerated and 20 percent of federal inmates—with Indigenous women representing the fastest-growing population of the imprisoned.

132. Nichols, "The Colonialism of Incarceration," 449.

133. Gilmore, *Golden Gulag*, 14.

134. Esp. see the superb book by Nick Estes, *Our History Is the Future* (New York: Verso Press, 2019).

135. Nichols, "The Colonialism of Incarceration," 446.

136. See Bruyneel, *Third Space of Sovereignty*.
137. Nichols, "The Colonialism of Incarceration," 437.
138. George Jackson, "Soledad Brother and Blood in My Eyes (Excerpts)," in *Warfare in the American Homeland: Policing and Prison in a Penal Democracy*, ed. Joy James (Durham, NC: Duke University Press, 2007), 129.
139. Jackson, "Soledad Brother," 129.
140. Jackson, "Soledad Brother," 131.
141. Jackson, "Soledad Brother," 131.
142. Jackson, "Soledad Brother," 132–133.
143. Jackson, "Soledad Brother," 135.
144. Jackson, "Soledad Brother," 135. Jackson quotes from Gerassi's *The Coming of the New International*.
145. Jackson, "Soledad Brother," 123.
146. Jackson, "Soledad Brother," 21.
147. See Ann Laura Stoler, *Race and the Education of Desire: Foucault's History of Sexuality and the Colonial Order of Things* (Durham, NC: Duke University Press, 1995); Alexander Weheliye, *Habeus Viscus: Racializing Assemblages, Biopolitics, and Black Feminist Theories of the Human* (Durham, NC: Duke University Press, 2014); Moreton-Robinson, *The White Possessive*, 125–137.
148. It is heartening that scholars have begun to confront this head-on. For an excellent analysis of Foucault's thinking as influenced by the Black Panthers, see Delio Vasquez, "Illegalist Foucault, Criminal Foucault," *Theory & Event* 23, no. 4 (October 2020): 935–972; see also Andrew Dilts and Peter Zurn, eds., *Active Intolerance: Michel Foucault, the Prisons Information Group and the Future of Abolition* (London: Palgrave, 2016).
149. The governmental powers of the state being the domain in which the criminal justice system was traditionally assumed to reside.
150. Ian Urbina, "Prison Labor Fuels the American War Machine," in Herivel and Wright, *Prison Profiteers*, 109–119.
151. Schrader, *Badges without Borders*, 24.
152. Schrader, *Badges without Borders*, 20–21. The book provides a rich account of how techniques of professionalization and technologies of proactive policing have been disseminated abroad through practices of "training trainers," weapons, and equipment—and then repatriated from the colonies and brought home.
153. Jeanne Morefield, *Empires without Imperialism: Anglo-American Decline and the Politics of Deflection* (New York: Oxford University Press, 2014); Eduardo Bonilla-Silva, *Racism without Racists: Colorblind Racism and the Persistence of Inequality in America* (Lanham, MD: Rowman & Littlefield, 2018).
154. Schrader, *Badges without Borders*, 50.
155. Schrader, *Badges without Borders*, 48.
156. Schrader, *Badges without Borders*, 267. "Professionalization [of police] also differed from modernization. Its itinerary and chronology were not 'bonded to the nation-state' whereas modernization presupposed and hypostatized the nation-state as a container for its unfolding stages. The presumption, however, occluded

the relationship of modernization to capitalism, as the itinerary of capitalism intersected but exceeded the nation-state. Unlike modernization, police professionalization addressed itself to a set of institutions and social problems at once smaller and greater than the nation-state."
157. I discuss this at length in Chapter 4.
158. Hence the familiar apologia that race is irrelevant to police violence because those violated should have just followed orders. The imperative to follow police directives no matter what applies to any dissident behavior coded as insurgency; including nonviolent protest, or simply being incredulous in the face of racist "stop and frisk" tactics. See Bernard Harcourt, *Illusion of Order: The False Promise of Broken Windows Policing* (Cambridge, MA: Harvard University Press, 2001).

Interlude 1

1. Grosz, *Nick of Time*, 249. "Indeed, the very notion of a model entails spatialization and resists duration; space is the ongoing metaphoric site for the representation of temporal qualities. Yet the 'logic' of temporality does not involve static self-identical terms, terms that can be laid side by side and compared, but those more appropriate to the self-changing, that which has no self-identity but continually differs from itself."
2. I am grateful to Rom Coles for the inspiration to turn to Rancière, and to Sam Chambers for generative conversations on the temporal aspects of the distribution of the sensible. See Samuel A. Chambers, *The Lessons of Rancière* (New York: Oxford University Press, 2013).
3. Jacques Rancière, "The Method of Equality: An Answer to Some Questions," in *Jacques Rancière: History, Politics, Aesthetics*, ed. Gabrielle Rockhill and Philip Watts (Durham, NC: Duke University Press, 2009), 282.
4. Rancière, "Method of Equality," 282.
5. Rancière, "Method of Equality," 282–283.
6. Jacques Rancière, *Dis-agreement* (Minneapolis: University of Minnesota Press, 1999), 9.
7. Rancière, *Dis-agreement*, 11.
8. Rancière, *Dis-agreement*, 18.
9. Rancière, *Dis-agreement*, 22–23.
10. Rancière, *Dis-agreement*, 24–26.
11. Rancière, *Dis-agreement*, 30.
12. With attention to the linguistic field, Dean Mathiowetz offers a related critique from a different angle and text. Reading Rancière's *Ten Theses on Politics*, Mathiowetz argues that Rancière reproduces the partition of the sensible that "repeatedly excludes *kairos*'s embodied dimension, its affective and extra-linguistic sensoria, from the field of politics." See Dean Mathiowetz, "*Kairos* and Affect in Rancière's *Ten Theses on Politics*," *Theory & Event* 20, no. 1 (2017): 90.

13. The status of the taxonomy in Plato's work is itself contestable. For a nuanced discussion of the Athenian myth of autochthony as it relates to the polis's naturalized boundaries of descent via the *gennaion pseudos* and "noble lie" in Plato's *Republic*, see Demetra Kasimis, "Plato's Open Secret," *Contemporary Political Theory* 15, no. 4 (November 2016): 339–357.
14. Rancière, *Dis-agreement*, 67.
15. Rancière, *Dis-agreement*, 29.
16. Robinson, "Slavery and the Platonic Origins of Anti-Democracy," 31.
17. This is Peter Euben's interpretation in *Platonic Noise*.
18. I reminded Euben that Wolin had said this, and he responded with the helpful corrective that "*The Laws* were Plato's revenge on all of us." For an intervention in debates over Wolin's thinking on the relationship between democracy and time that resists the easy dichotomies of fast vs. slow time and patience vs. impatience, see Mario Feit, "Wolin, Time and the Democratic Temperament," *Theory & Event* 15, no. 4 (2012).
19. Robinson, "Slavery and the Platonic Origins of Anti-Democracy," 26.
20. Robinson, "Slavery and the Platonic Origins of Anti-Democracy," 31.

Chapter 3

1. Oscar J. Martínez, *Border People: Life and Society in the U.S.-Mexico Borderlands* (Tucson: University of Arizona Press, 1994), 28.
2. Importantly, Mexicans are hardly the only group to be stigmatized as potential carriers of infirmities. Asian, Italian, and Irish immigrants, among others, were all suspected of putting the American public at risk at one time or another. See Natalia Molina, *Fit to Be Citizens: Public Health and Race in Los Angeles, 1879–1939* (Berkeley: University of California Press, 2006). For an overview of the correspondence between race and public health, see Thomas A. LaVeist and Lydia A. Isaac, eds., *Race, Ethnicity and Health: A Public Health Reader*, 2nd ed. (San Francisco: Jossey-Bass, 2012); Donald A. Barr, *Health Disparities in the United States: Social Class, Race, Ethnicity and Health* (Baltimore: Johns Hopkins University Press, 2008).
3. Ian Haney López, *Dog Whistle Politics: How Coded Racial Appeals Have Reinvented Racism and Wrecked the Middle Class* (New York: Oxford University Press, 2014).
4. McCarthy, *Race, Empire*, 118–120. Racism is "ethical" in the dual sense that it (a) partakes in the Greek notion of ethics (*ethos* or *ethoi*) as involving habit and acculturation and (b) is viewed as ethical (and thus not racist at all) in the sense of being morally righteous in the minds of those who make racially inflected judgments, since those judgments are ostensibly not being made on the basis of phenotype or genealogy. Rather, racial inequalities exist as just deserts resulting from the poor choices made by freely consenting individuals who just happen to be nonwhite. Despite these permutations in racial perceptions, however, it is virtually the same racial groups who were once stigmatized as biologically

anachronistic (or less evolved) that are still disproportionately rendered behind the times as a result of their alleged cultural backwardness. As a consequence, stigmatized groups are effectively cast out of time, exposed to slow death, excluded from the dominant temporal flows of economic privilege, and poised to experience a foreshortened lifespan, a denial of healthcare, and a lack of social/political standing.

5. Vann R. Newkirk II, "The Real Risk of Trump's Dehumanization of Immigrants," *The Atlantic*, May 19, 2018, online at https://www.theatlantic.com/politics/archive/2018/05/the-real-risk-of-trumps-dehumanization-of-immigrants/560762/.

6. See T. Tancredo, *In Mortal Danger: The Battle for America's Border and Security* (Nashville: WND, 2006); Patrick Buchanan, *State of Emergency: The Third World Invasion* (New York: St. Martin's Press, 2006).

7. Otto Santa Ana, *Brown Tide Rising: Metaphors of Latinos in Contemporary American Public Discourse* (Austin: University of Texas Press, 2002); Hage, *Is Racism an Environmental Threat?*; Eithe Luibheld, *Entry Denied: Controlling Sexuality at the Border* (Minneapolis: University of Minnesota Press, 2002); Arnoldo De Leon, *They Called Them Greasers: Anglo Attitudes towards Mexicans in Texas, 1821–1900* (Austin: University of Texas Press, 1983).

8. Leo R. Chavez, *The Latino Threat: Constructing Immigrants, Citizens and the Nation* (Stanford, CA: Stanford University Press, 2008).

9. For historical accounts of the relation between race and epidemiology, see Nancy Leys Stepan, *The Hour of Eugenics: Race, Gender and Nation in Latin America* (Ithaca, NY: Cornell University Press, 1996); Suman Seth, *Difference and Disease: Medicine, Race, and the Eighteen Century British Empire* (Cambridge: Cambridge University Press, 2018).

10. Reflecting on Donald Trump's flagrant fluency in eugenicist language, his biographer says the family subscribes to a racehorse theory of human development. See "The Choice," PBS *Frontline*, September 27, 2016, online at https://www.pbs.org/wgbh/frontline/film/the-choice-2016/. Those surprised at the uptick in the naked racism on the right, and even media who regarded the vulgarity as emerging ex nihilo, may have forgotten the more recent history of the GOP and the long career of then-senator (and future attorney general) Jefferson Beauregard Sessions III. In a 2013 event billed as the "DC March for Jobs Rally," Sessions worked the crowd as Ken Crow, the former president of the Tea Party of America, reminded those gathered of their incredible DNA and the need to protect it since "you cannot breed Secretariat to a donkey and expect to win the Kentucky Derby." The event was organized by John Tanton: a white nationalist who declared Black Americans a "retrograde species of humanity" and authored "The Case for Passive Eugenics." See George Zornick, "Ugly Opposition to Immigration Reform Comes Back to Capitol Hill," *The Nation*, July 15, 2013, online at http://www.thenation.com/blog/175276/ugly-opposition-immigration-reform-comes-back- capitol-hill#.

11. When Donald Trump publicly asserted that Haitians all had AIDS and associated inferior people with subprime land (shithole countries), he invoked a rather ancient form of proto-racialization whereby the toxicity of poor territory grows monstrous inhabitants. Such ancient notions of autochthony, depicted in the form of graphic

monsters by cartographers, eventually gave way to Jean Baptiste de Lamarck's notion of environmental influence on heredity. Forms of neo-Lamarckism were variously mixed with eugenicist logics to argue that improving the environment will improve people and produce a heartier "stock." Alternately, that logic also fueled arguments foreseeing human regression down the evolutionary ladder as inevitable. See Alexandra Minna Stern, *Eugenic Nation: Faults and Frontiers of Better Breeding in America* (Berkeley: University of California Press, 2015).

12. Malcolm X, Quoted in Lipsitz, *The Possessive Investment in Whiteness*, 183.
13. Unlike epidemics, endemic threats call for tactics of management, containment, and regularization over time and space such that their existence is kept at a baseline level, and even made useful for the health of the prevailing order. One analog is how a weakened virus becomes useful as a vaccine.
14. The turn to Foucault may seem strange given that his reflections on race and colonialism are sparse and insufficient, and his reference points largely restricted to continental Europe. Yet what I find intriguing, and problematic in illuminating ways, is his exposition of biopolitical power and race occurs in the context of *endemic* threats, while disciplinary power is elaborated relative to *epidemics* conceived in terms of the plague dream.
15. Ali Behdad, *A Forgetful Nation: On Immigration and Cultural Identity in the United States* (Durham, NC: Duke University Press, 2005).
16. This is not to say that all normalized perceptions of immigrants are (or have been) negative. Bonnie Honig offers useful nuance to the picture by theorizing the phenomena of the immigrant as the "supercitizen." See Bonnie Honig, *Democracy and the Foreigner* (Princeton, NJ: Princeton University Press, 2001). I take this up in the second Interlude on time travel.
17. Gloria Anzaldúa, *Borderlands / La Frontera: The New Mestiza* (San Francisco: Aunt Lute Books, 2007), 29.
18. Anzaldúa, *Borderlands*, 28. For historiographical work on this relationship, See Kathleen Davis, *Periodization and Sovereignty* (Philadelphia, PA: University of Pennsylvania Press, 2008). For a broader discussion of sovereign temporal borders and citizenship, see Cohen, *Political Value of Time*, 29–61.
19. Alicia Schmidt Camacho, *Migrant Imaginaries: Latino Cultural Politics in the U.S.-Mexico Borderlands* (New York: New York University Press, 2008), 2, 25.
20. Lina Newton, *Illegal, Alien, or Immigrant: The Politics of Immigration Reform* (New York: New York University Press, 2008), 151.
21. Edward E. Telles and Vilma Ortiz, *Generations of Exclusion* (New York: Russell Sage Foundations, 2008), 16–17.
22. Also see Laura E. Gomez, "Opposite One-Drop Rules: Mexican Americans, African Americans, and the Need to Reconceive Turn-of-the Twentieth-Century Race Relations," in *How the United States Racializes Latinos: White Hegemony and Its Consequences*, ed. Jose A. Cobas, Jorge Duany, and Joe R. Feagin (Boulder, CO: Paradigm Publishers, 2009), 87.
23. Telles and Ortiz, *Generations of Exclusion*, 16–17.
24. Schmidt Camacho, *Migrant Imaginaries*, 2.

25. Martha D. Escobar, *Captivity beyond Prisons:Criminalization Experiences of Latina (Im)migrants* (Austin: University of Texas Press, 2016), 8–15.
26. Hiroshi Motomoro, *Americans in Waiting* (New York: Oxford University Press, 2006).
27. Paul Apostolidis, *Breaks in the Chain* (Minneapolis: University of Minnesota Press, 2010), 86.
28. Apostolidis, *Breaks in the Chain*, 86.
29. Apostolidis, *Breaks in the Chain*, 86.
30. Schmidt Camacho, *Migrant Imaginaries*, 240; also see Apostolidis, *Breaks in the Chain*, 128. As a particularly unsettling example, immigrant workers on the "disassembly line" at Tyson Chicken in Washington reported that supervisors forced employees to wait so long for bathroom breaks that some would unintentionally wet themselves.
31. For an analysis of how this plays out in continental Europe, see Nicholas De Genova, ed., *The Borders of "Europe"* (Durham, NC: Duke University Press, 2017), esp. 6–8.
32. Although not yet framed as such, a struggle to intuit just how those different projects interact would resurface in Foucault's later work on ethics, biopolitics, and governmentality. For a lucid account of the latter concept, see William Walters, *Governmentality* (London: Routledge, 2012).
33. The capillary workings of panoptic self-surveillance and normalization radically destabilized the borderline between coercion and consent—which ignited no small amount of controversy. It seemed that, for some, Foucault himself represented an oncoming plague. Among the most potentially devastating aspects of Foucault's criticism was an open invitation to consider the possibility that the most insidious articulations of power cause modern subjects to imagine they are participating in free choice when even their *very idea* of freedom has been coerced. At bottom, if one's conception of freedom is indeed a function of discipline, then even one's thoughts about freedom cannot be entirely free. And the snapshot presented here does not begin to broach Foucault's assault on the sprawling assumptions of liberal sovereignty. Equally troubling, to critics it was not at all obvious what arts of resistance (if any) remained available to be learned, or even the extent to which we can count on the emancipatory power of Enlightenment learning at all. Simply put, Foucault made it much more difficult to trust that if you "know the truth," then "the truth shall set you free" (John 8:32). It is a suspicion that is especially unsettling if truth and freedom are both products of power, and the nature of that power—and its entailment—remains shrouded in mystery.
34. Michel Foucault, *Power/Knowledge: Selected Interviews and Writings, 1972–1977*, ed. Colin Gordan (New York: Vintage Books, 1980).
35. Locke's famous warning to rulers came enclosed in a reminder to the governed that they could revoke their consent—violently, if necessary. Should the government overstep its bounds, Locke contended, the social contract could be dissolved and people could ultimately "*appeal to heaven*" and overthrow the regime (*Second Treatise of Government*, 87).
36. Michael Dillon and Luis Lobo-Guerrero, "Biopolitics and Security in the 21st Century," *Review of International Studies* 34, no. 2 (2008): 265–292; Roberto Esposito,

Bios: Biopolitics and Philosophy (Minneapolis: University of Minnesota Press, 2008); Stoler, *Race and the Education of Desire*; Moreton-Robinson, *White Possessive*. Readers can plausibly surmise that at least part of this ambiguity is by design, both because of the provisional form and content of the ideas presented in the lectures, and the contingency that attaches to the various moving parts of the theoretical modes Foucault alternately parses and conjoins.

37. For instance, the phenomenon Foucault calls biopolitics was well underway before the time period he indexes.
38. Orlando Patterson, *Slavery and Social Death* (Cambridge, MA: Harvard University Press, 1985); Lisa Marie Cacho, *Social Death: Racialized Rightlessness and the Criminalization of the Unprotected* (New York: New York University Press, 2012).
39. As evidence of how the above points intersect politically, in the 2012 election cycle, former Speaker of the House and presidential candidate Newt Gingrich courted voters by promising to compel native Spanish speakers to learn English so they could learn "the language of prosperity" instead of the "language of the ghetto." The statement can at once convey the backwardness of a racial group, identify that group as subject to the control and management of governmental power, and reinforce a logic of power that renders such a population expendable. It might function to shore up the linguistic identity of the racially dominant group through disciplinary means (compulsory education, legal prohibition, an "official" language) while also advancing a biopolitical project whereby Latinx peoples can be silenced (by the pen or the sword) because brown lives matter less—to the point that, in some cases, they do not even count as lives. In Foucauldian terms, the stigma of being racialized as Hispanic functions as a marker of visibility subjecting Latinx peoples to surveillance, biometric analysis, forced segregation, deportation, sexual assault, sterilization, and death.
40. I discuss how the capacity to take the polity back in time has been framed as a positive quality in the second interlude.
41. This is not to suggest, however, that a fascist dictator or an official state policy must explicitly recognize a group of people as a plague or virus for the logics of epidemiology and biopolitics to become operative.
42. See Apostolidis, *Breaks in the Chain*. Foucault outlines relevant distinctions between the aims and workings of disciplinary panopticism and the biopolitical regulation of life and death. Yet my concern here is that parsing too strong a divide along the lines of disciplinary power as applicable to individuals and biopower to masses risks missing how disciplinary projects can be interpolated for biopolitical ends, and vice-versa.
43. David Liptak, "Court Splits Immigration Law Verdicts; Upholds Hotly Debated Centerpiece, 8–0," *New York Times*, June 26, 2012, A1. When legal challenges to Arizona's law were taken up by the Supreme Court in June 2012, the court rendered a split decision that nevertheless upheld the "show me your papers" provision.
44. David A. Fahrentold, "Self-Deportation Proponents Kris Kobach, Michael Hethmon, Facing Time of Trial," *Washington Post*, April 24, 2012, online at http://www.washingtonpost.com/politics/time-of-trial-for-proponents-of-self-deportation/2012/04/24/gIQAe6lheT_story.html. On April 24, 2012, attorney Michael Hethmon was interviewed by the *Washington Post* about his defining role in drafting the law and

commented on his motivations. Hethmon candidly confessed that he feared the United States was being overtaken by nonwhites.
45. The law presumably places the burden on citizens to demand papers before, say, giving a coworker a ride home.
46. Manuel A. Vasquez, "From Colonialism to Neo-liberal Capitalism: Latino/a Immigrants in the U.S. and the New Biopolitics," *JCRT: Journal for Cultural and Religious Theory* 13, no. 1 (2014): 83–84.
47. Instances of disciplinary spectacle in the service of white supremacy far exceed those recounted here. See Hartman, *Scenes of Subjection*; Brendese, "Worlds Neither New Nor Brave."
48. Chavez, *Latino Threat*, 144. For Chavez, the success of the Minutemen's initiative was not measured in the number of individual border crossers the group thwarts, but in its ability to draw attention to a nation under assault as part of a broader disciplinary project.
49. Chavez, *Latino Threat*, 135.
50. Chavez, *Latino Threat*, 151. In view of the government's vast resources relative to those of the Minutemen, the group's intended effect was to leverage public opinion and compel the government to mobilize its capacities on behalf of the Minutemen's goals.
51. Alexander Burns and Astead W. Herndon, "Trump and GOP Escalate Race and Fear as Election Ploys," *New York Times*, October 22, 2018, online at https://www.nytimes.com/2018/10/22/us/politics/republicans-race-divisions-elections-caravan.html.
52. Typically couched in criticisms of "hot Latinas," the pejorative term "anchor babies" denotes a perceived strategy by foreigners who migrate to the United States in order to take advantage of the Fourteenth Amendment's conferral of citizenship status to those born on American soil. A popular supposition is that the immigrant parents of US-born children will be more difficult to deport, thereby rendering them "anchored" to the birthplace of their offspring. The assumption persists despite harrowing accounts of families being forcibly separated. The danger ascribed to "anchor babies" is consonant with repeated depictions of Latinx peoples (particularly Mexicans) as sexually incontinent and hyperfertile. Recent scholarly analysis evinces Latino reproduction as frequently portrayed in the popular media as "dangerous, pathological, abnormal and even a threat to national security." Chavez, *Latino Threat*, 72; also see Marysol Ascencio, ed., *Latina/o Sexualities: Probing Powers, Passions, Practices and Politics* (New Brunswick, NJ: Rutgers University Press, 2010). Texas state representative Debbie Riddle took the neonatal security threat to the outer edges of absurdity, going so far as to tell CNN that pregnant women are coming to the United States to have babies "with the nefarious purpose of turning them into little terrorists who will then come back to the U.S. and do us harm." Vasquez, "From Colonialism to Neo-liberal Capitalism," 81.
53. Marc Silver, "Bodies on the Border," *New York Times*, August 17, 2013, online at https://www.nytimes.com/2013/08/18/opinion/bodies-on-the-border.html?searchResultPosition=1.

54. Jason De Leon, *The Land of Open Graves* (Oakland: University of California Press, 2015), 3–4.
55. See David Bacon, *Illegal People: How Globalization Creates Migration and Criminalizes Immigrants* (Boston: Beacon Press, 2008), 117. Critics who would argue that guest worker programs adequately address the brutal experiences of workers hired to maintain profits in the midst of such eventualities would do well to consult the Southern Policy Law Center's report entitled "Close to Slavery," so characterizing the H-2 guest worker program. As the title suggests, the report finds that workers are "systematically exploited and abused.... They are, in effect the disposable workers of the U.S. economy."
56. Joanne Grant, *Ella Baker: Freedom Bound* (United Kingdom: Wiley 1998), 12.
57. Honig, *Democracy and the Foreigner*, 77.
58. Rohy, *Anachronism and Its Others*.
59. Notice that some, but not all, fall into the oft-cited category of "slow death" that Berlant regards as the "temporality of the endemic." See Berlant, "Slow Death," 756. Distinct from her formulation, wars and necropolitical incursions make quick use of racial others to shore up the contingency of white temporality.
60. Rebecca Best, Kylean Hunter, Theresa Schroeder, and Jeremy Teigen, "Military Service Was Once a Fast Track to Citizenship: The Trump Administration Keeps Narrowing That Possibility," *Washington Post*, September 6, 2019, online at https://www.washingtonpost.com/politics/2019/09/06/military-service-was-once-fast-track-us-citizenship-trump-administration-keeps-narrowing-that-possibility/.
61. Amy Lutz, "Who Joins the Military? A Look at Race, Class and Immigration Status," *Journal of Political and Military Sociology* 36, no. 2 (2008): 170.
62. Lutz, "Who Joins the Military," 174.
63. See Mimi Thi Nguyen, *The Gift of Freedom: War, Debt and Other Refugee Passages* (Durham, NC: Duke University Press, 2012).
64. Abdelmalek Sayad, quoted by Kitty Calavita, "Immigration, Social Control, and Punishment in the Industrial Era," in *Race, Gender and Punishment: From Colonialism to the War on Terror*, ed. Mary Bosworth and Jeanne Flavin (New Brunswick, NJ: Rutgers University Press, 2006), 129.
65. Achille Mbembe, *Critique of Black Reason*, trans. Laurent Dubois (Durham, NC: Duke University Press, 2017).
66. Apostolidis, *Breaks in the Chain*, 127, 180.
67. Paul Apostolidis, *The Fight for Time: Migrant Day Laborers and the Politics of Precarity* (New York: Oxford University Press, 2019).
68. Apostolidis, *Fight for Time*, 189, 170.
69. Cristina Beltrán, *The Trouble with Unity* (New York: Oxford University Press, 2014).
70. Beltrán, *The Trouble with Unity*, 141.

Chapter 4

1. For an excellent analysis of this topic, see Nguyen, *Gift of Freedom*.

2. Gilles Deleuze, "Postscript on the Societies of Control," *October* 59 (Winter 1992): 6.
3. Maurizio Lazzarato, *The Making of the Indebted Man: An Essay on the Neoliberal Condition*, trans. Joshua David Jordan (Los Angeles: Semiotext(e), 2012), 49. Hereafter citations appear in the text as "MIM."
4. The phrase is Zygmunt Bauman's. See Chronis J. Polychroniou, "Globalization and Capitalism: An Interview with Zygmunt Bauman," *New Politics* 12, no. 3 (Summer 2009):110–116.
5. To be clear, the point is not to understate the capacity of the present order to inflict indebtedness on myriad populations of many backgrounds. Nor is it to diminish the injuries disseminated so widely by rendering the pain of some less real than others through what has been called "the suffering Olympics." Quite the contrary. By tracing the logics of power coursing through race and debt as temporal impositions, we attain a more refined acknowledgment of how debt functions as an engine of the proliferation of contemporary disposable populations.
6. Frank B. Wilderson III, "The Prison Slave as Hegemony's (Silent) Scandal," in *Warfare in the American Homeland*, ed. James, 31–32.
7. Fred Moten, "The Subprime and the Beautiful," *African Identities* 11, no. 2 (2013): 240.
8. See Du Bois's *Black Reconstruction in America*; Robinson, *Black Marxism*; Williams, *Capitalism and Slavery*; C.L.R. James, *The Black Jacobins: Toussaint L'Ouverture and the San Domingo Revolution* (New York: Vintage Books, 1963). For illuminating conversations on the entwinement of race and capital, I am indebted to Samuel Chambers, William E. Connolly, Michael Dawson, Chris Forster-Smith, Laura Grattan, Cheryl I. Harris, Aileen Moreton-Robinson, and Lester K. Spence. My thinking on the credit value of whiteness has been enlarged by Christopher Forster-Smith's illuminating dissertation "The Color of Creditworthiness: Debt, Race and Democracy in the 21st Century," Johns Hopkins University Department of Political Science (2018).
9. Jodi Melamed, "Racial Capitalism," *Critical Ethnic Studies* 1, no. 1 (Spring 2015): 77.
10. Marieke De Goode, *Virtue, Fortune, Faith: A Genealogy of Finance* (Minneapolis: University of Minnesota Press, 2005), 27.
11. Harris, "Whiteness as Property," 1734.
12. Nathan Connolly argues that neoliberalism's starting point bears a problematic racial marker. See N. D. B. Connolly, "A White Story," *Dissent*, January 28, 2018, online at https://www.dissentmagazine.org/blog/neoliberalism-forum-ndb-connolly.
13. Political theorists of neoliberalism have identified as distinctive its collapse of traditional liberal antagonisms: namely the tensions between government intervention and private enterprise, economic rationality and intellectual freedom, capitalist value and the self as the creator of values, and the free market and the free individual—to name but a few.
14. David Graeber, *Debt: The First 5000 Years* (New York: Melville House, 2014), 16. David Graeber notes that, during the colonial era those failing to pay their debts had their ears nailed to a tree. A ghastly warning to would-be debtors, the maimed body served as a highly public stigma of credit unworthiness. I note that the ancient Greeks employed the practice of cutting off ears to mark slaves who had attempted to escape

captivity. To them, stigmatization was a practical necessity since slavery was not racialized by phenotype.
15. The credit value of whiteness as subject to flux, fortification, and reappraisal relative to sociotemporal conditions is the topic of the next chapter.
16. I am deliberately employing the both the intentional and the financial meanings of interest.
17. Lazzarato's subsequent work, *Governing by Debt*, trans. Joshua David Jordan (Los Angeles: Semiotext(e), 2015), exemplifies the point.
18. Robert C. Tucker, ed., *The Marx-Engels Reader*, 2nd ed. (New York: Norton, 1978), 379. On the "always on" aspects of work on the self as a feature of neoliberal temporality, see Sarah Sharma, "The Biopolitical Economy of Time," *Journal of Communication Inquiry* 35, no. 4 (2011): 439–444.
19. For instance, in response to Sartre's early existentialist claims of "infinite responsibility," Foucault famously accused Sartre of being a terrorist.
20. With respect to the "we," note that the divide between being guilty before divinity and capital is often conflated rather than parsed as separate stages and entities. After all, the language of saving, redemption, and atonement is both theological and economic. Max Weber famously theorized how potent spiritual affinities can be simultaneously shared across Protestantism and capitalism. In the United States, evangelical Christians preach the prosperity gospel to rollicking megachurches, openly avowing the close connection between spiritual salvation and God's financial "favors." Wielding formidable political power, they form a potent voting block overwhelmingly supportive of the far-right, ethnonationalist policies committed to eroding economic protections and civil rights. See William E. Connolly, *Capitalism & Christianity American Style* (Durham, NC: Duke University Press, 2008).
21. For a sustained exposition of this dynamic, see Joel Soss, Richard C. Fording, and Sanford F. Schram, *Disciplining the Poor: Neoliberal Paternalism and the Persistent Power of Race* (Chicago: University of Chicago Press, 2011).
22. Melamed, "Racial Capitalism," 77.
23. Again, my purpose is not just to mark an oversight, nor is it to fine-tune the periodicity demarking the neoliberal turn.
24. Du Bois, *Black Reconstruction in America*. Note that a version of that myth-history is still visible in the 2012 movie *Lincoln*. The film acknowledges the presence of Black soldiers in the Civil War, but it omits prominent Black abolitionist luminaries whose counsel Lincoln sought—namely Frederick Douglass. Instead, emancipation is largely figured as the largesse of brilliant white political entrepreneurs.
25. James Baldwin, "The American Dream and the American Negro," in *Price of the Ticket*, 404.
26. Joseph, *Debt to Society*, 53.
27. Hartman, *Scenes of Subjection*, 131.
28. See Isaac Brinckerhoff and J.B. Waterbury, *Advice to Freedmen*, Freedmen's School and Textbooks, vol. 4 (New York: AMS Press, 1980), 7. In a section entitled "How You Became Free," Brinckerhoff insisted freedmen remember their outstanding debt to "the government that has spent many millions of dollars, many parents have given up

their sons, many wives lost their husbands. . . . With treasure and precious blood your freedom has been purchased."
29. Hartman, *Scenes of Subjection*, 145.
30. Hartman, *Scenes of Subjection*, 146.
31. Hartman, *Scenes of Subjection*, 136, 132.
32. Booker T. Washington, *Up from Slavery*, quoted in David W. Blight, *Race and Reunion: The Civil War in American Memory* (Cambridge, MA: Belknap Press of Harvard University Press, 2001), 322.
33. In the context of whites' demand for gratitude, what "proper conduct" looks like can take a variety of forms when viewed through a temporal lens. Today, respectability politics wastes the time and energy of people of color with the psychic weight of having to avoid anything that mirrors behavior that might be seen as racially stereotypical. Consider how such avoidance can come with the felt compulsion to perform whiteness by emulating white civic norms, a phenomenon Claude M. Steele evocatively terms "whistling Vivaldi." Nevertheless, whistling classical music as a means of rhythmically keeping (white) time proves futile in disarming racist projections. Claude M. Steele, *Whistling Vivaldi: How Stereotypes Affect Us and What We Can Do* (New York: W.W. Norton & Co., 2010).
34. Fanon, *Wretched of the Earth*, 135.
35. There is the violent history of white rage in the face of Black failure to express gratitude for their oppression. The insurgent rebellions of Nat Turner and Denmark Vesey come to mind. And the Haitian Revolution famously sent shockwaves across Europe and the Americas at the so-called monstrous ingratitude expressed by African servants toward their white benefactors.
36. Ta-Nehisi Coates, *Between the World and Me* (New York: Spiegel & Grau, 2015). For an example of the critique, see David Brooks, "Listening to Ta-Nehisi Coates while White," *New York Times*, July 17, 2015, online at https://www.nytimes.com/2015/07/17/opinion/listening-to-ta-nehisi-coates-while-white.html?searchResultPosition=5.
37. Coates, *Between the World and Me*, 131–133.
38. See McClanahan, *Dead Pledges*, 126. McClanahan explains mortgage as dead pledges as follows: "As collateral for a loan, property can be either 'dead' to the lender, if the loan was paid, or 'dead' to the borrower, if he defaulted. What this etymology suggests is that the house is a kind of liminal status while the loan is still owed; neither living nor dead, the mortgaged home has a strange ontology."
39. King, *A Testament of Hope*, 217.
40. McClanahan, *Dead Pledges*, 99. Interestingly, I note that *oikos* can also refer to family, family lineage, or the family's wealth.
41. Katznelson, *When Affirmative Action Was White*.
42. Karl Marx, *Economic and Philosophical Manuscripts of 1844*, Marxists.org, online at https://www.marxists.org/archive/marx/works/1844/manuscripts/needs.htm. Accessed November 8, 2020. It is telling that Marx speaks of the poor cellar dweller as evidence of human regression and estrangement beneath even the savage in his cave.
43. McClanahan, *Dead Pledges*, 100.

44. This does not presume a uniformity of experience across Black communities, plural. See Lester K. Spence, *Knocking the Hustle: Against the Neoliberal Turn in Black Politics* (New York: Punctum Books, 2015), xv–xxv. Referencing the mortgage crisis in Baltimore specifically, Spence calls attention to the inequalities of financial wealth and social networks within Black communities that allow some to recover faster than others, or simply maintain their position. From the perspective of my argument, Spence's point suggests an intraracial segregation of time that iterates intersectionally across entanglements of class, gender, (social) capital, and so on.

45. Ta-Nehisi Coates, "The Case for Reparations," *The Atlantic*, June 2014, online at https://www.theatlantic.com/magazine/archive/2014/06/the-case-for-reparations/361631/

46. Coates, "The Case for Reparations": "In 2009, half the properties in Baltimore whose owners had been granted loans by Wells Fargo between 2005 and 2008 were vacant; 71 percent of these properties were in predominantly black neighborhoods."

47. McClanahan, *Dead Pledges*, 100. Note: these numbers refer to median wealth as an aggregate, not a suggestion that *all* African American households lost all their wealth. McClanahan cites Charles Nier and Maureen R. St. Cyr, "A Racial Financial Crisis," *Temple Law Review* 83 (2011): 941–978.

48. McClanahan, *Dead Pledges*, 79–80. McClanahan holds that Lazzarato overplays the psychological aspects of debt and diminishes the very real material consequences for failing to repay. While I do not disagree, my intervention proceeds along somewhat different terrain. McClanahan's account recenters the discussion on the material conditions of extracting payment and a novel scenario where Americans now go into debt to maintain a standard of living they were once able to afford. Yet, as her own work suggests, both the capacity to afford that standard of living and the expectation that it would be maintained through time are hardly equal across racial groups.

49. Connolly, "A White Story." Connolly also notes that 60 percent of all Black wealth in the United States was wiped out when white managers rewrote the charter of the Freedman's Savings Bank and squandered the funds on junk railroad stock. For a historical account of the equity in the bodies of the enslaved, see Diana Ramey Berry, *The Price for Their Pound of Flesh: The Value of the Enslaved from Womb to Grave in the Building of a Nation* (Boston: Beacon Press, 2017) esp. 12, 117–119, 142–143.

50. Moten, "The Subprime and the Beautiful," 240.

51. Deleuze, "Postscript," 6.

52. Ruth Wilson Gilmore, "Fatal Couplings of Power and Difference: Notes on Racism and Geography," *Professional Geographer* 54, no. 1 (2002): 16.

53. Joseph, *Debt to Society*, 25. See also page 18, where Joseph critiques Graeber for dichotomizing "particularity and abstraction, demonizing only abstraction, as if it could be disentangled from processes of particularization, and offers particularization as a cure."

54. K-Sue Park, "Money, Mortgages and the Conquest of America," *Law & Social Inquiry* 41 (Fall 2016): 1006–1035. Hereafter citations appear in the text as "MMCA."

55. According to twelfth-century descriptions, there were two types of gages: a *vif* gage and a *mort* gage—live and dead pledges. The difference between the two was that in

a *vif* gage a creditor exacting rents and fruits of the land applied them toward the outstanding principal of the loan, thereby reducing the debt accordingly. Through the "dead pledge" of the *mort* gage, however, those same collections would not count toward repayment but added profit to the loan through what amounted to interest in disguise. Unsurprisingly, the ability to use the mortgage to sidestep prohibitions against interest made the mortgage the more frequently used gage.

56. The predatory nature of the debt structure was not lost on Indigenous nations. King Philip (aka Metacom) borrowed against his nation's land to purchase guns and supplies for war. As more of his people's land was taken, he became painfully aware of the violence that underwrote the contact economy and the white mortgage trap. Case in point; Philip was only willing to borrow against his people's land because he intended to kill the whites who held the lien on it with the weapons he bought with the proceeds. In what became known as King Philip's War, he vowed to reclaim the land in hock along with the rest of his territory the whites had taken—and almost succeeded. With regard to debt, gratitude, and salvation, Philip's story is a uniquely remarkable in another respect. It was his own father, Massasoit, who had allied with the Plymouth settlers and came to their rescue mere decades prior. See Jill Lepore, *The Name of War: King Philip's War and the Origins of American Identity* (New York: Knopf, 1998).
57. Alexander Hamilton, James Madison, and John Jay, *The Federalist Papers* (New York: Quarto Publishing Group, 2017), 45.
58. O'Brien, *Firsting and Lasting*.
59. Michael Ralph, *Forensics of Capital* (Chicago: University of Chicago Press, 2015), 14.
60. Bauman, *Liquid Modernity*. To his credit, Lazzarato parts company with social theorists like Bauman who view contemporary society as "liquid," since the relays of capital do not liquefy without also solidifying social and property relations by fortifying structures of inequality and intensifying exploitation. See *Governing by Debt*, 174–175.
61. In general, my view is that Bauman's fatalism presumes to know the future too well and, in so doing, exercises a kind of conceptual temporal sovereignty I critique in the epilogue. Further, his notion of fluid identities constantly available for disposal in favor of new facades fails to consider Indigenous peoples whose sense of self, collectivity, and cosmology might not be as fungible as their colonial counterparts. His perspective aligns uncomfortably with settler-colonials who have a vested interest in shedding the past in favor of notions of identity unbounded by time and space, tensions that potentially call into question constructivism's points of departure—and its limits.
62. Nixon, *Slow Violence*, 176.
63. Time is borrowed time in the colloquial sense of being vulnerable to the creeping uncertainty of dreading when the other shoe will drop on the one hand and the certainty that it will on the other.
64. White refusal to apprehend native resistance as a counter to colonial powers, but rather as just another example of the essential savagery of Indigenous peoples, is a tactic that predates the reservation system. Native savagery, long believed to be

timeless, provided further justification for Indigenous subjugation by the pastoral powers of white presence.

65. Sherman Alexie, *The Absolutely True Diary of a Part-Time Indian* (Boston: Little, Brown, 2007), 31. That overlap between segregated time and segregated memory was painfully clear to a young Sherman Alexie when he saw that his school textbook had his own mother's name printed in the inside cover. Realizing that she had owned it three decades prior was the final push compelling Alexie to leave his reservation's school. In place of knowledge *about* the past, he was given the past's knowledge—literally what had previously passed for knowledge a generation prior. More than a desire to be unstuck from a present space, Alexie's account reads as an escape from a compulsory captivity to a past time that refuses to recede.
66. Wolfe, *Traces of History*, 2.
67. Dunbar-Ortiz, *Indigenous People's History*, 49–50.
68. Schoolchildren learn of Massasoit as the famous Indian at the first Thanksgiving who allied with the Plymouth settlers and came to their rescue. In truth, that celebrated event was not yet an official holiday. In reality, Massasoit's son, Philip (Metacom), would be the Indian at the first official Thanksgiving. After he failed to recapture his land in what was known as King Philip's War, the colonists butchered him, divided his body as plunder, and brought his head to Plymouth on a pike. An icon of payback, his skull remained on display for decades as a macabre trophy—a warning to would-be offenders and an omen of the extermination to come. See Lepore, *Name of War*.
69. To be abundantly clear, I am not implying that reservations should be abolished.
70. Justin B. Richland and Sarah Deer, *Introduction to Tribal Legal Studies*, 3rd ed. (Lanham, MD: Rowman & Littlefield, 2016), 86.
71. Dunbar-Ortiz and Gilio-Whitaker, *All the Real Indians*, 28–29.
72. Wolfe, *Traces of History*, 143. If you are wondering how the Court could "assert a title" while simultaneously using that title as a vehicle of dispossession, the answer lies in the prerogative of assertion. The tortured logic held that sovereignty proceeded from the king's dominion, whose prerogative allowed the right of possession and occupancy of land to be distributed unequally. By separating sovereignty from ownership and occupancy, the right to define "legitimate" land transfer could revert back to its European definers. Since Christian monarchs had ultimate title to land, individuals' ownership of it had to be traceable to an original transfer from the Crown (or, after the Revolutionary War, from the US government). Given a legitimate transfer from the sovereign, landownership came to participate in the quality of sovereignty, conferring rights that the state was committed to defending. These rights, which were available to Europeans or their creole successors, were categorically superior to Natives' rights over the land that they occupied.
73. Smith, *Conquest*, 58.
74. Gabriel Schwab, *Radioactive Ghosts* (Minneapolis: University of Minnesota Press, 2020). This has prompted even some whites to rethink the half-life of Native American prophecy.
75. Durrenberger, quoted in Traci Brynne Voyles, *Wastelanding: Legacies of Uranium Mining in Navajo Country* (Minneapolis: University of Minnesota Press, 2015), 1.

76. Locke, *Second Treatise of Government*, 19–22.
77. Simpson, *Mohawk Interruptus*, 12.
78. Through practices like DNA tests, the settler state reserves the right to determine who can pass as Indian, versus who has passed into whiteness to the point that their Indianness is past. In a virtually mind-bending weaponization of segregated time, the US government employs Native American DNA to measure whether one's genetic makeup is substantial enough for Indian identity. Consanguinity through DNA is not a prerequisite for membership in any Indigenous nation of which I am aware. Nevertheless, the use of state-of-the-art genetic tests adapts the logic of the nineteenth-century blood quantum "one drop rule," along with its biological racism. See Kim Tall Bear, *Native American DNA*.
79. Graeber, *Debt*, 6. As recently as 2010 France still collected debt for the "theft" of the property and land of Saint Domingue. The Republic of Haiti is an instructive (and arguably an archetypical) exemplar of the relays between colonialism, race, and sovereign debt.
80. Lila Abu-Lughod, "Do Muslim Women Really Need Saving? Anthropological Reflections on Cultural Relativism and Its Others," *American Anthropologist* 104, no. 3 (2002): 788–789.
81. Jacques Derrida, *Given Time 1. Counterfeit Money*, trans. Peggy Kamuf (Chicago: University of Chicago Press, 1994), 41. Even a gift that comes with an expectation of gratitude, in whatever form gratitude may take, is to some extent an exchange.
82. Nguyen, *Gift of Freedom*, 20.
83. It may convey a sense of indefinite existence *on someone else's time*. See Alexie, *Absolutely True Story*, 102. In a fictionalized version of himself as a youth on Willpinit Reservation, Alexie recounts the irony of Indian families celebrating Thanksgiving, asking: "Hey Dad, . . . What do Indians have to be so thankful for?" "We should be thankful that they didn't kill us all. We laughed like crazy. It was a good day."
84. Du Bois, "Souls of White Folk," 17.
85. Harris, "Whiteness as Property," 1734.
86. De Goode, *Virtue, Fortune, Faith*, 27.
87. Bentham, "Security and Equality in Property," 51–52, quoted in Harris, "Whiteness as Property," 1729; emphasis mine.
88. Harris, "Whiteness as Property," 1729.
89. This is effectively a legal expression of Bergson's point that when we speak time, it is space that answers the call.
90. I return to this theme in the epilogue.
91. Harris, "Whiteness as Property," 1734.
92. Carole Pateman has termed this the "settler contract." See Carole Pateman and Charles Mills, *Contract and Domination* (Malden, MA: Polity Press, 2007), 56.
93. Bob Drury and Tom Clavin, *The Heart of Everything That Is: The Untold Story of Red Cloud, an American Legend* (New York: Simon & Schuster, 2013), 351.
94. From this vantage, it becomes easier to see how the notion of Indian land as held in trust by the demonstrably untrustworthy US government gained its currency.
95. Wolfe, *Traces of History*, 145.

96. Joseph, *Debt to Society*, 88.
97. Colonialism keeps company with capitalism and racism insofar as none exists as a discrete event, but they are contiguous structures that imbue time racially with whiteness. Just as accumulation is not an historical stage, but an "ever-renewed actuality" (MIM, 44), the same goes for colonialism. As Indigenous political theorist Glen Coulthard argues via his rejection of Marx's primitive accumulation as a discrete historical epoch, colonialism is acquisitive of territory in perpetuity. See Coulthard, *Red Skin / White Masks*, esp. 6–15.
98. For an illuminating account of this resistance from the perspective of American political development, see Chloe Thurston, *At the Boundaries of Home Ownership: Credit Discrimination and the American State* (Cambridge: Cambridge University Press, 2018), 25.
99. Moten, "The Subprime and the Beautiful," 241.
100. My suspicion is that the "other timeline" refers to the lie of progress and linearity of what I have been calling white time, whereas "the broken circle" gestures to the brute reality of segregated time whose burdens include demands on present time in the form of efforts to stave off future uncertainties.
101. Coates, *Between the World and Me*, 132.
102. Harris, "Whiteness as Property," 1733–1734.
103. Criticized as started by and for white people, the movement's participants often seemed unaware that figures such as Huey P. Newton, the Black Panther Party, and James Foreman (among *many* others) had mounted powerful critiques of capitalism without significant buy-in from whites. See Stacey Patton, "Why Blacks Aren't Embracing Occupy Wall Street," *Washington Post*, November 25, 2011, online at https://www.washingtonpost.com/opinions/why-blacks-arent-embracing-occupy-wall-street/2011/11/16/gIQAwc3FwN_story.html.
104. Mbembe, *Critique of Black Reason*, 137. "Racial capitalism is the equivalent of a giant necropolis. It rests on the traffic of the dead and human bones. To evoke and summon the dead demands that we know how to dispose of the remains or relics of the bodies of those killed so that their spirits can be captured."
105. And here lies the limit of the canary and the coal mine analogy for climate debt and biopolitics. While the unmistakably dehumanizing aspect of the bird metaphor captures the inherent racism of biopolitics as a whole, the analogy is ultimately inadequate to climate debt and the ongoing ecological crisis. After all, it presumes that when the bird dies, the miners will have the sense to stop digging—if only to save themselves. Such is the high price of being color-blind in white time.
106. John Trudell, quoted in Naomi Klein, *No Is Not Enough: Resisting Trump's Shock Politics and Winning the World We Need* (Chicago: Haymarket Books, 2017), epigraph.

Interlude 2

1. The myriad practices of racialization as a vector of temporal transcendence, paralysis, or epochal reconfiguration merit a full-length study in their own right.
2. I discuss Turner's particular form of racial time travel in the next chapter.
3. He also speaks to a tacit fixation in liberal humanism that ultimate progress can happen without loss; all will be reconciled and redeemed in the end.
4. Georgie Anne Geyer, *Americans No More: The Death of Citizenship* (New York: Atlantic Monthly Press, 1996), 305.
5. Geyer, *Americans No More*, 305. Regarding Geyer's viewpoint, she thinks the poor will suffer most because there will be no elite culture "anymore to inspire them or help them up the ladder" (330); she cites Charles Murray, thinks America is a "generally classless society" (333), and calls *The Economist* "always prescient and ever provocative."
6. Honig, *Democracy and the Foreigner*, 76.
7. Honig, *Democracy and the Foreigner*, 76.
8. Honig, *Democracy and the Foreigner*, 77.
9. Honig, *Democracy and the Foreigner*, 74.
10. As Honig notes, "proimmigrant" logic stirs unease among those holding onto the incremental gains in matters of gender and sex equality.
11. Niccolò Machiavelli, "Discourses on Livy," in *The Portable Machiavelli*, ed. Peter Bondanella and Mark Musa (New York: Penguin Books, 1979), 203.
12. See Hannah Fenichel Pitkin, *Fortune Is a Woman: Gender and Politics in the Thought of Niccolò Machiavelli* (Chicago: University of Chicago Press, 1999). Effectively ripping a page from Cicero's political playbook, Machiavelli is not alone in conflating politics and religion to the point that they are virtually indistinguishable in his reading of Livy.
13. Machiavelli, *The Portable Machiavelli*, 203.
14. Arendt, *Between Past and Future*, 121.
15. Robbie Shilliam, personal communication, October 2018.
16. In different ways, Honig and Behdad share a well-founded suspicion that the xenophobic and xenophilic aspects of American liberal democracy are twinned in ways that are ultimately more problematic than progressives would allow. The toxicity of such imbrications are visible in the transition of Asian immigrants from repositories of contagious backwardness, promiscuity, and infection, to recent celebrations of Asian youth as instrumental to future national prosperity. Once pilloried as disease-ridden dangers whom in 1862 railroad baron and Stanford University benefactor Leland Stanford ridiculed as "a degraded and distinct people" that will "exercise a deleterious influence upon the superior race," Asian immigrants came to be extolled as a "model minority." See Jane Junn, "From Coolie to Model Minority," *Du Bois Review: Social Science Research on Race* 4, no. 2 (2007): 357–358. With respect to the disciplinary function of the Asian as a model minority, it is striking that critics across the spectrum figure Asian temporal progress in terms of assimilation into whiteness. In this vernacular, racial "progress" looks like "honorary whiteness"

or "becoming white," both of which suppose a "catching up" to white time, as required by its imposed metric. In its weaponized, disciplinary form is a logic of power that appears as a racial timeline arching toward terminal whiteness for those with their priorities straight, meaning in synch with dominant norms and values. Taken to the extreme, the timeline takes the shape of a discourse of inevitability operative when disciplinary figures point to the spectacle of exemplary Asians in order to say: "See, everyone becomes white in the end."

17. Octavia Butler, *Kindred* (Boston: Beacon Press, [1979] 2003, Kindle ed.). Hereafter citations appear in the text as "K."
18. Interestingly, this happens as she is sorting her books by dividing nonfiction from fiction.
19. After they have endured the hardships of being an economically struggling, interracial couple, it is hard to overlook the symbolism of Dana's being pulled back in time precisely when they've bought a house and are making a home together—finally able to buy into the American Dream of homeownership and pluralism. Not incidentally, they live in Los Angeles, which has long been associated with the construction of futures unmoored to the past.
20. If the enslaved Alice does not give birth to Hagar by mating with Rufus, Dana's own line of descent will not come into being. In the context of the brutal racial dynamics of the time, this effectively means that Dana will have to be implicated in rape. This is not to suggest, however, that the plot turns on her decision as if Alice's fate were in Dana's hands alone. Rather, the sociohistorical conditions of the era function as an impossibly complex set of actors and forces in their own right. The impossibility of importing twentieth-century moral and ethical guideposts into nineteenth-century plantation life lends amplitude to the text.
21. This is not to imply that Butler had no predecessors. W. E. B. Du Bois's short story *The Comet* is typically credited as being a pathbreaking text laying the groundwork for what would become known as Afrofuturism. See also Sheree R. Thomas, *Dark Matter: A Century of Speculative Fiction from the African Diaspora* (New York: Warner Books, 2000). With respect to the historical context out of which *Kindred* emerged, George Clinton's Parliament-Funkadelic *Mothership Connection* landed in 1975, drawing inspiration from science fiction. The cosmic stylings of pathbreaking artists like Sun Ra had been available to those with their ears to the ground since the midcentury, and visual artists such as Jean-Michel Basquiat were gaining cultural currency, with Butler as his contemporary.
22. Robert Crossley, *Kindred: Critical Essay* (K, 265).
23. The notion that marginal figures will return to the fore and push history forward by way of salvation is arguably a popular philosophy of history and temporality. Depending on its incarnation, it can also take on psychosocial dimensions, such as an interpretation of Christianity's appearance conveyed by the phrase that "when Caesar becomes God, God becomes a Jew."
24. Butler herself has said that the book does not really qualify as science fiction as it has no science in it. While the genre of science fiction is widely regarded as understood to have begun in the early nineteenth century with Mary Shelly's

Frankenstein, its authors and its readership are disproportionately associated with white males. My view is that *Kindred* is also a work of horror with the implication that horror is the genre of African American history. Ultimately, I am less interested in classification debates over the novel's place in literary genre than its (un)timely commentary on the role of African Americans and their white counterparts with respect to time travel.

25. I note how that which "plays in the dark," as Toni Morrison put it, is assumed to catalyze the conjunctural transitions between the past and future of mainstream (white) character development—and even history as a whole. Morrison and Butler speak to how racial otherness shapes time as well as prevailing assumptions about time's machinations. See Toni Morrison, *Playing in the Dark: Whiteness and the Literary Imagination* (New York: Vintage, 1993).

26. *Kindred* also appeared before the term "Magic Negro" became a commonplace after filmmaker Spike Lee popularized the deliberately anachronistic term in 2001, criticizing the use of what he referred to as "super-duper magical Negroes" as plot lubricants. Lee was calling out an enduring filmmaking trope whereby white protagonists realize their potential with the help of an African American character who plays a supporting role in the service of white self-actualization. Typically, such figures appear without a past, have mystic/supernatural powers or wisdom, and exist primarily as grateful servants furthering the interests of white heroes on their epic journeys. Lee's critique identified a contemporary incarnation of historically entrenched technique of emplotment that was so conventional it had become virtually undetected among white audiences. The use of a Black savior is hardly exclusive to film and partakes of a broader presumption, particularly among whites, that figures marginal to the polity will return at the right moment to perform a salvific function. See Matthew Seitz, "The Offensive Movie Cliché That Won't Die," *Salon*, September 14, 2010, online at https://www.salon.com/2010/09/14/magical_negro_trope/.

27. One might rightly object that the realities of chattel slavery did not admit such a stark division between space and time. And this is what I take to be Butler's point by way of Dana's capacity for time travel in *Kindred* relative to her ancestor and doppelgänger Alice (K, 228). Alice tells Dana, "He likes me in bed, and you out of bed, and you and I look alike if you can believe what people say." Dana responds, "We look alike if we can believe our own eyes!" To which Alice replies, "I guess so. Anyway, all that means we're two halves of the same woman—at least in his crazy head" (also see K, 256). Alice's sentiment is confirmed when, in a prelude to an attempted rape, Rufus tells Dana, "You were one woman... You and her. Two halves of a whole."

28. Contra Hegel, Fanon memorably retorted the master does not want recognition from the slave, but work. In this fight to the death, the enslaved (Isaac) does not want the master's recognition but his death.

29. Baldwin, "Many Thousands Gone," in *The Price of the Ticket*, 77.

30. Randall Kenan, "An Interview with Octavia E. Butler," *Callaloo* 14 (Spring 1991): 498.

31. Hortense Spillers, "Mama's Baby, Papa's Maybe: An American Grammar Book," *Diacritics* 17, no.2, (Summer 1987): 67.

32. Katherine Lawrie Balfour, "Vexed Genealogy: Octavia Butler and the Political Memories of Slavery," in *Politics and Fiction in America*, ed. Patrick Deneen and Joseph Romance (Lanham, MD: Rowman & Littlefield, 2005), 178.
33. See Walidah Imarisha and adrienne marie brown, eds., *Octavia's Brood: Science Fiction Stories from Social Justice Movements* (Oakland, CA: AK Press, 2015).
34. Quoted in Sandra Y. Govan, "Connections, Links, and Extended Networks: Patterns in Octavia Butler's Science Fiction," *Black American Literature Forum* 18 (Fall 1984): 87 n. 12.

Chapter 5

1. Some Islamic radicals intend to foment the apocalypse by enticing the West into all-out war. The contemporary ubiquity of millennial themes in political discourse and popular culture suggests we would do well to consider how the storied historical legacy of apocalyptic thinking inhabits the present in ways that exceed the scope of this chapter.
2. Invoking the biblical apocalypse, Al Gore warns that our collective inaction on global warming has set us on a temporal path that could look "like a nature hike through the book of Revelations [*sic*]." Quoted in Allison McQueen, *Political Realism in Apocalyptic Times* (New York: Cambridge University Press, 2018), 6.
3. Jacques Derrida, "No Apocalypse, Not Now (Full Speed Ahead, Seven Missiles, Seven Missives)," with Catherine Porter and Philip Lewis, *Diacritics* 14, no. 2 (Summer 1984): 24.
4. The newly empty time (*tempus nullius*) is fertile to give way to abundance (*tempus plentitudinus*), much like the land Europeans fictionalized as unproductive wilderness and empty wasted space (*terra nullius*) and hence subject to Anglo possession. I am indebted to Romand Coles for the formulation of *tempus plentitudenus*.
5. Harold Bloom, *The American Religion: The Emergence of the Post-Christian Nation* (UK: Simon & Schuster, 1992).
6. Christopher Columbus, Roberto Rusconi, and Blair Sullivan, eds., *The Book of Prophecies* (Eugene, OR: Wipf & Stock, 1997), 5.
7. I am grateful to Sam Okoth Opondo for drawing my attention to Columbus's millennialism.
8. Pauline Moffatt Watts, "Prophecy and Discovery: On the Spiritual Origins of Christopher Columbus—Enterprise of the Indies," *American Historical Review* 90, no. 1 (1985): 73–102, 74.
9. Tiffany Lethabo King, *The Black Shoals: Offshore Formations of Black and Native Studies* (Durham, NC, & London: Duke University Press, 2019), 16.
10. As a mapmaker-merchant from the European underclass, he favored the kind of upward social mobility that would allow him to rise in power through imperial conquest. With respect to the infra-European social hierarchy, Columbus's brand of millennial Christianity departed from the prevailing orthodoxy that Sylvia Wynter

calls "the medieval-aristocratic order" of Christian humanism. Sylvia Wynter, interview with David Scott, "The Re-enchantment of Humanism," 194–195.

11. In popular culture, the end of time often looks like an end to a *particular period* of time, a bookend on a historical epoch, or the close of a specific way of life—as opposed to a cosmological end of time itself akin to another Big Bang, an asteroid strike, planetary absorption into a black hole, and so forth. Theistic stories of beginnings tend to come prewired with their own respective end times, the subject of *eschatology*, which the Oxford English Dictionary defines as "the part of theology concerned with death, judgement and the final judgement of the soul and of humankind." To a certain degree, the antiquity of apocalypse as an anticipated time worth thinking about should make its prevalence unsurprising. According to the Gospels, Jesus's disciples believed he would return in their lifetimes to bring an end to human time on earth and inaugurate a reconciliation with the almighty in Eternal time.

12. The question throws into relief the willful extinction of lifeways wrought by colonial legacies evoked by *Apocalypse Now*, Francis Ford Coppola's cinematic take on Joseph Conrad's *Heart of Darkness*.

13. Jonathan Lear, *Radical Hope: Ethics in the Face of Cultural Devastation* (Cambridge, MA: Harvard University Press, 2006), 2. Part of the challenge of grappling with apocalypse is that statements of Indigenous extinction are themselves vehicles of disappearing and dispossessing First Nations. When Plenty Coups says, "After this nothing happened," one can hear it as a declaration that Crow lifeways without whites ended without necessarily taking it to mean that there are no longer Crow people (like Plenty Coups himself) who have a claim to stolen land.

14. Catherine Keller, *Apocalypse Now and Then: A Feminist Guide to the End of the World* (Minneapolis: Fortress Press, 2005), 87.

15. The terrorist Dylann Roof embraces this philosophy. Broadly stated, the conspiracy theory of white genocide is associated with neo-Nazi groups and the American alt-right, which conflate antiracism with white extermination, understanding diversity and interracial procreation as threating white supremacy. Increasingly, the theory has been mainstreamed by conservative media outlets. In August 2018, Trump drew widespread recrimination for amplifying the false claim that the South African government was participating in the "large-scale killing" of white farmers, and ordered Secretary of State Mike Pompeo to monitor the situation.

16. Baldwin participates in a tradition of what Michael Hanchard calls "eschatological renderings of racial time" that keeps company with Nat Turner and John Brown as well as the voodoo of Boukman in the Haitian insurrection. See Hanchard, "Afro-Modernity," 257.

17. Baldwin, "The Fire Next Time," in *The Price of the Ticket*, 336.

18. Baldwin, "The Fire Next Time," in *The Price of the Ticket*, 336. In an apparent oversight, Baldwin's locution implies that there once *was* a time when their racial/metaphysical grasp was actually secure. Still, his expression of the centrality of Black subordination in white cosmology and metaphysics—that which anchors the white world and its sense of reality—is on point.

19. Moving too fast through a white neighborhood risks suspicions of running away from a past crime. Stopping, or moving too slowly, through that same neighborhood raises alarm at the prospect of a future crime.
20. Jonathan Metzl, *Dying of Whiteness: How the Politics of Racial Resentment Is Killing America's Heartland* (New York: Basic Books, 2019). Hereafter citations appear in the text as "DW."
21. Painter, *History of White People*, 42.
22. Nancy Isenberg, *White Trash: The 400-Year Untold History of Class in America* (New York: Viking, 2016).
23. Isenberg, *White Trash* XXVIII.
24. For additional commentary on Locke's illiberalism, see James Farr, "Locke, Natural Law and New World Slavery," *Political Theory* 36, no. 4 (August 2008): 495–522.
25. See for example, Charles W. Mills, *The Racial Contract* (Ithaca, NY: Cornell University Press, 1999); Carole Pateman, *The Sexual Contract* (Stanford, CA: Stanford University Press, 1988); Susan Moller Okin, "Political Liberalism, Justice and Gender," *Ethics* 105 (1994): 23–43; McCarthy, *Race, Empire*.
26. Isenberg, *White Trash*, 44, 46–47.
27. James Tully, *An Approach to Political Philosophy: Locke in Contexts* (Cambridge: Cambridge University Press, 1993), 155.
28. Isenberg, *White Trash*, 45. I am grateful to the historian John Marshall for conversations on the context out of which these ideas emerged, and for pointing out that Locke did not invoke the poor as a separate breed.
29. Some scholars speculate the epithet "white trash" originated with Black Baltimoreans who deployed it against the indentured in the early nineteenth century. See Matt Wray, "White Trash: The Social Origins of a Stigmatype," *The Society Pages*, June 21, 2013, https://thesocietypages.org/specials/white-trash/.
30. Painter, *History of White People*; Isenberg, *White Trash*, 56, 55–60. Examples are numerous. In the Americas, William Byrd, for one, insisted that the idle "lubbers" had sloth in their blood that was contagious, making them both lethargic and anarchic, sexually incontinent, and hideous to behold, with a "cadaverous complexion" and living like animals and worse than "the bogtrotting Irish"—with "bogtrotting" connoting a swamp vagrant.
31. I am grateful to Michael Hanchard for this insight.
32. Isenberg, *White Trash*, 135–154; Carl A. Zimring, *Clean and White: A History of Environmental Racism in the United States* (New York: New York University Press 2015).
33. Connery Bolton Valenčius, *The Health of the Country: How American Settlers Understood Themselves and Their Land* (New York: Basic Books, 2002), 99.
34. Rather, Charles Lyall's injunction that the end is prefigured in the beginning might be more appropriate.
35. W.E.B. Du Bois, "The Evolution of the Race Problem," Proceedings of the National Negro Conference (New York, 1909), online at http://www.webdubois.org/dbEvo1OfRaceProb.html.
36. Du Bois, "Evolution of the Race Problem."

37. Dion Million, "We Are the Land and the Land Is Us," in *Racial Ecologies*, ed. Leilani Nisheme and Kim D. Hester Williams (Seattle: University of Washington Press, 2018), 31–32.
38. Bolton Valenčius, *Health of the Country*, 230.
39. Frederick Jackson Turner, *The Frontier in American History* (Huntington, NY: Robert E. Krieger Publishing Company, 1976), 4.
40. Turner, *Frontier in American History*, 3.
41. Turner, *Frontier in American History*, 2. He regarded this dynamic as building off the "germ theory of politics."
42. The highly devout abolitionist John Brown was also deeply invested in the latter narrative. See Stephen B. Oates, *To Purge This Land with Blood: A Biography of John Brown* (Amherst: University of Massachusetts Press, 1984).
43. Turner, *Frontier in American History*, 11.
44. The disastrous human and ecological consequences of such erasures point to why figures such as William Cronon and Charles C. Mann (among others) have expended considerable energy and erudition on dispelling myths of a virgin, untamed wilderness prior to colonization. See Cronon, *Changes in the Land*; Mann, *1491*.
45. Kennan, quoted by Nikhil Pal Singh, "Race Realism and US Globalism," Public Lecture at Johns Hopkins University, March 24, 2019.
46. George W. Bush, October 6, 2001. Quoted in Nikhil Pal Singh, *Race and America's Long War* (Oakland: University of California Press, 2017), 98. Recall the mission was named "Infinite Justice," and apparently infinite justice does not like to wait. And the rhetoric of scalps and crusades to defend American sovereignty à la "If we don't fight them there, we'll fight them here" was not the *only* kind deployed. After the failure to find WMD in Iraq, the Official Public Memory was rewritten by the administration as one of missionary colonialism not at all hostile to Islam, which Bush called a "religion of peace." In the revised historical memory, the United States was always already invading Iraq with the intention of beneficently spreading the gifts of democracy and freedom. Any connection to oil, and the use of American guns, bombs, money, and lives (aka "collateral damage") was entirely ancillary—along with thousands of dead Iraqis who never counted in the first place.
47. Keller, *Apocalypse Now and Then*, vii, 86. Keller contends that the widespread belief in the immanence of the apocalypse represents the social force of what she calls "apocalyptic literalism" that "underlines the paradox of a stubbornly nonlinear text founding caricatures of Western linear time."
48. Anne Case and Angus Deaton, "Rising Morbidity and Mortality in Midlife among White Non-Hispanic Americans in the 21st Century," *PNAS* 112, no. 49 (2015), online at https://www.pnas.org/content/pnas/112/49/15078.full.pdf.
49. Carol Anderson, *White Rage: The Unspoken Truth of Our Racial Divide* (New York: Bloomsbury Press, 2016); Justin Gest, *The New Minority: White Working Class Politics in an Age of Immigration and Inequality* (New York: Oxford University Press, 2016).
50. For instance, contrary to many mainstream explanations that immediately followed Trump's election, we now know that economic standing does not explain his ascent; the median income of his voters was $70,000. Also see Melamed, "Racial Capitalism."

51. Gest, *The New Minority*, 16. Gest bases his analysis on ethnographic fieldwork and quantitative survey data.
52. Gest, *The New Minority*, 17. See also Ashley Jardina, *White Identity Politics* (Cambridge: Cambridge University Press, 2019).
53. More than twice as likely to own firearms, whites disproportionately oppose gun control, despite being most susceptible to gun suicides (DW, 69). "Broadly put, a white person in the United States is five times as likely to die by suicide using a gun as to be shot with a gun; for each African American who uses a gun to commit suicide, five are killed by other people with guns" (DW, 48).
54. Africana philosopher Lewis Gordon registers this theme in Fanon's plays and letters. See Lewis Gordon, *What Fanon Said: A Philosophical Introduction to His Life and Thought* (New York: Fordham University Press, 2015).
55. On the international histories of race war, see Jacob Kripp, "The Creative Advance Must Be Defended: Miscegenation, Metaphysics, and Race War in Jan Smuts's Vision of the League of Nations," *American Political Science Review* 116, no. 3 (August 2022): 940–953.
56. Note that the refusal of Medicaid expansion at the state level largely maps onto the antebellum divide between the Union and Confederacy.
57. Recall that white temporalities are riven with the frenetic desire to securitize the future. This apprehension is not *just* a will to future privilege and stability—though such a will is certainly operative. Also at stake is an affective sense of time, experiencing any present moment as a precursor to an expected future of status and power.
58. "Pat Buchanan's Real Agenda," *Searchlight*, April 1996, 22; my emphasis. Quoted in Daniel Schlozman and Sam Rosenfeld, "The Long New Right and the World It Made," American Political Science Association paper, 2018, 68. Cited with permission. I am grateful to Danny Schlozman for bringing this to my attention and for generative conversations on the subject.
59. Samuel Francis, "The Education of David Duke," *Chronicles*, (February 1992): "The Fire Next Time," in 7–9.
60. For a discussion of Buchanan's segregated memory, see P.J. Brendese, "The Race of a More Perfect Union: James Baldwin, Segregated Memory and the Presidential Race," *Theory & Event* 15, no. 1 (March 2012). Over a decade ago, I argued Pat Buchanan's positions were resonant for the Right by way of James Baldwin on segregated memory. Some critics branded me anachronistic for invoking both men. Baldwin is now the subject of feature films and an inspiration for the movement for Black lives, and Trump became most powerful human on the planet. He professes a debt to none other than—wait for it—Pat Buchanan.
61. Patrick J. Buchanan, *Suicide of a Superpower: Will America Survive to 2025?* (New York: St. Martin's Press, 2011).
62. Patrick J. Buchanan, *The Death of the West: How Dying Populations and Immigrant Invasions Imperil Our Country and Civilization* (New York: St. Martins Griffin, 2002). To be sure, Trump himself is far too undisciplined, opportunistic, and transactional to be considered a dogmatist. But Buchanan is arguably the closest ideological forebear to Trump*ism*.

63. While he thinks that Trump is the last, best shot for his brand of white nationalism, Buchanan is not optimistic. Rather, the "America we knew and grew up with, it's gone. And it's not coming back." Buchanan's avowed nostalgia for the postwar, early 1950s America is conjoined to an armchair philosophy of history where most everything that has happened since amounts to a jeremiad, or story of decline. Tim Alberta, "The Ideas Made It, but I Didn't," *Politico*, May/June 2017. Online at https://www.politico.com/magazine/story/2017/04/22/pat-buchanan-trump-president-history-profile-215042/.

64. Schlozman and Rosenfeld, "Long New Right." I am doubtful that Trump is the last chance for those ideas, but Buchanan's claim to them is accurate. He even pre-engineered two Trump slogans in one with "Make America First," though he also used "America First." Before Trump accused African Americans of being ungrateful, Buchanan had been stoking controversy for decades with a willfully amnesiac history that made him utterly incapable of comprehending why, for instance, Blacks express grievance and not gratitude in the aftermath of slavery. Trump's fluency in the rhetoric of immigrant "invasion" and "infestation" is textbook Buchanan, who decries what he terms a Third World invasion. When it became obvious Buchanan would beat him when the two ran against each other in the 2000 GOP primary, Trump exited the contest having learned to amplify his already well-established racism, misogyny, and nativism. The next time Trump emerged on the stage of national politics, it was to foment the racist lie of "birtherism" that Barack Obama was not an American and his presidency illegitimate.

65. David Corn, "Trump's Campaign Enlists Commentator He Once Slammed as a Bigot and Hitler 'Fan,'" *Mother Jones*, October 11, 2016. Online at https://www.motherjones.com/politics/2016/10/donald-trump-pat-buchanan-hitler/.

66. Benjamin Weiser, "5 Exonerated in Central Park Jogger Case Agree to Settle Suit for $40 Million," *New York Times*, June 19, 2014, online at https://www.nytimes.com/2014/06/20/nyregion/5-exonerated-in-central-park-jogger-case-are-to-settle-suit-for-40-million.html.

67. Let me be clear, by referencing understated histories that follow, my purpose is not to imply that Trump's ascent was inevitable, but that his defeat was not. Windsor Mann, "How Pat Buchanan Made President Trump Possible," *The Week*, July 26, 2019. Online at https://theweek.com/articles/853163/how-pat-buchanan-made-president-trump-possible.

68. Roxanne A. Dunbar, "Bloody Footprints: Reflections on Growing Up Poor White," in *White Trash: Race and Class in America*, ed. Matt Wray and Annalee Newitz (New York: Routledge, 1997), 77.

69. That Trump's loyal followers still overwhelmingly support him despite his failure to lift them up economically is further evidence of the power of racial resentment to explain his sustained popularity.

70. Sullivan, *Good White People: The Problem with Middle Class Anti-racism* (Albany: SUNY Press, 2014), 46.

71. Bill Kristol, a former student of Harvey Mansfield (who introduced him to the philosophy of Leo Strauss) is well known for being wrong in his predictions—not least about the Iraq war. A Trump scold, Kristol's occasional self-reproach allowed him to

brand himself as an employable conservative pundit outside of Trumpism's immediate thrall.
72. Nancy S. Love, *Trendy Fascism* (Albany: SUNY Press, 2016), 131.
73. Note a disturbing transhistorical symmetry: the early planter class would often let poor white settlers fight it out with the Native people, and then move in and take their newly stolen land.
74. It is also undercut by his own sporadic admissions that some privileged peoples get "lifeboats" on the sinking ship, and that certain benefits accrue to whites as a result of segregation (DW, 19, 15–16). Metzl's generalizations may well hold true on the state level, but it is the broader extrapolation I contest.
75. Furthermore, remaining uncritical of how racial anachronism is (re)produced and projected upon marginal whites is a perilous political oversight. Self-proclaimed progressives who bristle at epithets of nonwhites as backward savages would do well to reflect on how they unwittingly advance neocolonial race-making projects by partaking in a politics of trashing marginal whites as disposable inbred troglodytes. To be clear, the point is not to suggest that making all whites coeval amounts to some fantasy panacea.
76. On the right, the maintenance of a cross-class white coalition hinges on a racial bribe whose fragility can be exploited by contesting the conservative divide between the neoconservative elite who condescendingly rely on the aforementioned neo-Confederate "cavemen" whom they need to advance their racist wars and plutocratic policies.
77. Keller, *Apocalypse Now and Then*, 91.
78. Baldwin, "The Fire Next Time," in *Price of the Ticket*, 371.
79. I am in agreement with Jairus Grove that "the genre is also dangerous because images that depict the loss of a manageable world do not remain in the world of fiction." See Grove, *Savage Ecology*, 231.
80. I develop this argument in Brendese, "A Race of Devils."
81. As a story of Eastern European insurgency, Stoker's *Dracula* belongs in this category as well. For a broader discussion of fantasies of reverse colonialism, see Hage, *Is Racism an Environmental Threat*, 68–77.
82. Jean Raspail, *Camp of the Saints*, trans. Norman R. Shapiro (Petoskey, MI: Social Contract Press, 1995).

Epilogue

1. King, "Remaining Awake," in *A Testament of Hope*, 270.
2. Baldwin, "The Fire Next Time," in *The Price of the Ticket*, 374.
3. Among these are the embeddedness of rights-based liberal discourse, the perils of universalisms too tightly tethered to European descent, and the present-centered orientation of liberalism more generally. From there, a raft of temporal issues surface around the politics of what it means to be recognized as existing in time.

4. Wendy Brown, *Walled States / Waning Sovereignty* (New York: Zone Books, 2010). Also see Pauline Ochoa Espejo, *The Time of Popular Sovereignty: Process and the Democratic State* (University Park Pennsylvania State University Press, 2011). I am sympathetic to Ochoa's processual view of "the people" as in flux. My view is that the implications of such dynamism ultimately challenge liberalism rather than necessarily compelling us toward it.
5. Michael O'Malley, *Keeping Watch: A History of American Time* (New York: Penguin, 1990), 46–47.
6. See Singh, *Race and America's Long War*, 45, 140–150; Gorup, "Strange Fruit."
7. Mark Rifkin, *Beyond Settler Time: Temporal Sovereignty and Indigenous Self-Determination* (Durham, NC: Duke University Press, 2017). Hereafter citations appear in text as "BST."
8. This is in contrast to the modalities of settler time and the African American "emancipation sublime" (BST, 94) and other modes of temporality inhabited by nonwhite others, which he leaves as "an open question."
9. See also Smith, *Conquest*; and Kim Tall Bear, *Native American DNA*.
10. I quote at length for textual fidelity and to capture Rifkin's sense of what he calls his study's "negative dialectical" and "inherently speculative quality" that purports to unpack and "lay bare from the perspective of a non-Native, highlighting the violence of extant forms of temporal recognition (and their de-facto modes of translation)" (BST, 4).
11. This temporal trap gives rise to his call to rethink continuity as a dynamic process that is continually adaptive, with regenerative capacities such that a continuous identity does not suppose stasis or an imposed "anthropological minimum" as a requisite shared background for recognition, but figures identity in terms of particular manifold "frames of reference" that include affective connections to land, people, climate, and transgenerational modes of storytelling (BST, 33–47). In a wide-ranging discussion that spans the work of Kevin Bruyneel, Jean O'Brien, Joanne Barker, and Vine Deloria (among others), Rifkin rightly details how the supposed inevitability of extermination facilitates Indigenous erasure. He is likewise attentive to how what I call "white time" functions to perniciously trap Native peoples in an impossible bind where Indigenous reinvention and change is necessary for the survival of a people across time and space, but also that which provides the ground for the liberal state to declare that a people no longer exists. Note that Rifkin's invocation of "white forms of existence" marks another distinction between his work and my own. Since not all colonialism is settler colonialism, his focus is on settler time rather than the more expansive category of whiteness.
12. His attention to the affective dimensions of temporal duration allows him to nuance his discussion with the sensibility that time is not merely thought but experienced, and that the temporal impositions over time represent forms of chrononormativity, routines, and rhythms (BST, 37, 95–128).
13. In the concluding pages, Rifkin offers the following: "Unlike juridical assertions of sovereignty, the characterization of time in these terms does not really speak to expressions of authority or claims to jurisdiction" (BST, 186).

14. This is especially true of Bergson. Merleau-Ponty's phenomenology can tend toward universality, but the flux of the dynamism of perception (his object of analysis) arguably escapes the stasis associated with temporal sovereignty. Bergson's durational sense of time is processual, and he openly resists the stasis that comes with spatialized notions of time. With respect to Einstein, the theory of general relativity might be said to have disparate spacetime distinctions, without necessarily implying ownership over time.
15. Coulthard, *Red Skin / White Masks* quoted in BST, 187.
16. Because my objection to "temporal sovereignty" exceeds an elementary exposition of a performative contradiction, I forgo a belabored hairsplitting over the conceptual uses of sovereignty.
17. Aimé Césaire, "Culture and Colonialism," *Social Text* 28, no. 2 (Summer 2010): 133.
18. Elizabeth Kolbert, *The Sixth Extinction* (New York: Picador, 2015).
19. See Zerubavel, *Time Maps*, 89–92. As Jairus Grove notes, even secularist political theorists like John Rawls follow a "Christian literalist view of the planet.... There was creation and now there is the age of man" ("Apocalyptic Tone").
20. Dipesh Chakrabarty, "The Climate of History: Four Theses," *Critical Inquiry* 35 (Winter 2009): 197–222; Connolly, *The Fragility of Things*.
21. Those familiar with the breadth of outright climate denial in the United States know that Americans exhibit an exceptional capacity to be inured to the "reality based" scientific community written off as so much "fake news." When even those inundated by storms of never-before-seen magnitude deny the reality of climate change, one might be given to expletive and exasperation. It would seem these Americans can deny water is wet even as they are drowning in it.
22. Dipesh Chakrabarty, "Climate and Capital," *Critical Inquiry* 41 (Autumn 2014): 4–5.
23. Chakrabarty, "Climate and Capital," 5.
24. Chakrabarty, "Climate and Capital," 5.
25. Chakrabarty, "Climate and Capital," 21.
26. A rather obvious, if underappreciated, aspect of the shift to the "planetary" is that of scale. For contemporary theorists of the planetary, this entails a shift toward a position destabilizing the centrality of the human in time and space. Interplanetary research, for example, is deeply concerned with cosmic forces vastly exceeding even earth-centered approaches—let alone anthropocentricism(s).
27. Connolly, *Facing the Planetary*.
28. Slavoj Žižek, *Living in the End Times* (New York: Verso, 2010); John Bellamy Foster, Richard York, and Brett Clark, *The Ecological Rift: Capitalism's War on the Earth* (New York: Monthly Review Press, 2010).
29. Chakrabarty, "Climate and Capital," 10. Chakrabarty takes exception to the notion that what Foster, York, and Clark call *The Ecological Rift* is "at bottom the product of a social rift: the domination of human being by human being. The driving force is a society based on class, inequality and acquisition without end." He critiques Žižek for essentially putting "capitalism in the drivers' seat" and overdetermining its role in climate change. For Connolly, such positions represent what he terms "sociocentrism" that typically plays out to the exclusion of the relays between human and nonhuman forces.

30. Connolly, *Facing the Planetary*, 158–174.
31. Chakrabarty, "Climate and Capital," 6.
32. My brief remarks do not treat accelerationism as an ideology complete with a flag and army, but are focused on what I take to be some its more dangerous and widely shared undercurrents.
33. Alex William and Nick Srnicek, "#Accelerate: Manifesto for an Accelerationist Politics," in *#Accelerate: The Accelerationist Reader*, ed. Armen Avanessian and Robin Mackay (Falmouth, UK: Urbanomic, 2014).
34. Déborah Danowski and Eduardo Vivieros De Castro, *The Ends of the World* (Malden, MA: Polity Press, 2017), 113–114.
35. Williams and Srnicek, "#Accelerate."
36. With respect to right accelerationism, among the most prominent incarnations are religious fundamentalists such as ISIS who seek to hasten the onset of the apocalypse through war.
37. Robert Hassan, "The Sovereignty of Time," in Critical Exchange: Robert Hassan, P.J. Brendese, and Nathan Widder, "Time and the Politics of Sovereignty," *Contemporary Political Theory* 12 (2013): 222. Hassan advances temporal sovereignty on "what are necessarily only provisional observations, but they seem at least to furnish the basis for plausible arguments." On that basis, I thought it unfair to critique it as if his was a grand theory, or even a completed argument since he never advertised it as such.
38. Hassan, "The Sovereignty of Time." Also see Robert Hassan and Ronald E. Purser, eds., *24/7: Time and Temporality in the Network Society* (Stanford, CA: Stanford University Press, 2007), 37–61.
39. Ryan Gunderson, Brian Petersen, and Diana Stuart, "A Critical Examination of Geoengineering: Economic and Technological Rationality in Social Context," *Sustainability* 10, no. 1 (2018): 269. I am grateful to Nicole Kiker for bringing this to my attention and for insightful conversations around these themes.
40. Mark W. Driscoll, *The Whites Are Enemies of Heaven: Climate Caucasianism and Asian Ecological Protection* (Durham, NC: Duke University Press, 2020), 3. I only became aware of Driscoll's work as this was going to press, so I do not discuss it at length.
41. Driscoll, *The Whites Are Enemies of Heaven*, 3.
42. Mark Reinhardt, *The Art of Being Free* (Ithaca, NY: Cornell University Press, 1997).
43. E.g., see Alexander G. Weheliye, "The Grooves of Temporality," *Public Culture* 17, no. 2 (Spring 2005): 319–338.

Index

For the benefit of digital users, indexed terms that span two pages (e.g., 52–53) may, on occasion, appear on only one of those pages.

Abu-Lughod, Lila, 127–28
accelerationism, 183
Adam, Barbara, 21–22, 192n.59
Adenauer, Konrad, 9–10
Afrofuturism, 136–37, 141, 142–43
Alexander, Michelle, 45–46, 47, 51, 52–53, 202n.22
Alexie, Sherman, 124, 225n.65, 226n.83
Ana, Otto Santa, 80
Anderson, Carol, 160
Anderson, Jessica, 204n.44
Anthropocene, 26–27
Anzaldúa, Gloria, 82–83
apocalypse, 149–51, 156–60, 168, 231n.1
Apostolidis, Paul, 85–86, 101–3, 217n.42
apprehension, 38–41, 62, 105, 143, 173–74
Arendt, Hannah, 47–48, 139
Aristotle, 24, 195n.20
Auyero, Javier, 189n.18

Bacon, David, 97–98
Baker, Ella, 54, 97–98
Baldwin, James, 7, 31–32, 34, 60, 80, 113–14, 130, 144, 151, 168, 173, 208n.102, 232n.18
Balfour, Lawrie, 145–46
Baltimore, 19–20, 46, 117–18
Banhart, Bruce, 208n.98
Barr, Donald A, 213n.2
Basquiat, Jean-Michel, 229n.21
Bauman, Zygmunt, 63–64, 123–24, 189n.21, 190n.37, 224n.60
Behdad, Ali, 82
Beltrán, Cristina, 103
Benjamin, Ruha, 45–46, 206n.71
Benjamin, Walter, 193n.67
Bentham, Jeremy, 36–37, 129–30

Bergson, Henri, 19–20, 194n.3, 239n.14
Berlant, Lauren, 52–53, 57–59, 190n.40, 219n.59
Berry, Diana Ramey, 223n.49
Best, Rebecca, 99
Best, Stephen, 59–60, 65, 193n.71
Bhabha, Homi K., 67
biopolitics, 7–8, 67–68, 90–94, 97–100, 162, 163–64, 199n.69, 217n.37, 217n.41, 227n.105
Black, Earle and Merle, 203n.36
Black Lives Matter, 56–57, 62–63, 89–90, 101–2
Black Panther Party, 67–69
Blackmon, Douglas A., 206n.55
Blight, David W., 115–16
Bloom, Harold, 149
Bobo, Lawrence, 51, 52
Bonilla-Silva, Eduardo, 70–71
Booth, W. James, 192n.61
borders, 79, 81–83, 84, 85–86, 93, 95–97, 100, 137–40, 153
borrowed time, 5, 38–39, 107, 108–9, 115–16, 118, 123–24, 128–29, 131–32, 133, 167, 177
Bourdieu, Pierre, 44–45
Brendese, P.J., 9, 11–12, 188n.15, 192n.62, 199n.68, 201n.14, 203n.27, 218n.47, 235n.60
Brinckerhoff, Isaac, 221n.28
Brooks, David, 222n.36
Brooks, Meagan Parker, 56–57
brown, adrienne marie, 231n.33
Brown, Lawrence, 46
Brown, Wendy, 174–75
Bruyneel, Kevin, 67–68, 198n.55
Buchanan, Patrick, 165–66, 214n.6

Buonomano, Dean, 22
Burns, Alexander, 96
Bush, George W., 159, 188n.9
Butler, Judith, 19, 38–39
Butler, Octavia E., 140–46
Butler, Paul, 39
Byrd, Jodi A., 32–33

Cacho, Lisa Marie, 93–94
Calavita, Kitty, 101
Camacho, Alicia Schmidt, 82–83, 84, 86
Canales, Jimena, 194n.9
Carceral Temporality, 43–46, 52–54, 65–66, 85, 174
Case, Anne, 160
Césaire, Aimé, 27–28, 35–36, 180, 185
Chakrabarty, Dipesh, 2, 67, 181–83, 190n.38, 240n.31
Chambers, Samuel A., 197n.47
Chappell, Bill, 56
Chavez, Leo R., 80, 95–96
Cherokee v. Georgia, 31–32
Christian, David, 26–27
chronobiopolitical, 56, 171, 173–74
chronos, 5, 8–9, 22, 25–28, 29–30, 37–38, 55, 93–94, 146, 159–60, 174, 178, 180
Churchill, Ward, 188n.17
Ciccariello-Maher, George, 200n.78, 210n.130
citizenship, 51–52, 53, 82–83, 84, 85, 88, 89–90, 95–96, 98, 99, 101, 138–39
Clark, Brett, 182–83
Clavin, Tom, 130
climate change, 5, 27, 151, 181–83, 184
Clinton, George, 229n.21
clock time, 5–6, 21–22, 183–84
Coates, Ta-Nehisi, 116–18, 131
Cohen, Elizabeth, 188n.18, 215n.18
Coles, Romand, 188n.16, 231n.4
colonialism, 9–10, 16–17, 25–29, 67–68, 109, 169–70, 180, 202n.20
Columbus, Christopher, 149
Connolly, N.D.B., 107, 118, 220n.8, 223n.49
Connolly, William E., 26–27, 28, 182–83, 221n.20, 240n.30
Cook, Captain James, 22, 32–33
Corn, David, 166

cosmology, 23, 125, 152
Coulthard, Glen S., 64–65, 179–80, 197n.46, 227n.97
creditworthiness, 108, 130–31
Cronon, William, 199n.64, 234n.44
Crossley, Robert, 141
Culotta, Carmen M., 54

Danowski, Deborah, 240n.34
Davis, Angela, 43, 45–46, 58, 67, 208n.86
Davis, Kathleen, 215n.18
De Castro, Eduardo Vivieros, 240n.34
De Genova, Nicholas, 216n.32
De Goode, Marieke, 108, 129–30
De Leon, Arnoldo, 80
De Leon, Jason, 96–97
Deaton, Angus, 160
decolonial, 29–30, 63–64, 100, 109, 175–76
Deer, Sarah, 125
Deleuze, Gilles, 105–6, 113–14, 118–19
Deloria, Philip J., 208–9n.111
DeLoughrey, Elizabeth, 6
democracy, 2, 76, 158
Derrida, Jacques, 128–29, 149–50
Descartes, René, 195n.19
Diamond, Neil, 208–9n.111
Dillon, Michael, 93
Dilts, Andrew, 211n.148
disavowal, 7, 8, 10–11, 32, 59, 61, 82–83, 122, 123–24, 126–27, 133, 181
discovery doctrine, 30–31, 126, 198nn.50–54
disposability, 5, 126, 153–56, 167
DiTomasso, Natalie A., 54
Douglas, Mary, 171
Douglass, Frederick, 51–52, 60, 208n.99
Driscoll, Mark W., 184
Droit, Roger-Pol, 50, 63–64, 204n.10, 209n.117
Drury, Bob, 130
Du Bois, W. E. B., 6, 20–21, 35–36, 43, 101–2, 113–14, 129, 155–56, 173–74, 185, 220n.8, 221n.24
Dunbar-Ortiz, Roxanne, 2, 33–34, 125, 126, 166–67

Edelman, Lee, 197n.38
Edsall, Thomas and Mary, 47–48, 49–50

Einstein, Albert 21, 24, 28, 179–80, 194n.9, 239n.14
Ellison, Ralph, 61, 209n.106
endemic, 80–82, 90–94, 97–99, 103, 133, 162–63
environmental racism, 27, 126–27, 133, 171, 184–85
epidemic, 79–82, 87–90, 98–99, 215nn.13–14
Escobar, Martha D., 84
Esposito, Roberto, 93
Estes, Nick, 67
Euben, J. Peter, 59–60, 61, 208n.90

Fabian, Johannes, 2, 7–8, 43–44
Fahrentold, David A., 94–95
Fanon, Frantz, 3, 4, 10–11, 20–21, 34, 35–36, 46, 115–16, 131, 135–36, 151, 170–71, 173–74, 185, 190nn.33–34, 200n.79, 222n.34
Farr, James, 233n.24
Fassin, Didier, 8, 190n.42
Feit, Mario, 213n.18
Feldman, Allen, 51–52
Foner, Philip S., 51–52
Fording, Richard C., 221n.21
Forester-Smith, Christopher, 220n.8
Foster, John Bellamy, 182–83
Foucault, Michel, 7–8, 35, 50, 63–64, 66, 81, 87–95, 97–98, 99–100, 101, 162–63, 199n.69, 204n.29, 210n.119, 216n.32
Francis, Sam, 164
freedom, 9–10, 35, 85–86, 105, 112–13, 114–15, 116–17, 128–29, 149, 184–85, 199n.69
Freeman, Elizabeth, 8–9, 44–45
Friedman, Thomas, 26, 189n.22
frontlash, 48, 49–50

Gest, Justin, 160
Geyer, Georgie Ann, 137, 228n.4
Gibson, William, 189n.24
Gilmore, Ruth Wilson, 4, 45–46, 50, 51–52, 67, 119, 205n.49
Glezos, Simon, 189n.23
Glissant, Edouard, 8–9, 25, 40, 195n.26
Goff, Phillip, 54
Gomez, Laura E., 83–84

Gopnik, Adam, 43
Gordon, Lewis, 235n.54
Gorup, Michael, 53, 238n.6
Gottschalk, Marie, 52, 54
Govan, Sandra Y., 146
Graeber, David, 108, 127
Grant, Joanne, 97–98
Green, Alice, 206n.67
Grosz, Elizabeth, 67, 73, 210n.129
Grove, Jairus, 26–27, 237n.79, 239n.19
Grovougi, Siba N., 28–29
Gunderson, Ryan, 184
Gunnell, John G., 24–25, 195n.22

Hage, Ghasson, 7, 80, 237n.82
Halberstam, Judith, 197n.38
Hall, Stuart, 9–10
Hamilton, Alexander, 122
Hammer, Fannie Lou, 56–57
Hanchard, Michael, 1, 29, 62–63, 67, 155, 187n.2, 190n.38, 207n.83, 232n.16
Handley, George B., 6
Harcourt, Bernard, 55, 207n.71
Harris, Cheryl I., 33–34, 35–38, 108, 129–30, 131–32
Hartman, Saidiya, 59–61, 65, 114–15, 193n.71, 208n.100, 218n.47
Harvery, David, 197n.46
Hassan, Robert, 183–84, 240n.37
Hayes, Chris, 202n.20
Hegel, G. W. F., 25, 158–59
Heidegger, Martin, 11–12, 192n.56
Herndon, Astead W., 96
Hill, Mark Lamont, 32
Hobbes, Thomas, 11–12, 91
Honig, Bonnie, 98, 138–40, 215n.16
Hoy, David Couzens, 29, 195n.24
humanism, 26–27, 28–29, 92, 136, 150, 232n.10
Hunter, Gary, 205n.55
Hunter, Kylean, 99
Hutchings, Kimberly, 25–26, 196n.27, 196n.30

Idle No More, 56–57, 130–31
Imarisba, Walidah, 231n.33
immigration, 82–86, 94–98, 100–1, 139–40, 193n.72, 216n.30

integrated time, 173–74
Isaac, Lydia A., 213n.2
Isenberg, Nancy, 153–55
Iton, Richard, 39, 67

Jackson, George, 67–70
Jackson, Matthew C., 54
James, C.L.R., 220n.6
Jardina, Ashley, 235n.52
Jay, John, 122
Johnson v. McIntosh, 30–31, 198n.54
Johnson, Kevin R., 50–51
Joseph, Miranda, 114, 119, 130–31, 223n.53
Junn, Jane, 228n.16

kairos, 25–29, 196n.29, 212n.12
Kant, Immanuel, 24–25, 195nn.24–25
Kasimis, Demetra, 201n.13
Katznelson, Ira, 117, 204n.42
Keller, Catherine, 151, 159–60, 168, 234n.47
Kenan, Randall, 144–45
Kennan, George, 159
Kham, Muqtedar, 196n.31
King, Desmond, 52
King Jr., Martin Luther, 1–2, 34, 35–36, 62–63, 117, 173
King, Tiffany Lethabo, 231n.9
Klein, Naomi, 133
Kolbert, Elizabeth, 181
Kripp, Jacob, 235n.55

LaDuke, Winona, 210n.128
Latinx politics, 45, 79–80, 85–86, 98–101, 217n.39, 218n.52
Lauritsen, Janet, 51, 204n.45
LaVeist, Thomas A, 213n.2
Lazzarato, Maurizio, 105–6, 109–13, 220n.3
Lear, Jonathan, 232n.13
Lederach, John Paul, 12–13, 192n.63
Lee, Spike, 230n.26
Leone, Brooke Allison Lewis Di, 54
Lepore, Jill, 225n.68
Lerman, Amy, 43, 201n.3, 202n.23
liberalism, 1–2, 3–4, 9–12, 31, 34, 35, 65, 71–72, 91, 98–99, 105, 109–10, 123–24, 128–29, 139–40, 153–54, 163, 188n.11

linear time, 13, 38–39, 79–80, 81, 108–9, 146, 178, 181–82
Lipsitz, George, 36, 80
Liptak, David, 94–95
Lobo-Guerrero, Luis, 93
Locke, John, 12, 91, 153–55, 188n.10
López, Ian Haney, 79–80
Loury, Glen, 43
Love, Nancy S., 167
Lowe, Lisa, 197n.46
Lowndes, Joseph, 47–48
Luibheid, Eithe, 80
Lukacs, Georg, 37
Lutz, Amy, 99

Machiavelli, Niccolò, 139
Mackinnon, Catherine A., 27–28
Madison, James, 122
Malcolm X, 80
Mann, Charles C., 199n.64, 234n.44
Manza, Jeff, 53
Marshall, John, 30–31
Martinez, Oscar J., 79
Marx, Karl, 29–30, 110–11, 117, 183, 184, 222n.42
mass incarceration, 43–44, 53, 58, 70, 118
Mathiowetz, Dean, 212n.12
Mauer, Marc, 205n.47
Mbembe, Achille, 28, 101, 131–32, 197n.40, 200n.93, 227n.104
McCarthy, Thomas, 2, 79–80, 190n.37, 233n.25
McClanahan, Annie, 16–17, 117–18, 222n.38, 223n.47
McKittrick, Katherine, 7–8
McQueen, Allison, 231n.2
Mehta, Uday Sinha, 188n.11
Melamed, Jodi, 107, 234n.50
Mendelsohn, Jennifer, 19–20
Metzl, Jonathan, 152–53, 160–64, 167, 237n.74
Milbank, Dana, 191n.54
Mill, J.S., 188n.10
Million, Dion, 155–56
Mills, Charles W., 34, 192n.58, 226n.92, 233n.25
Mills, Mike, 201n.12
Mitchell, Timothy, 28
Mohawk, 12–13
Molina, Natalia, 213n.2

INDEX

Moore, Barington, 39
Morefield, Jeanne, 70–71, 188n.11
Moreton-Robinson, Aileen, 20–21, 32–33, 36, 40, 93, 211n.147
Morison, Tracey, 61
Morris, Errol, 56
Morrison, Toni, 230n.25
mortgage, 106–8, 116–19, 120–21, 123
Moten, Fred, 38–39, 106, 118–19, 130–31
Motomoro, Hiroshi, 85
Muhammad, Khalil Gibran, 50–51, 55–56
Munoz, José Esteban, 197n.38
Murukawa, Naomi, 205n.51
Myers, Ella, 35–36

Nanni, Giordano, 6, 22
nativism, 79–80, 82, 85, 97–98
Nelson, Scott Reynolds, 206n.55
neoliberalism, 70, 108, 113
Newkirk II, Vann R., 79–80
Newton, Isaac, 21–22, 23–25, 179–80
Newton, Lina, 83
Nguyen, Dan Thu, 20–21
Nguyen, Mimi Thi, 128–29, 219 n.63, 219n.1
Nichols, Robert, 67–68
Nier, Charles, 223n.47
Nietzsche, Friedrich, 29, 56, 62, 110–11, 114–15, 169
Nixon, Rob, 5, 123–24
Noble, Safiya Umoja, 207n.71
Nobles III, Wilborn P., 202n.18
Northrup, Solomon, 209n.106

O'Brien, Jean M., 33, 122–23
O'Malley, Michael, 176–77
O'Neil, Cathay, 55
Oates, Stephen B., 158
Ochoa, Pauline Espejo, 238n.4
Okin, Susan Moller, 192n.58, 233n.25
Olson, Joel, 191n.53
Ortiz, Vilma, 83–84
Osborne, Peter, 56–57

Painter, Nell Irvin, 14–15, 153, 155
Park, K-Sue, 120–22, 123
Pateman, Carole, 226n.92, 233n.25
paternalism, 1–2, 30–31, 34, 64, 71, 109, 125, 127, 129
Patterson, Orlando, 93–94

Patton, Stacey, 227n.103
Petersen, Brian, 184
Pitkin, Hannah Fenichel, 228n.12
plague dream, 80–81, 86, 87–90, 96, 168
planetary time, 182–83
Plato, 22–23, 76–77
precarity, 5, 19, 45, 92, 107, 118, 128–29, 130–31, 160
predictive policing, 55, 207n.76
predictive technology, 45–46, 49–50, 55, 108–9, 174
primitive accumulation, 29–30
prison abolition, 65–66, 69–70, 202n.17
Purser, Ronald E., 240n.38

race, 5–8, 19–21, 48, 49–51, 55–57, 61–62, 106, 150, 156–60, 173–75, 213n.2
racial amnesia, 11–12, 59, 103, 126–27
racial capitalism, 44–45, 63–64, 68–69, 106–7, 155–56, 220n.9
racial debt, 38–39, 71, 103, 113–19, 127, 145, 220n.5
racial inequality, 1, 9, 62–63
racial stigma, 5, 106, 108–9, 113–14, 127, 130–31
Radin, Margaret, 37–38
Ralph, Michael, 122–23
Rancière, Jacques, 73–76
Rankine, Claudia, 209n.106
Raspail, Jean, 169–70
Reagon, Bernice Johnson, 206n.67
Reinhardt, Mark, 184–85
Resendez, Andres, 189n.31
Richland, Justin B., 125
Rifkin, Mark, 175–76, 177–81, 238nn.10–13
Roberts, Dorothy, 54
Roberts, Neil, 67
Robinson, Cedric, 22–23, 76–77, 197n.46
Roediger, David R., 199n.66, 203n.36
Rogin, Michael Paul, 198n.56, 208n.94, 209n.111
Rohy, Valerie, 27–28, 57–58, 98, 189n.19
Rose, Deborah Bird, 189n.28
Rosenfeld, Sam, 165, 204n.45
Rovelli, Carlo, 21, 23–24

Sachs, Joe, 24
Sampson, Robert J., 51, 204n.42
Sayad, Abdelmalek, 101

Schlozman, Daniel, 165, 235n.58
Schrader, Stuart, 50, 70–71, 211n.151, 211n.156
Schram, Sanford F., 221n.21
Schroeder, Theresa, 99
Schwab, Gabriel, 126
Scott, David, 190n.37
Segregated Apocalypse, 131–32, 149–53
segregated memory, 8–13, 59–60, 77, 82–83, 107, 122–23, 125, 141, 153–56, 191n.54
segregated temporality, 1, 2, 45, 52–53, 55, 59, 61, 65, 67, 75–76, 79, 202n.15
segregated time, 1, 3–5, 8–13, 21–25, 52–57, 101–3, 105–6, 116, 118, 124, 141–42, 149, 173–75, 192n.63, 201n.13
Seth, Sanjay, 28–29
Seth, Suman, 214n.9
settler colonialism, 12, 67–68, 124
settler time, 177–78
Sharma, Sarah, 221n.18
Sharpe, Christina, 209n.106
Shelby, Tommie, 12
Shilliam, Robbie, 139–40
Silver, Marc, 96–97
Simpson, Audra, 13, 32–33, 126–27
Singh, Nikhil Pal, 53, 159, 202n.20, 238n.6
slavery, 1, 6, 9–11, 22–23, 39, 45–46, 60, 76, 114–16, 141–42, 145, 155, 193n.73
Smith, Adam, 29–30
Smith, Andrea, 64, 210 n.124, 126, 238n.9
Smith, Mark M., 6
Smith, Rogers, 52
Snyder, Benjamin H., 194n.14
Soss, Joel, 221n.21
spectrality, 13, 32, 57–58, 59, 64, 74, 80, 83, 102–3, 105, 126–27, 158
Spence, Lester, 223n.44
Spillers, Hortense, 145
Srnicek, Nick, 183
St. Cyr, Maureen R., 223n.47
Stepan, Nancy Leys, 214n.9
Stern, Alexandra Minna, 215n.11
Stevens, Jacqueline, 26–27
Stevenson, Bryan, 51, 52–53
Stoler, Ann Laura, 93, 211n.147
Stuart, Diana, 184

subprime, 106–8, 117–23, 130–31
subprime time, 107, 119–23, 131
Sullivan, Shannon, 40, 167, 201n.96

Tall Bear, Kim, 40, 226n.78, 238n.9
Tancredo, Thomas, 214n.6
Teigen, Jeremy, 99
Telles, Edward E., 83–84
temporal refugee, 5
temporal sovereignty, 129–30, 142–43, 146, 151, 173–81, 183–84, 240n.37
temporal theft, 4, 44, 46–47, 52–53, 56–57, 81, 145, 175
tempus nullius, 32–34, 158, 231n.4
Thomas, Sheree R., 229n.21
Thompson, E.P., 194n.14
Thompson, Victor, 51, 52
Thorpe, David, 59–60
Thurston, Chloe, 227n.98
time travel, 98, 105, 135–36, 137–40, 141, 142–43, 146, 157–58, 174
Tinker, George E., 198n.50
Tonry, Michael, 47, 51
Trudell, John, 133
Trump, Donald J., 117–18, 165–66, 190n.43, 214nn.10–11, 236n.71
Tully, James, 154–55
Turner, Fredrick Jackson, 156–59

Uggen, Christopher, 53
Urbina, Ian, 70

Valenčius, Conevery Bolton, 155, 156–57
Vásquez, Delio, 211n.148
Vasquez, Manuel A., 94–95
Verges, Francoise, 196n.36
Virilio, Paul, 189n.23
Vitale, Alex S., 53–54
Voyles, Traci Brynne, 126–27

Wacquant, Loïc, 43
Wagner, Peter, 205n.55
Walters, William, 216n.32
Wang, Jackie, 55–56
Washington, Booker T., 115–16
Watts, Pauline Moffatt, 231n.8
Weaver, Vesla, 43, 48–50, 201n.3, 202n.23, 203 n.31

Weheliye, Alexander, 211n.147, 240n.43
Weil, Simone, 19
Weiser, Benjamin, 166
Western, Bruce, 53
white noise, 46–47, 57–63, 73, 75
white supremacy, 4–5, 41, 61, 117–18, 131, 145, 150, 162–63, 167, 169–70, 184–85, 232n.15
white time, 29–34, 55–56, 57–63, 66, 81–82, 102–3, 109, 113–14, 125, 127–28, 141, 160, 168–69, 173–74, 176–77
white temporality, 34–41, 44–45, 129, 131–32, 163–64, 235n.57
white trash, 143–44, 153–56, 166–67, 233n.29
whiteness as credit, 106, 108–9, 119, 123, 128, 150, 165, 177
whiteness as property, 62–63, 108, 129, 131–32
Whitman, James Q., 9–10
Widder, Nathan, 195n.20
Wilder, Gary, 200n.93

Wilderson, Frank B., 106, 209n.112
Wilkins, Kimberly, 209n.108
William, Alex, 183
Williams, Eric, 202n.20, 220n.8
Williams Jr., Robert A., 198n.50
Wolfe, Patrick, 30, 31–32, 124, 126, 130, 189n.31
Wolin, Sheldon S., 192n.58
Wray, Matt, 233n.29
Wynter, Sylvia, 190n.40, 231n.10

xenophobia, 82, 100, 170–71

York, Richard, 182–83
Younis, Musab, 28–29
Yusoff, Katheryn, 27

Zerubavel, Eviatar, 194n.13, 198n.51, 239n.19
Zimring, Carl A., 155
Zizek, Slavoj, 182–83
Zurn, Perry, 211n.148